George Whitefield, Andrew Gifford

Eighteen Sermons Preached by the Late Rev. George Whitefield

George Whitefield, Andrew Gifford

Eighteen Sermons Preached by the Late Rev. George Whitefield

ISBN/EAN: 9783337087418

Printed in Europe, USA, Canada, Australia, Japan

Cover: Foto ©Lupo / pixelio.de

More available books at **www.hansebooks.com**

TO THE

RIGHT HONOURABLE

SELINA

COUNTESS DOWAGER OF

HUNTINGDON

THESE SERMONS
ARE MOST HUMBLY INSCRIBED

BY HER LADYSHIP's

MOST DEVOTED

AND OBEDIENT

HUMBLE SERVANT

JOSEPH GURNEY.

TO THE
READER.

POsthumous publications generally need an apology. This poor Orphan's plea is, that it attempts to preserve the genuine remains of One who has incontestibly proved himself the destitute helpless Orphan's friend yet speaking to a serious auditory hanging on his lips for instruction, and comfort, though in a fainter light, as the glorious luminary of the heavens, the ruler of the day, seems visible, even after it is set, by the refraction of its resplendent rays. As to its spots, if such there are, let them be put down to the account of the editor.

A. G.

ERRATA.

Page 51, line 24, for *to* read *for*
- 82, - 11 and 16, for *needy* read *naughty*
- 220, - 10 and 11, for *stars* read *palms*

THE CONTENTS.

SERMON I.
A Faithful Minister's parting Blessing.
A Farewell Sermon, February 23, 1763.

REVEL. xxii. 21.

THE grace of our Lord Jesus Christ be with you all. Amen. page 1

SERMON II.
CHRIST, the Believer's Refuge.
On the Death of Mr. BECKMAN.

PSALM xlvi. 1—6.

GOD *is our refuge and strength, a very present help in trouble; therefore will we not fear, though the earth be removed, and the mountains be carried into the midst of the sea, though the waters thereof roar, and be troubled, though the mountains shake with the swelling thereof,* Selah. *There is a river, the streams whereof shall* make glad the city of God, the holy place of the tabernacles of the Most-High: God is in the midst of her, she shall not be moved;

The CONTENTS.

moved; God shall help her, and that right early.   26

SERMON III.
Soul Prosperity.

3 Ep. JOHN ver. 2.

Beloved, I wish above all things that thou mayst prosper, and be in health, even as thy soul prospereth.   54

SERMON IV.
The Gospel a dying Saint's Triumph.
A Funeral Sermon.

MARK xvi. 15, 16.

And he said unto them, Go ye into all the world, and preach the gospel to every creature. He that believeth, and is baptised, shall be saved, but he that believeth not, shall be damned.   78

SERMON V.
Repentance and Conversion.

ACTS iii. 19.

Repent ye therefore and be converted, that your sins may be blotted out, when the times of refreshing shall come from the presence of the Lord.   103

The CONTENTS.

SERMON VI.
Glorifying GOD in the Fire; or, the right Improvement of Affliction.

ISAIAH xxiv. 15.

Wherefore glorify ye the Lord in the fires. 134

SERMON VII.
The Beloved of GOD.

DEUT. xxxiii. 12.

And of Benjamin he said, The beloved of the Lord shall dwell in safety by *him; and the Lord shall cover him all the day long, and he shall* dwell *between his shoulders.* 155

SERMON VIII.
The Furnace of Affliction.
On the Death of the Rev. Mr. MIDDLETON.

ISAIAH xlviii. 10.

I have chosen thee in the furnace of Affliction. 179

SERMON IX.
The LORD our Light.

ISAIAH lx. 19, 20.

The sun shall be no more thy light by day, neither for brightness shall the moon give light unto thee, but the Lord shall be unto thee an everlasting

The CONTENTS.

everlasting light, and thy God thy glory. Thy sun shall no more go down, neither shall thy moon withdraw itself, for the Lord shall be thine everlasting light, and the days of thy mourning shall be ended. 202

SERMON X.
Self-Enquiry concerning the Work of GOD.

NUMB. xxiii. 23.
According to this time it shall be said of Jacob, and of Israel, What hath God wrought! 225

SERMON XI.
The burning Bush.

EXOD. iii. 2, 3.
And he looked, and behold the bush burned with fire, and the bush was not consumed; and Moses said, I will now turn aside, and see this great sight, why the bush is not burnt. 250

SERMON XII.
Soul Dejection.

PSALM xlii. 5.
Why art thou cast down, O my soul? and why art thou disquieted within me? hope thou in God, for I shall yet praise him for the help of his countenance. 272

The CONTENTS.

SERMON XIII.
Spiritual Baptism.

ROM. vi. 3, 4.

Know ye not, that so many of us as were baptized into Jesus Christ, were baptized into his death? Therefore we are buried with him by baptism into death: that like as Christ was raised up from the dead by the glory of the Father, even so we also should walk in newness of life. 293

SERMON XIV.
Neglect of CHRIST the killing Sin.

JOHN v. 40.

And ye will not come to me that ye may have life. 317

SERMON XV.
All Men's Place.

ECCLES. vi. 6.

Do not all go to one place? 345

SERMON XVI.
GOD a Believer's Glory.

ISAIAH lx. 19.

And thy God thy Glory. 373

The CONTENTS.

SERMON XVII.
Jacob's Ladder.

A Farewell Sermon at Tottenham-Court-Road Chapel, Sunday, August 27, 1769.

GEN. xxviii. 12, &c.

And he dreamed, and behold, a ladder set upon the earth, and the top of it reached to heaven: and behold, the angels of God ascending and descending *on it. And behold, the Lord stood above it, and said,* I am the Lord God of Abraham thy father, *and the God of Isaac: the land whereon thou liest, to thee will I give it and to thy seed. And thy seed shall be as the dust of the earth; and thou shalt spread abroad to the west, and to the east, and to the north, and to the south: and in thee, and in thy seed, shall all the families of the earth be blessed. And behold, I am with thee, and will keep thee in all places, whither thou goest, and will bring thee again into this land: for I will not leave thee, until I have done that which I have spoken to thee of.* 397

SERMON XVIII.
The Good Shepherd.

A Farewell Sermon at the Tabernacle, Wednesday, August 30, 1769.

JOHN x. 27, 28.

My sheep hear my voice, and I know them, and they follow me. *And I give* unto them eternal life, *and they shall never perish, neither shall* any pluck them out of my hand. 427

SERMON I.

A Faithful Minister's Parting Blessing.

REVELATIONS xxii. 21.

The grace of our Lord Jesus Christ be with you all. Amen.

IT is very remarkable that the old testament ends with the word curse; whereby we are taught, that the law made nothing perfect: but blessed be God, the new testament ends otherwise, even a precious blessing, that glorious grace put into the heart, and dropt by the pen of the disciple whom Jesus loved.

My brethren, as the providence of God calls us now to bid each other a long farewel, can I part from you better than in enlarging a little upon this short but glorious prayer; can I wish

B   you,

you, or you me, better in time and eternity, than that the words of our text may be fulfilled in our hearts, *the grace of our Lord Jesus Christ be with you all, Amen.* In opening which,

First, it will be proper to explain what we are to understand by the word grace.

Secondly, what by the grace of our Lord Jesus Christ, and its being with us all; and then to observe upon the word Amen: shewing you why it is that every one of us may wish, that the grace of our Lord Jesus Christ may be with us all.

Perhaps, there is not a word in the book of God that has a greater variety of interpretations put upon it than this little, this great word grace: I don't intend to spin out, or waste the time by giving you all. It will be enough in general to observe, that the word grace signifies favour, or may imply the general kindness that God bears to the world; but it signifies that here which I pray God we may all experience, I mean the grace, the special grace of the blessed God communicated to his people; not only his favour displayed to us outwardly, but the work of the blessed Spirit imparted and conveyed inwardly and most powerfully to our souls, and this is what our

church

church in the catechism calls special grace; for though Jesus Christ in one respect is the Saviour of all, and we are to offer * Jesus Christ universally to all, yet he is said in a special manner to be the saviour of them that believe; so that the word grace is a very complex word, and takes in all that the blessed Spirit of God does for a poor sinner, from the moment he first draws his breath, and brings him to Jesus Christ, till he is pleased to call him by death; and as it is begun in grace, it will be swallowed up in an endless eternity of glory hereafter; this is called the grace of our Lord Jesus Christ: why so? because it is purchased † for us by the Lord Jesus Christ: the law was given by Moses, but grace and truth, in the most emphatical manner, came by Jesus Christ the Son of God. If it was not for the purchase of a Mediator's blood, if it was not that Jesus Christ had bought us with a price, even with the price of his own blood, you and I should never have had, you and I could never have had the grace of God manifested at all to our souls. The covenant of works being broken, our first parents stood convicted before God: they were criminals, though they did

* Preach.   † Procured.

not care to own it; condemn'd before God, and in themselves, so that like their children they made excuses for their sin. Man by nature had but one neck, and if God had pleased to have done it, he might justly have cut it off at one blow; but no sooner had man incurred the curse of the law, but behold a Mediator is provided under the character of the seed of the woman, which should bruise the serpent's head; implying what the Redeemer was first to do without, and afterwards to do in the hearts of all his people: well therefore are we taught in our church collects to end all our prayers with the words, *through Jesus Christ our Lord*.

Moreover, brethren, this grace may be called the grace of our Lord Jesus Christ, because it is not only purchased * by him, but it is conveyed into our hearts through Christ; the federal head of his glorious body, is a head of influence to those for whom he shed his blood: thus his disciples said, he was full of grace and truth, and out of his fulness we, all that are true believers, receive grace for grace; grace upon grace, says Mr. Blackwall, in his Sacred Classicks: grace for grace, that is,

* Procured.

is, says Luther, every grace that is in Christ Jesus, will be by his blessed Spirit transcribed into every believer's heart, even as the warm wax receives the impress of the seal upon it; as there is line upon line upon the seal left upon the wax, so in a degree, though we come greatly short of what the law requires, the grace that is in Jesus Christ is, in a measure, implanted in our souls; but the Lord Jesus Christ, blessed be God, has our stock in his hands. God trusted man once, but never will more; he set Adam up, gave him a blessed stock, placed him in a paradise of love, and he soon became a bankrupt, some think in twenty-four hours, however, all agree it was in six or seven days, and that he never had but one sabbath; but now, blessed be God, we are under a better dispensation, our stock is put into Christ's hands, he knows how to keep it, and us too; so this grace may be said to be the grace of our Lord Jesus Christ, secured by his blood, and conveyed to our souls by his being the head of his church and people.

This grace has a variety of epithets put to it, and I question whether there is any kind of grace but what the Lord Jesus Christ exercises towards his people some way or other, every hour, every moment of the day. First,

First, His restraining grace; why, if it was not for this, God's people would be just as weak and wicked as other folks are: remember what David said when Abigail came to him; he was going to kill a neighbour for affronting him, forgot that he was a Psalmist, and was only acting as a creature: blessed be God, says he, that has sent thee to meet and keep me: My brethren, we may talk what we please, and build upon our own stock; we are just like little children that will walk by themselves; well, says the father, walk alone then, they tumble down, get a broken brow, and then are glad to take hold of the father: thus Jesus Christ is always acting in a restraining way to his people; if it was not so, by the blindness of their understandings, the corruptions of their hearts and affections, together with the perverseness of their will, alas! alas! there is not a child of God that would not run away every day, if Christ did not restrain him!

Secondly, There is convicting grace, which from the Lord Jesus Christ acts every day and hour. Oh! it is a blessed thing to be under the Redeemer's convicting grace! a man may speak to the ear, but it is the Spirit of God alone

alone can speak to the heart: I am not speaking of convicting grace that wounds before conversion, and gives us a sense of our sin and misery; no, I mean convicting grace that follows the believer from time to time. If a heathen Socrates could say, that he had always a monitor with him to check him when he did amiss, and direct him when he went right, surely the Christian may say, and blessed be God for it, that he has got a Jesus that kindly shews him when he goes astray, and by his grace puts him into the way of righteousness, that his feet may not slip; this is what the shepherd does to his sheep when they have wandered; what does the shepherd do, but sends some little cur, his dog, after them, to bring them to the fold again? what does Jesus Christ do in temptations, trials, and afflictions? he fetches his people home, and convinces them that they have done amiss.

Then, thirdly, There is the converting grace of our Lord Jesus Christ. Oh! what poor unhappy creatures are they, that think they can turn to God when they please, to which abominable principle it is owing, that they leave it till they cannot turn in their beds: Satan tells them then, it is too late, their consciences

sciences are filled with horror, and they go off in a whirlwind; may this be the case of none here! That is a most excellent prayer in our Communion Office, *Turn us, O good Lord, and we shall be turned*; we can no more turn our hearts than we can turn the world upside down; it is the Redeemer, by his Spirit, must take away the heart of stone, and by the influence of the holy Spirit give us a heart of flesh. I might as well attempt to reach the heavens with my hand; I might as well go to some church-yard and command the dead to rise; I might as soon shake my handkerchief and bid the streams divide, and they give way, as to expect a soul to turn to God without the grace of the Mediator. Come, my dear hearers, I am of a good man's opinion, that prayed he might be converted every day. In the divine life, not to go forwards is to go backwards; and it is one great part of the work of the Spirit of God, to convert the soul from something that is wrong to something that is right, every day, hour, and moment of the believer's life, so that in short his life is one continued act of converting grace: there is not a day but there is something wrong; there is something we want to have taken away; we

want

want to get rid of the old man, and to get more of the new man, and so the Spirit of God works every day: O! my brethren, God give us more of this converting grace!

Then there is establishing grace. David prays, *Create in me a new heart, and renew a right spirit within me*; in the margin, it is constant spirit; and you hear of some that are rooted and grounded in the love of God, and the apostle prays, that they may always abound in the work of the Lord: again, it is good to have the heart established with grace: there is a good many people have some religion in them, but they are not established; hence they are mere weather-cocks, turned about by every wind of doctrine; and you may as soon measure the moon for a suit of clothes, as some people that are always changing; this is for want of more grace, more of the Spirit of God; and as children grow that are got stronger and riper, so as people grow in grace, and in the knowledge of the Lord Jesus Christ, they will be more settled, more confirmed: on first setting out they prattle, but they will be more manly, more firm, more steady: young Christians are like little rivulets that make a large noise, and have shallow water; old Christians are like deep water that makes little noise, carries a good load, and gives not way.

What think you, my brethren, of the Redeemer's comforting grace? O! what can you do without it? *In the multitude of my thoughts within me,* says the Psalmist, *thy comforts have refreshed my soul.* I believe you will all find what lord Bolinbrooke, in spite of all his fine learning, and deistical principles, found when under affliction; he sent a letter which I saw and heard read to me, at least that part of it in which he says: *Now I am under this affliction, I find my philosophy fails me.* With all our philosophy and striving, it is too hard to work ourselves into a passive state: alas! it is commendable to strive, but we shall never be content, we shall never be chearful under sufferings, but through the assistance of the Redeemer. Even now, in respect of parting from one another, what can comfort friends when separated but the Spirit of God. Paul, when going away for Jerusalem, said, *What mean ye to weep and to break my heart?* he also says, *I am ready not to be bound only, but also to die at Jerusalem, for the name of the Lord Jesus,* which he could not have said, had he not felt the comforting grace of Jesus Christ.

Our

Our Lord, when going away, says, *I will send the Comforter*; I will not leave you comfortless and helpless, I will come again: the Lord helps the believer from time to time. We can easily, my brethren, talk when not under the rod ourselves; there is not a physician or apothecary in London but can give good advice, but when they are sick themselves, poor souls! they are just like their patients, and many times are more impatient than those they used to preach patience to; so it is with the greatest Christian, we are all men of like passions, there is not one of us when under the rod, if left to ourselves, but would curse God, and, Ephraim like, *be as a bullock unaccustomed to the yoke*; and there are many here, I do not doubt, that have said to the Redeemer, *What dost thou?* or, perhaps, with Jonah, *We do well to be angry*; if the Lord does but take away his goard from us, if he is pleased to baulk us in regard to the creatures, how uncomfortable are we? and there are so many afflictions and trials, that if it was not for the Lord Jesus Christ's comfortings, no flesh could bear them.

In a word, what think you, my brethren, of the quickning grace of our Lord Jesus Christ?

Chrift? Remember David fays, *Quicken me according to thy word, quicken me in thy way, quicken me in thy righteoufnefs:* God's people want quickening every day; this is trimming our lamps, girding up the loins of our minds, ftirring up the gift of God that is in us. It is juft with a foul as it is with the plants and trees; how would it be with them if the Lord did not command quickening life to them after the winter? the believer has his frofty and winter days, and wo be to them that think they have always a fummer; the believer at times can fay, *The winter is paft, the rain is over and gone, the flowers appear on the earth, the time of the finging of birds is come, and the voice of the turtle is heard in our land, the fig-tree putteth forth her green figs, and the vines with the tender grapes give a good fmell,* Cant. ii. 12. What is all this but God's quickening grace, reftoring the believer to his bleffed joy. Oh! my brethren, I have not time to fhow you in how many ways the Redeemer's grace is difplayed; but wherever this grace is, what reafon have you that are partakers of it, and I, to pray that it may be with us all; *the grace of our Lord Jefus Chrift*, fays John here, *be with you all:* it is not faid all minifters, it is not faid all of

this

this or that particular people, but with all believers. O! my friends, remember what Mr. Henry said, he desired to be a Catholic, but not a Roman Catholic. I have often thought since I went to see the water-works, that it was an emblem of Christ; there is a great reservoir of water from which this great city is supplied; but how is it supplied from that reservoir? why by hundreds and hundreds of pipes: but where does this water go, does it go only to the dissenters or to the church people, only to this or that people? no, the pipes convey the water to all; and I remember when I saw it, it put me in mind of the great reservoir of grace, that living water that is in Christ Jesus, and the pipes are the ordinances by which his grace is conveyed to all believing souls, God grant we may be of that happy number. O what a mercy it is that Christ has said, *I will be with you always even to the end of the world*, Matt. xxviii. 20. and therefore we must look upon this prayer to be as efficacious now, as it was the moment the words dropt from the apostle's pen. I believe the most minute philosophers, and those that have the greatest skill in astronomy, cannot perceive there has been any abatement in the heat of the sun, since God first commanded it to rule the day, then surely, if my God can make a sun that for so many thousands of years shall irradiate, enlighten, and warm the world, without losing any of its light and heat, so does the sun of righteousness, the Son of God, arise upon the children of God with healing under his wings; he raises, warms, nourishes, and comforts his people, and we have the gospel on the ends of the earth, as well as those who had the honour of conversing with him in the days of his flesh. I mention this in answer to all those who have wrote against the Methodists, and represented them as fanatics; there is no other way of talking against the divine influence, but by allowing it was so formerly, but that it is not so now; they say the primitive Christians had it, but it is not to be so with us now as it was formerly. O my brethren, what fools these great men are when they talk about things they know nothing of; give them a polyglot, give them a lexicon, give them a geographical text, or the chronological part of the scripture, they have something to say; but when they come to talk of the Spirit of God, they see the word Spirit, and they read the word grace, but while they read it their hearts cry, because

their

their knowledge puffs them up, surely if it was so, we great men that have been in the university should have it, God would give it us; and because they find it not in themselves, their abominable pride will not own it may be in any. Pray what was Peter, James, and John, I don't mean to speak disrespectfully of them, they were as weak, as blind, as obstinate, and worldly-minded as others, till Jesus Christ changed their hearts; and that same grace that changed their hearts, changes now the hearts of God's people; and blessed be God, that same grace is with all his people.

It is so in his ordinances. Here is the difference between a Formalist and a Christian; the Formalist goes to ordinances, but then he does not feel the God of ordinances, and that is the reason most formal people don't care to go to church very often: who cares to go to the house of a person he does not love? they will only just knock at the door, and ask if such a person is at home, and are very glad to hear the servants say their master or mistress is not at home; the visit is paid; so it is with many people that go to church and meeting; and I do not doubt but there are many Methodists, hundreds and hundreds, that have been

at

at the ordinances, who never felt the God of ordinances converting them to this day.

The grace of our Lord Jesus Christ is with his people in prayer. Who can pray without grace? they may laugh at it as will, but God give you and I a spirit of prayer; let them laugh as they please; what profit will it be to us to read this book without the grace of God. What a horrid blunder has the bishop of G--r been guilty of? What do you think his lordship says, in order to expose the fanaticism of the Methodists? Why, says he, they say they cannot understand the scriptures without the Spirit of God. Can any man understand the scriptures without the Spirit of God helps him? Jesus Christ must open our understanding to understand the scriptures, and the Spirit of God must take of the things of Christ and show them unto us; as we are taught to pray, *O Lord, thou hast caused thy holy scriptures to be written,* &c. as in the second Sunday in Advent; and here the b—p pretends to tell us, there is no need of it; here our collect and b——p disagree very much. So with respect to all ordinances it is the same: what signifies my preaching, and your hearing, if the Spirit of God does not enlighten? Formal ministers can steal a sermon,

mon, and add a little out of their own heads, but a minister of the gospel cannot preach to purpose without the assistance of the Spirit of God, no more than a ship can sail without wind. As for a carnal man he may take his sermon in his pocket, and you will find his sermons always the same; but spiritual preachers are seldom so; sometimes they are in darkness, so as to speak to those that are in darkness; sometimes they are tempted, so as to speak to those that are tempted; sometimes they have a full gale, and go before the wind, and this is all by the assistance of the Spirit of God, and without this a man may preach like an angel, and do no good at all. So in respect to hearing the word of God, I declare I would not preach again, if I did not think that God would accompany the word by his Spirit: what are we but *sounding brass and tinkling cymbals?* If the word is preached in the strength of the Spirit, it will be attended with convictions, and conversions, and the grace of God will be both with preacher and hearer.

The grace of God is with his people in *his providence*. Oh! says bishop Hall, a little aid is not enough for me. My going on the waters puts me in mind of what I have seen many times: if the sailors perceive a storm a coming, they do not chuse to speak to the passengers for fear of frightening them, they will go quietly on deck, and give orders for proper care to be taken; and if a sailor can tell of storms approaching by the clouds, why can't God's people tell why God does so and so with them? The people of God eye him in his providence; the very hairs of their heads are all numbered, and the grace of God is with them in the common business of life. Some people think that the Methodists preach so and so to make them neglect their business, and we preach at unseasonable times: we would not preach at this time, but that we are going to part from one another; no, we preach that the grace of God may attend them in their counting-houses, and wo be to those persons that do not take the grace of God with them into their counting-houses, and in their common business. O what blessed times would it be if every one made the grace of God their employ, that when the Lord comes he may say, Lord, here I am waiting for thee.

The grace of the Lord Jesus Christ is with his people when *sick* and when *dying*. O my dear souls, what shall we do when death comes? What

What a mercy it is that we have got a good master to carry us through that time! As a poor converted Negro that saw a believer who was dying in comfort, said, Master don't fear, Jesus Christ will carry you safe through the dark valley of the shadow of death.—But the time would fail, if I was to shew you in how many respects *the grace of the Lord Jesus Christ* helps us; but what I have said will shew, that we need all join in a hearty Amen; Amen, I pray God it may be so, so it is, so may it be! May be what? why that *the grace of the Lord Jesus Christ, convicting, restraining, converting, establishing* and *comforting grace*, may be with us in his ordinances, in his providences, in sickness, and when dying: then, blessed be God, we shall carry it with us after time. And now, my dear hearers, by the help of my God, in whose strength I desire once more to go upon the waters, I shall pray wherever I am, that this *grace of the Lord Jesus Christ may be with you all.*

To whom shall I speak first by way of improvement? Are there any of you here unconverted? no doubt too many. Are there any of you here this morning come out of curiosity to hear what the babler has to say? Many, perhaps

haps, are glad it is my last sermon, and that London is to be rid of such a monster: I don't doubt but it has been a pleasant paragraph for many to read; but whoever there are of you that are unconverted, or whatever you may think, sure you cannot be angry for my wishing that the *grace of God may be with you*. O that it may be with every unconverted soul. O pray for me, my dear friends, that the Lord may bless me to some unconverted soul; what wilt thou do if the grace of God is not with thee? what wilt thou do with the favour of man if thou hast not got the grace of God? you will find, my brethren, it will not do, you cannot do without the grace of God when you come to die. There was a nobleman that kept a deistical chaplain, and his lady a christian one; when he was dying, he says to his chaplain, I liked you very well when I was in health, but it is my lady's chaplain I must have when I am sick. Do you know that you are nothing but devils incarnate? Do you know that every moment you are liable to eternal pains? The Lord help thee to awake O sinner, awake, awake thou stupid soul, if the grace of God was never with thee before, God grant it may now. Don't say I part with you in

an

an ill humour; don't say that a madman left you with a curse. Blessed be God that when first I entered into the field, (and blessed be God that honoured me with being a field-preacher) I proclaimed the grace of God to the worst of sinners, and I proclaim it now to the vilest sinner under heaven; could I speak so loud as that the whole world might hear me, I would declare that the grace of God is free for all poor souls that are willing to accept of it by Christ; God make you all willing this day.

There are many of you, I doubt not, but have got this grace, and I believe there are many of you that can say that this poor despised place was that which God honoured first with giving it you: but whether you were converted here, or elsewhere, if you have got the grace of God, the Lord grant you more grace; *grace, mercy and peace be multiplied unto you all.* My brethren, they that have got Christ never have enough of him; you want more grace every day, and hour, and moment: I see for my part more of my want of grace than I did ten or twenty years ago; may be that is because I don't grow in grace; but those that grow in grace will grow every day more sensible of their want of grace, they will feel their

weak-

weakness more and more every day. Some who are called Christians are a most foul-mouth people, they abuse their neighbours, but real believers abuse themselves most, and call themselves, *i. e.* what is in themselves, the worst of neighbours. O my brethren, may the Lord Jesus Christ's grace be with you more and more, that you may be transformed into the divine likeness, and pass from glory to glory by the Spirit of the Lord. May God grant that this grace may be with you all, particularly those young men that have given up their souls to Christ. It delights my soul when I go round the communion table, to see how many young souls have given themselves to Christ, the Lord grant that you may not return again to folly. O young men, flee youthful lusts; O young women, the Lord Jesus Christ grant that grace may be with you all, that you may study the beauties of the mind, shine in the beauties of holiness, and be wise to everlasting salvation.

May the grace of the Lord Jesus Christ be with you all that are in the marriage state. It needs much grace to bear with heavy trials, much grace to deal with servants, children, and under disappointments in trade; to walk with God with a pure heart. Some people think

think it clever to have wives and children, but they want a thousand times more grace than they had when they were single; you have need of much grace to honor God in your houses, much grace to teach you to be prophets, much grace to teach you to be kings in the family; to know, when to be pleased; to know, when to be silent; to know, when to be angry: but the greatest grace is to be angry when called to it, to be angry without sin. O! may the grace of God be with you all in your closets, every time you pray, every time you come to an ordinance; O! may the grace of God be with you all when you frequent this despised place! blessed be God some may say, that ever it was built; though as soon as it was built I was called away. As soon also as the chapel was built I was then called away, and so am now; and when I came out of my chamber, I could hardly support it. I would as lieve go to an execution, if my way was not very clear; what is dying? that is but for a moment. O may the grace of God be with all, that preach the gospel here. Blessed be God his grace has been with them; don't let the world say, he is gone, and all the people are gone now;

don't

don't weaken the hands of those that shall labour here; I should not mention such a word if I was not going away. The Lord Jesus Christ grant that you may keep steady, and honor the preachers more and more; there will be good Mr. Adams, blessed be God, from time to time, with Mr. Beridge, and so there will be a blessed change: may the Spirit of God be with them, and you, more and more! and O my dear friends, if the Lord God has vouchsafed to own these labours to any of you, do remember me in a particular manner, when gone; for though my body has been weak, yet I thank God that he has enabled me to speak when called to it.

And so I must go, whether well or ill; pray, that if it should please God to spare me, that I may speak more effectually to you, when I come back again; pray, that the grace of the Lord Jesus Christ may be with me in a restraining, comforting, supporting, and transforming way, that it may be with me when I am sick, and when I die. O my brethren, I see I want the grace of the Lord Jesus Christ, in every one of these respects, every moment; O may the Lord God bless you all that have been kind to me, and forgive

give every thing that I have done amiss. I am ashamed of myself, so much of the man comes up with me, though I humbly hope, and dare to say, that at the bottom my heart is upright towards God; I would employ it to his praise, but there is so much sin mixed with all I do, that was not the blood of Christ constantly applied to my soul, and the grace of God continually manifested to me, I could not preach any more. You may see a thousand things wrong in me, but I see ten thousand more, O may *the Grace of God be with you all*. Now, dear friends, farewel! dear tabernacle, farewel! if I never preach here any more; O that we may meet in a better tabernacle, when these tabernacles are taken down, when these bodies shall drop, when we shall be for ever with the Lord. I must have done, I can't bear it; *the Lord bless you, the Lord God cause his face to shine upon you.* I cannot say more, I dare not: *The Grace of our Lord Jesus be with you all, Amen.*

SERMON II.

Christ the Believer's Refuge.

PSALM xlvi. 1—6.

God is our refuge and strength, a very present help in trouble; therefore will we not fear, though the earth be removed, and the mountains be carried into the midst of the sea, though the waters thereof roar, and be troubled, though the mountains shake with the swelling thereof, Selah. There is a river, the streams whereof shall make glad the city of God, the holy place of the tabernacles of the Most High: God is in the midst of her, she shall not be moved; God shall help her, and that right early.

THERE was a tradition among the ancient Jews, that the manna which came down from heaven, though it was a little grain like coriander-seed, yet suited every taste; as milk unto babes, and

strong

strong meat to grown persons. Whether this supposition be founded on fact or not, the observation will hold good in a great measure respecting the sayings of David; for if we have eyes to see, and ears to hear, if God has been pleased to take away the veil from our hearts, we shall find, by happy experience, that let our circumstances be what they will, the book of Psalms may serve as a spiritual magazine, out of which we may draw spiritual weapons in the time of the hottest fight, especially those that are under trouble, *when the hand of the Lord is gone* seemingly *forth against them*; when unbelief is apt to make them say, *all these things are against me!* if we can have the presence of mind to turn to the book of Psalms, we may find something there suitable to our case, a word to refresh us in pursuing our spiritual enemy. This is true of the 46th Psalm in particular, part of which I have just now read to you, and which I pray the blessed Spirit of God to apply to every one of our hearts. It is uncertain at what time, or upon what occasion, David wrote it; probably under some sharp affliction, which made him eloquent; or when the affliction was over, when his heart was swiming with gratitude and love, and when out of the fulness of it his pen was made *the pen of a ready writer*. It was a favourite Pſalm with Luther; for whenever Melancthon, who was of a melancholy turn, or any other of his friends, told him ſome ſad news, he uſed to ſay, come, come, let us ſing the 46th Pſalm; and when he had ſung that, his heart was quiet. May every true mourner here, and afflicted perſon, experience the ſame! I know not when I read it which to admire moſt, the piety, or the poetry; the matter, or the manner; and I believe I may venture to defy all the criticks on earth to ſhew me any compoſition of Pindar, or Horace, that any way comes up to the diction of this Pſalm conſidered only as human: he that hath an ear to hear, let him hear, *God is our refuge and ſtrength, a very preſent help in trouble*. Stop here, my friends, let us pauſe a while, and before we go further, may the Lord help us to draw ſome comfort from this very firſt verſe: for obſerve, it is not ſaid, *God is* my *refuge*; David ſays ſo in another Pſalm, but he ſays here, *God is* our *refuge*: he ſpeaks in the plural number, implying, that this Pſalm was of no private interpretation, but was intended

tended for the comfort and encouragement of all believers, till time shall be no more. Observe the climax, *God is our refuge,* is one degree; *God is our strength,* another; *God is our help,* and not only so, but is a *present help,* yea, *is a very present help,* and at a time when we want it most, *in the time of trouble.* It is here supposed, that all God's people will have their troubles, *man is born to trouble, as the sparks fly upward;* and if we are born to trouble as men, we are much more so as christians. We forget ourselves, and the station in which God has placed us, when we so much as begin to dream of having much respite from trouble while we are here below. The decree is gone forth like the laws of the Medes and Persians, it alters not; through tribulation, through much tribulation, we must all go; but blessed be God we are to be carried through it; and blessed be God, glory is to be the end of it: may God give us to know this by happy experience! *in the world,* says our blessed Lord, *ye shall have tribulation,* tribulation and trouble of different kinds; and in another place, *if any man will come after me,* says he, *let him take up his cross daily, and follow me;* so that the day, when we take up no cross, we may say as Titus did,

when

when he reflected that he had done no good that day, I have loſt a day! But then what ſhall we do, my dear hearers, when trouble comes, when one trouble comes after another, and afflictions ſeem to purſue us wherever we go, ſeem to ariſe up out of the ground, meet us as we are walking along? why bleſſed be God, if we have an intereſt in Chriſt, mind that, if we have an intereſt in Chriſt, God is our help, God is our aſylum, our city of refuge, a place appointed by God himſelf, to which the purſued ſaints may fly by faith, and be ſafe. The wicked have no notion of this; when they are in trouble, what is their refuge? let a ſoul be under ſpiritual trouble, and cry out *what ſhall I do to be ſaved?* let him go to a carnal miniſter, an unconverted wretch that knows nothing about the matter, he ſhall be told, oh! go, and play an innocent game at cards, and divert yourſelf; that is to ſay, the devil muſt be your refuge. Wordly people have worldly refuges; and Cain would ſeem as if he was in earneſt when he ſaid, *my puniſhment is greater than I can bear:* what does he do, he goes and diverts himſelf by building a city, goes and amuſes himſelf by building. The devil, my brethren, will give

you

you leave to amuse yourselves; you may have your choice of diversions, only take care to be diverted from God, and the devil is sure of you; but the believer has something better: faith *sweeps away the refuge of lies*, and the believer turns to his God, and says *O my God, thou shalt be my refuge.* The devil pursues me, my false friends have designs against me, my own wicked heart itself molests me, *my foes are those of my own house*; but do thou, O God, be my refuge I will fly there; by these it may be said, *God is our refuge.* The question is, what shall I do to make him my refuge? how shall I be helped to do so? you bid me fly; you say, I may fly there, but where shall I get wings? how shall I be supported? Here is a blessed word, *God shall not only be our refuge,* but *God shall be our strength* also. Strength, what is strength? why, my brethren, to make every day of trouble so easy to us by his power, as to carry us through it; God has said, and will stand to it, *as thy day is, so shall thy strength be.* Afflictions even at a distance will appear very formidable, when viewed by unbelief. Our fears say, O my God, if I come to be tried this or that way, how shall I bear it? but we don't know what

we

we can bear till the trial comes, and we do not know what strength God can give us, or what a strong God he will be, till he is pleased to put us into a furnace of affliction; and therefore it is said, not only that *God is our refuge and our strength*, but that *God is our help* also. What help? why, my dear friends, help to support us under the trouble; help so as to comfort us as long as the trouble lasts; and blessed be God, that the help will never leave us, till we are helped quite over and quite through it. But what kind of an help is it? O blessed be God, *he is a very present help*. We may have an helper, but he may be afar off; I may be sick, I may want a physician, and may be obliged to send miles for one; he might be a help if he was here, but what shall I do now he is at a distance. This cannot be said of God, he is not only a help, but he is a *present help: the gates of the new Jerusalem are open night and day*. We need not be afraid to cry unto God; we cannot say of our God as Elijah does of Baal, *perhaps he is asleep, or talking, or gone a journey:* it is not so with our God, *he is a present help*; he is likewise a sufficient help, that is, *a very present help*, and that too *in the time of trouble*.

It

It is but to send a short letter, I mean a short prayer, upon the wings of faith and love, and God, my brethren, will come down and help us. Now to this David affixes his *probatum est*, David proves it by his own experience, and therefore if *God is our refuge*, therefore if *God is our strength*, if *God is our help*, if *God is a present help*, if *God is a very present help*, and that too *in a time of trouble*, what then? *therefore will we not fear.*—Therefore, is an inference, and it is a very natural one, a conclusion naturally drawn from the foregoing premisses; for Paul says, *if God be for us, who can be against us?* There is not a greater enemy to faith than servile fear and unbelief. My brethren, the devil has got an advantage over us when he has brought us into a state of fear; indeed in one sense we should always fear, I mean with a filial fear; *blessed is the man*, in this sense, *that feareth always:* but, my brethren, have we strong faith in a God of refuge? this forbids us to fear; says Nehemiah, *shall such a man as I flee?* and the Christian may say, shall a believer in Jesus Christ fear? shall I fear that my God will leave me? shall I fear that my God will not succour me? no, says David, *we will not fear*; how so? why *though*

F

the

the mountains be carried into the midst of the sea, though the waters thereof roar and be troubled, though the mountains shake with the swelling thereof. Where is Horace, where is Pindar, now? let them come here and throw their palms down before the sweet singer of Israel. There is not such a bold piece of imagery in any human composition in the world. Can any thing appear more great, more considerable than this? Imagine how it was with us some years ago, when an enthusiastic fool threatened us with a third earthquake; imagine how it was with us when God sent us the same year two dreadful earthquakes; had the earth been at that time not only shook, but removed, had the fountains of the sea been permitted to break in upon us, and carry all the mountains of England before it, what a dreadful tremor must we all unavoidably have been in? David supposes that this may be the case, and I believe at the great day it will be something like it: the earth and all things therein, are to be burnt up; and, my brethren, what shall we do then if God is not our refuge, if God is not our strength?

We may apply it to civil commotions: David had lately been beset with the Philistines,

tines, and other enemies, that threatened to deprive him of his life; and there are certain times when we shall be left alone. This also, my brethren, may be applied to creature-comforts: sometimes the earth seems to be removed, what then? why all the friends we take delight in, our most familiar friends, our soul-friends, friends by nature, and friends by grace, may be removed from us by the stroke of death; we know not how soon that stroke may come, it may come at an hour we thought not of; the mountains themselves, all the things that seem to surround and promise us a lasting scene of comfort, they themselves may soon be removed out of our sight, what then shall we do? *they may be carried into the midst of the sea;* what is that? our friends may be laid in the silent grave, and *the places that knew them may know them no more.* It is easy talking, but it is not so easy to bear up under these things: but faith, my brethren, teaches us to say, though all friends are gone, blessed be God, God is not gone. As a noble lady's daughter told her mother, when she was weeping for the death of one of her little children, a daughter four years old said, Dear mamma, is God Almighty dead, that you cry so long after my sister? No, he is not dead, neither does he sleep. But here the imagery grows bolder, the painting stronger, and the resemblance more striking, *though the waters thereof roar and be troubled, though the mountains shake with the swelling thereof*; what won't this make us fearful? will not this shake us off our bottom, our foundation, and take up the roots? No, no, even then the believer need not fear; why, *God is in the midst of her*. Don't you remember God spoke to Moses out of the bush? did he stand at a distance, and call to him at a distance from the bush? no, the voice came out of the bush, *Moses! Moses!* as Mr. Ainsworth, who was a spiritual critic, says.

Learn from hence, *that in all our afflictions God is afflicted; he is in the midst of the bush*; and oh! it is a sweet time with the soul when God speaks to him out of the bush, when he is under affliction, and talks to him all the while. Though it was threatened by the fire which surrounded it with immediate and total desolation; *yet the bush burned, and was not consumed*. I do not know whether I told you, but I believe I told them at Tottenham-court, and perhaps here, that every christian has got a coat of arms, and I will give it you out of Chrift's heraldry, that is the *burning bufh*; every chriftian is burned, but not confumed. But how is it the faint is held up, whence does he get this ftrength; or how is this ftrength, this fupporting, comforting ftrength, conveyed to his heart? read a little further, you fhall find David fay, *there is a river*, mind that, *there is a river the ftreams whereof make glad the city of God, the holy place of the tabernacles of the Moft High*; need I tell you, that probably here is an allufion to the fituation of Jerufalem, and the waters of Shiloah, that flowed gently through the city of Jerufalem, which the people found fweet and refrefhing in the time of its being befieged. So the rivers run through moft of the cities in Holland, and bring their commodities even to the doors of the inhabitants. Pray, what do you think this river is? why, I believe it means the covenant of grace; O that is a river, the fprings of which firft burft out in Paradife, when God faid, *the feed of the woman fhall bruife the ferpent's head*; then God made this river vifit the habitation of man, as the firft opening of his everlafting covenant.

No sooner had the devil betrayed man, and thought he was sure to get him into the pit, even when he was laughing at man's misery, and thinking he was revenged of God for driving him out of heaven; at that very time did the great God open this river, and made it flow down in that blessed stream to mankind, implyed in those words, *it shall bruise thy head.* O this is a stream which, I pray, may this night *make glad* this part of *the city of God.* If by the river we understand the covenant of grace, then, my brethren, the *promises* of God are the streams that flow from it. There is no promise in the Bible made to an unbeliever, but to a believer; all the promises of God are his, and no one knows, but the poor believer that experiences it, how glad it makes his heart. God only speaks one single word, or applies one single promise; for if when one's heart is overwhelmed with sorrow, we find relief by unfolding ourselves to a faithful disinterested friend; if a word of comfort sometimes gives us such support from a minister of Christ, O! my friends, what support must a promise from God applied to the soul give? and this made a good woman say, I have oft had a blessed meal on the promises, when I have had no bread to make a meal for my body.

But by the river we may likewise understand, the *Spirit* of the living God. If you remember, Jesus Christ declared at the great day of the feast, *if any man believe on me, out of his belly shall flow rivers of living water;* this, saith the beloved disciple, *spake he of the Spirit, which they that believe on him should receive.* My brethren, the divine influences are not only a conduit, but a deep river, a river of broad waters. Here is room for the babes to walk, and for the man of God to bathe and swim in from time to time; and supposing that the river means the Spirit of God, as I believe really it does, why then the streams that flow from this river are the means of grace, the ordinances of God, which God makes use of as channels, whereby to convey his blessed Spirit to the soul. Nay, by the river we may understand, *God himself* who is the believer's river, the Three-one, Father, Son, and Holy Ghost. This river is in the midst of the city, not at the court-end of the town only, or one corner, or end, but quite through, in a variety of streams, so that high and low may come to it for supply; and not only be
supported,

supported, but have their hearts made glad daily thereby; God help us to drink afresh of this river. If this be the case, well may David triumph and say, *glorious things are spoken of the city of God*; are spoken of *her*, in the feminine gender. The church is spoken of in that sense, because Eve, the first woman, was the mother of all believers; we may apply this to a single saint, as well as to a community, under trouble, *she shall not be moved*; not moved? pray, would you have them stupid? do you love when you strike a child, to see it hardened and regardless? do you not like the child should smart under it and cry, and when it is a little penitent, you almost wish you had not struck it at all. God expects, when he strikes, that we should be moved; and there is not a greater sign in a reprobate heart of a soul given over by God, to have affliction upon affliction, and yet *come out like a fool brayed in a mortar*, unmoved and hardened. My brethren, this is the worst sign of a man or woman's being given over by God. Jesus was moved, when he was under the rod; he cries, *father! if it be possible, let this cup pass from me!* he was moved so as to shed tears, tears of blood, falling to the ground.

Wo

Woe, woe, woe be to us, if when God knocks at the door by some shocking domestic or foreign trial, we don't say, *my God! my God! wherefore dost thou strike?* When we are sick we allow physicians to feel our pulse, whether it be high or languid; and when we are sick, and tried with affliction, it is time to feel our pulse, to see if we were not going into a high fever, and do not want some salutary purge. It is expected therefore that we should be moved; we may speak, but not in a murmuring way: Job was moved, and God knows when we are under the rod, we are all moved more than we ought to be in a wrong way; but when it is said here, *she shall not be moved,* it implies, not totally removed; *perplexed,* says the apostle, *but not in despair; persecuted, but not forsaken; cast down, but not destroyed;* therefore removal means destruction: *when the earth is moved, the mountains shake, and the waters roar,* where can we flee? what can we see but destruction all round us? But, my brethren, since *there is a river the streams whereof make glad the city of God,* since God is our refuge, since God is our strength, since God is our help, since God is a present help, since God is a very present help in the time of trouble,

trouble, since *God is in the midst of her*, since *God causes the streams to make her glad*, blessed be God, we shall not, my brethren, be totally moved; nay, though death itself does remove our bodies, though the king of terrors, that grisly king, should come armed with all his shafts, yet *in the midst of death we are in life*, even then *we shall not be moved*, even though the body is removed in sleep, the soul is gone where it shall be sorrowful no more. One would have imagined that David had said enough, but pray observe how he goes on, he repeats it again, for when we are in an unbelieving frame we have need of *line upon line, words upon words, God shall help her*; ah! but when? when? when will he help her? when will he help her? why, *right early*; *God shall help her, and that right early*. Why sometimes we knock for a friend, but he will not get up early in the morning, but *God shall help us, and that right early*, in the morning. Ah! but, say you, I have been under trouble a long while; why God's morning is not come: you said right early; yes, but you are not yet prepared for it, you must wait till the precious right moment comes, and you may be assured of it. God never gives you one doubt more

than

than you want, or even defers help one moment longer than it ought to be.

Now, my dear hearers, if these things are so, who dares call the Christian a madman? If these things are so, who would but be a believer? who would not be a faithful follower of the son of God? My brethren, did you ever hear any of the devil's children compose an ode, that the devil is our refuge; the God of this world, whom we have served so heartily, we have found to be a present help in time of trouble? ah! a present help to help us after the devil: or did you ever hear, since the creation, of one single man that dared to say, that all the forty-sixth psalm was founded on a lie? No, it is founded on matters of fact, and therefore believer, believer, I wish you joy, although it is a tautology. I pray God, that from this time forth till we die, you and I, when under trouble, may say with Luther, come let us sing the forty-sixth psalm.

As for you that are wicked, what shall I say to you? are you in high spirits to night; has curiosity brought you here to hear what the babler has to say on a funeral occasion? well, I am glad to see you here, though I have scarce strength to speak for the violence of the heat, yet I pray God to magnify his strength in my weakness; and may the God of all mercy over-rule curiosity for good to you. I intend to speak about this death to the surviving friends; but, my dear hearers, the grand intention of having the funeral sermon to night, is to teach the living how to die. Give me leave to tell you, that however brisk you may be now, there will a time come when you will want God to be your help. Some pulpit may e'er long be hung in mourning for you; the black, the dreary appendages of death may e'er long be brought to your home; and if you move in a high sphere, some such escutcheon as this, some atchievement may be placed at your door, and woe, woe, woe be to those who in an hour of death cannot say, *God is my refuge.* You may form schemes as you please; after you have been driven out of one fool's paradise, you may retreat into another; you may say, now I will sing a requiem to my heart, and now I shall have some pleasant season; but if God loves you he will knock off your hands from that, you shall have thorns even in roses, and it will imbitter your comforts. O what will you do when the elements shall melt with fervent heat;

heat; when this earth, with all its fine furniture, shall be burnt up; when the archangel shall cry, *time shall be no more!* whither then, ye wicked ones, ye unconverted ones, will ye flee for refuge? O, says one, I will fly to the mountains: O silly fool, O silly fool, fly to the mountains, that are themselves to be burnt up and moved. O, says you, I will flee to the sea; O you fool, that will be boiling like a pot: O then I will flee to the elements; they will be melting with fervent heat. I can scarce bear this hot day, and how can you bear a hot element? there is no fan there, not a drop of water to cool your tongue. Will you fly to the moon? that will be turned into blood: will you stand by one of the stars? they will fall away: I know but of one place you can go to, that is to the devil; God keep you from that! Happy they that draw this inference; since every thing else will be a refuge of lies, God help me from this moment, God help me to make God my refuge! here you can never fail; your expectations here can never be raised too high; but if you stop short of this, *as the Lord liveth*, in whose name I speak, you will only be a sport for devils; a day of judgment will be no day of refuge to you,

you, you will only be summoned like a criminal that has been cast already, to the bar to receive the dreadful sentence, *Depart, ye cursed, into everlasting fire, prepared for the devil and his angels.* There is no river to make glad the inhabitants of hell, no streams to cool them in that scorching element: were those who are in hell to have such an offer of mercy as you have, how would their chains rattle! how would they come with the flames of hell about their ears! how would they rejoice even there, if a minister was to tell them, Come, come, after you have been here millions and millions of years, there shall come a river here to make you glad. But the day is over; God help us to take warning: and oh! with what gratitude should we approach him to night, for bearing with, and for for-bearing us so long; let each say to night, why am I out of hell? how came I not to be damned, when I have made every thing else my God, my refuge, for so many years? May goodness lead every unconverted soul to repentance, and may love constrain us to obedience: fly, fly, God help thee to fly, sinner; hark! hear the word of the Lord, see the world consumed, the avenger of blood, this grim death, is just at thy heels,

heels, and if thou doſt not this moment take refuge in God, to-night before to-morrow, you may be damned for ever; the arms of Jeſus yet lie open, his loving heart yet ſtreams with love, and bids a hearty welcome to every poor ſoul that is ſeeking happineſs in God. May God grant that every unconverted ſoul may be of the happy number.

But, my brethren, the moſt heavy taſk of this night yet lies unperformed; indeed, if my friendſhip for the deceaſed did not lead me to it, I ſhould pray to be excuſed; my body is ſo weak, my nerves ſo unſtrung, and the heat beats too intenſely on this tottering frame, for me to give ſuch a vent to my affections as I am ſure I ſhould give if I was in vigorous health; you may eaſily ſee, though I have not made that application, with what deſign I have choſe this Pſalm; you may eaſily ſee by the turn, I hope no unnatural one, that has been given to the text as we have paſſed along, that I have had in my view a mournful widow here before me. Did I think when this black furniture was taken from the pulpit when two branches were lopt off within about a year one after another, both lopt off from on earth, I hope and believe to be planted for ever in

hea-

heaven, little did I think that the axe was in a few months time to be laid to the root of the father; little did I think that this pulpit was then to be hung in mourning for the dear, the generous, the valuable, the univerfally benevolent, Mr. Beckman; a benefactor to every body, a benefactor to the Tabernacle; he has largely contributed both to the Chapel and Tabernacle, and, my dear hearers, now his works follow him, for he is gone beyond the grave. Such a fingular circumftance I believe rarely happens, that though I was laft night at near eleven o'clock dead almoft with heat, I thought if death was the confequence, I would go to the grave and have the laft look at my dear departed friend; to fee a new vault opened; to fee a place of which he has been, in a great meafure, the founder; to fee a place which he was enlarging at the very time he died; to fee a new vault there firft inhabited by the father, and two only fons, and all put there in the fpace of two years time, Oh! it was almoft too much for me, it weighed me down, it kept me in my bed all this day; and now I have rifen, God grant it may be to give a feafonable word to your fouls. Oh! my friends, put yourfelves in the ftate of a furviving

ving widow, and then see who is secure from cutting providences. The very children when they are young are a trial; but the young man for whom a handsome fortune awaited; for a tender loving father to have his son taken away; for the widow to have the husband taken away soon after; indeed, dear madam, you had need read the forty-sixth Psalm; you may well say, *call me no more Naomi*, that signifies pleasant, but *call me Marah, for the Lord hath dealt bitterly with me.* These are strokes that are not always given to the greatest saints. Such sudden strokes, such blow upon blow, Oh! if God is not a strength and refuge, how can the believer support under it? but blessed be the living God, I am a witness God has been your strength, I am witness that God has been your refuge; you have found, I know you have, already, that *there is a river*, a river in which you have swam now for some years, *the streams whereof make glad* your waiting heart. Surely I shall never forget the moment in which I visited your deceased husband, when the hiccoughs came, and death was supposed to be really come, to see the disconsolate widow flying out of the room, unable to bear the sight of a departing husband:

husband: I know that God was then your refuge, and God will continue to be your refuge. You are now God's peculiar care, and as a proof that you will make God your refuge, you have chosen to make your first appearance in the house of God, in the Tabernacle, where I hope God delights to dwell, and where you met with God, and which I hope you will never leave till God removes you hence. Whatever trials may yet await you, remember you are now become God's peculiar care. You had before a husband to plead for you; he is gone, but your pleader is not dead, he lives, and will plead your cause; may you find him better to you than ten thousand husbands; may he make up the awful chasm that death has made, and may the Lord God be your refuge in time, and your portion to all eternity; and then you will have a blessed change. You are properly a *Naomi*; I would humbly hope that your daughter-in-law, which so lately met with a stroke of the same nature, will prove a *Ruth* to you, and though young, and having a fortune, she may be tempted to take a walk in the world, yet I hope she will say, *where thou goest, I will go; where thou lodgest, I will lodge; thy peo-*

ple shall be my people, and thy God my God; where thou diest, will I die, and there will I be buried; the Lord do so to me, and more also, if ought but death part thee and me. It is to your honour, madam, and I think it right to speak of it, you had the smiles of your departing father-in-law, you had behaved with deference and love; he was very fond of you; God make you a comfort to your surviving mother, who has adopted you, and may the Lord Jesus Christ enable you to take God to be your portion.

As for you that are the relations of the deceased, there is one of you that has been honourably called to the service of the ministry: you, sir, was sent for over by an endearing uncle, you have been a stranger in a strange land: the Palatines will bless your ministry; God has, I hope, blessed it, and provided you a place to preach in. May God grant that that church may be filled with his presence and his glory; and you, madam, be made the instrument of sending the news to heaven to your husband, that *this and that man was born of God there.* As for you, the other friends of the deceased, may God grant that when you die, and when you are buried, the people may follow you with tears as they did dear Mr. Beckman last night. I was told by one this morning that walked along with the funeral, that it was delightful to hear what the people said when the coffin passed by; they blessed the person contained therein, Oh! he was a father to the poor. The poor have indeed lost a friend; and I believe there has not been a man, a tradesman in London, for these many years, that has been more lamented than the dear man who now, I hope, is at rest. You well know how mindful he has been of you, and that soon after the decease of his disconsolate widow, his substance will be divided among some of you. Give me leave to charge and intreat you, by the mercies of God in Jesus Christ, to be kind to the honoured widow. Don't say, Mr. Beckman my uncle is dead, come pluck up, let us plague her now she is living, we shall have all when she is dead. The plague of God will follow you if you do: if you valued your dear uncle, do all you can to make her life easy; pay her that respect which you would pay the deceased was he now living; this will shew your love is genuine, and not counterfeit, and do not *lay up wrath against the day of wrath*. Follow the ex-

example of your dear deceased uncle; the gentleman was visible in him as well as the christian; he would be in his warehouse early in the morning, that he might come soon to his country-house, and there employ himself in his friendly life, and open the door to the disciples of Jesus. It is time to draw to an end, but I will speak a word to the servants of the family, who have lost a good and a dear master. May the Lord Jesus Christ be your master for ever, that you may be the Lord's servants, however you may be disposed of in this world; that you may meet your master, your mistress, and all the family, in the kingdom of the living God, then we shall have a whole eternity to reflect upon the goodness of a gracious God. O may God help us to sing the forty-sixth Psalm; may we find him to be *our strength and our refuge, a very present help in the time of trouble*; may the river of the living God make glad your hearts, and may you be with God to all eternity; even so, Lord Jesus, Amen and Amen.

SERMON III.

Soul Prosperity.

3 Epistle JOHN ii.

Beloved, I wish above all things that thou mayst prosper, and be in health, even as thy soul prospereth.

WHAT a horrid blunder has one of the famous, or rather infamous, deistical writers made, when he says, that the gospel cannot be of God, because there is no such thing as friendship mentioned in it. Surely if he ever read the gospel, *having eyes he saw not, having ears he heard not*; but I believe the chief reason is, his heart being waxen gross, he could not understand; for this is so far from being the case, that the world never yet saw such a specimen of steady and disinterested friendship, as was displayed in the life, example, and conduct of Jesus of Nazareth.

John,

John, the writer of this epistle, had the honour of leaning on his bosom, and of being called, by way of emphasis, *the disciple whom Jesus loved*; and that very disciple, which is very remarkable concerning him, though he was one of those whom the Lord himself named Sons of Thunder, *Mark* iv. 17. and was so suddenly, as bishop Hall observes, turned into a son of lightning, that he would have called down fire from heaven to consume his Master's enemies; consequently, though he was of a natural fiery temper, yet the change in his heart was so remarkable, that if a judgment may be formed by his writings, he seems as full of love, if not fuller, than any of his fellow apostles. He learned pity and benevolence of the father of mercies; and to show how christian friendship is to be cultivated, he not only wrote letters to churches in general, even to those he never saw in the flesh, but private letters to particular saints, friends to whom he was attached, and wealthy rich friends, whom God had, by his Spirit, raised up to be helpers of the distressed. Happy would it be for us, if we could all learn that simplicity of heart which is displayed in these particular words; happy if we could learn this

one

one rule, never to write a letter without something of Jesus Christ in it; for, as Mr. Henry observes, if we are to answer for idle words, much more for idle letters; and if God has given us our pens, especially if he has given us *the pen of a ready writer*, it will be happy if we can improve our literary correspondence for his glory and one another's good. But what an unfashionable stile, if compared to our modern ones, is that of the apostle to Gaius. The superscription *from the elder to the well-beloved Gaius, whom I love in the truth*; there is fine language for you! Many who call themselves Christ's disciples, would be ashamed to write so now. *I send this, and that, and the other; I send my compliments.* Observe what he stiles himself, not as the pope;* but he stiles himself the elder. A judicious expositor is of opinion, that all the other apostles were dead, and only poor John left behind. I remember a remark of his, " the taller we grow, the lower we shall " stoop." The apostle puts himself upon a level with the common elders of a church,

that

---

* Whether Universal Bishop, or Vicar of Christ, Supreme Head, Lord or Governor of the World, or a more blasphemous title, is uncertain, the writer not hearing distinctly the Latin words in which it was expressed.

that he might not seem to take state upon him, not to rule as a lion, but with a rod of love; *the elder to the well-beloved Gaius, whom I love in the truth.* This Gaius seems to be in our modern language, what we call a gentleman, particularly remarkable for his hospitality, *Gaius mine host;* and this Gaius was well-beloved, not only beloved, but well-beloved; that is, one who I greatly esteem and am fond of; but then he shows us likewise upon what this fondness is founded, *whom I love in the truth.* There are a great many people in writing say, *dear sir,* or *good sir,* and subscribe *your humble servant, sir;* and not one word of truth either in the beginning or end; but John and Gaius's love was in truth, not only in words, *but in deed and in truth;* as if he had said, my heart goes along with my hand while I am writing, and it gives me pleasure in such a correspondence as this, or *whom I love for the truth's sake,* that is, whom I love for being particularly attached to the truth; and then our friendship has a proper foundation, when the love of God, and the Spirit of the Lord Jesus, is the basis and bond of it. One would think this was enough now; the epistles originally were not divided into verses as now that people

ple may the better find out particular places, though perhaps not altogether so properly as they might. The apostle's saying *beloved* is not needless tautology, but proves the strength of his affection; *I wish that thou mayst prosper, and be in health, even as thy soul prospereth.* Gaius, it seems, at this time felt a weak constitution, or a bad habit of body; this may show, that the most useful persons, the choicest favourites of heaven, must not expect to be without the common infirmities of the human frame; so far from this, that it is often found that a thousand useful Christians have weakly constitutions. That great and sweet singer of Israel, Dr. Watts, I remember about two and thirty years ago told me that he had got no sleep for three months, but what was procured by the most exquisite art of the most eminent physicians; and, my dear hearers, none but those that have such habits of body can sympathize with those that are under them. When we are in high spirits we think people might do if they would, but when brought down ourselves we cannot; but notwithstanding his body was in this condition, his soul prospered so eminently, so very eminently, that the apostle could not think it a greater mercy,

or

or the church a greater blessing, than that his bodily health might be as vigorous as the health of his soul. I remember the great colonel Gardiner, who had the honour of being killed in his country's cause, closes one of his last letters to me, with wishing I might enjoy a thriving soul in a healthy body; but this is peculiar to the followers of Jesus, they find the soul prospers most when the body is worst; and observe, he wishes him a prospering body above all things, that he might have joy and health with a prosperous soul; for if we have a good heart, and good health at the same time, and our hearts are alive to God, we go on with a fresh gale. I observe, that the soul of man in general must be made a partaker of a divine life before it can be said to prosper at all. The words of our text are particularly applicable to a renewed heart, to one that is really alive to God. When a tree is dead we don't so much as expect leaves from it, nor to see any beauty at all in a plant or flower that we know is absolutely dead; and therefore the foundation of the apostle's wish lies here, that the soul of Gaius, and consequently the souls of all true believers, have life communicated to them from the Spirit of the living God.

Such a life may God of his infinite mercy impart to each of us! and I think, if I am not mistaken, and I believe I may venture to say that I am not, that where the divine life is implanted by the Spirit of the living God, that life admits of decrease and increase, admits of dreadful decays, and also of some blessed revivings. The rays of the divine life being once implanted, it will grow up to eternal life; the new creation is just like the old when God said *let there be light, there was light*, which never ceased since the universe was made, and the favourite creature man was born. Upon a survey of his own works, God pronounced *every thing good, and entered into his rest*; so it will be with all those who are made partakers of the divine nature. *The water that I shall give him, shall be a well of water springing up into everlasting life.*

My brethren, from our first coming into the world, till our passing out of it to *the spirits of just men made perfect*, all the Lord's Children have found, some more, and others less, that they have had dreadful as well as blessed times, and all has been over-ruled to bring them nearer unto God: but I believe, I am sure, I speak to some this night, that if it

was

was put to their choice, had rather know that their souls prospered, than to have ten thousand pounds left them: and it is supposed that we may not only know it ourselves, but that others may know it, *that their profiting*, as Paul says, *may appear to all.* Because John says, *I wish above all things, that thy body may be in health, as thy soul prospers.* O may all that converse with us see it in us! We may frequently sit under the gospel, but if we don't take a great deal of care, however orthodox we are, we shall fall into practical Antinomianism, and be contented that we were converted twenty or thirty years ago, and learn, as some Antinomians, *to live by faith.* Thank God, say some, we met with God so many months ago, but are not at all solicitous whether they meet with him any more; and there is not a single individual here that is savingly acquainted with Jesus Christ, but wishes his soul prospered more than his body.

The great question is, how shall I know that my soul prospers? I have been told that there is such a thing as knowing this, and that I can be conscious of it myself, and others too. It may not be mispending an hour, to lay down some marks whereby we may know
whe-

whether our souls prosper or no. If there be any of you of an Antinomian turn of mind, (I don't know there are any of you) I don't know but you will be of the same mind of the man that came to me in Leadenhall twenty-five years ago: Sir, says he, you preached upon the marks of the new birth. Marks, says I, yes, sir: O thank God, says he, I am above marks, I don't mind marks at all: and you may be assured persons are upon the brink of Antinomianism, that say away with your legal preaching. I wonder they don't say as they go along the streets, away with your dials, away with your dials, we don't want marks, we know what it is o'clock without any. If the marks upon the soul of a believer are like the sun-dial, there are marks to prove that we are upon the right foundation: if the sun does not shine on the sun-dial, there is no knowing what o'clock it is; but let it shine, and instantaneously you know the time of the day; this is not known when it is cloudy; and who dare to say but that a child of God, for want of the sun of righteousness shining upon his heart, may write bitter things against himself. A good man may have the vapours, as one Mr. Brown had, that wrote

a book

a book of good hymns, who was so vapourish, that no body could make him believe he had a soul at all. Let the sun shine, the believer can see whether the sun is in the meridian at the sixth, ninth, or twelfth hour. O that there might be great searching of heart. I have been looking up to God for direction; I hope the preaching of this may be to awaken some, to call back some backsliders, to awaken some sinners that don't care whether their souls prosper or no. I don't mean the Tabernacle comers, or the Foundery comers, or the church, or dissenters, but I speak to all of you, of whatever denomination you are; God of his infinite mercy give you his Spirit. You that are believers, come, let us have that common name among us all; if we have got it, we go off well. If you want to know whether your souls prosper, that is, whether they are healthy; you know what a person means when he wishes your body to prosper; let me ask you how it is between you and God, with respect to secret prayer? Good Mr. Bunyan says, if we are prayerless, we are Christless. None of God's people, says he, come into the world still-born. Good Mr. Birket (whose commentary has gone through

five

five or six-and-twenty editions; and yet I think if he was now alive, and to preach once or twice a day, they would cry, Away with his commentary, and preaching and all) speaks to the same purpose. *Come into the world still-born!* what language is that in a preacher's mouth? but it will do for those that like to use marks and signs. *I will pour out a Spirit of grace and supplication*, says the Lord; and I will venture to say, if the Spirit of grace resides in the heart, the Spirit of supplication will not be wanting. Persons under their first love dare not go without God; they go to God, not as the formalist does, not for fear of going to hell, or being damned. It is a mercy any thing drives to prayer; and a person under the spirit of bondage, that has been just brought to the liberty of the sons of God, goes freely to his heavenly father, under the discoveries and constraints of divine love. Come, I will appeal to yourselves; did not you, like a dear fond mother, if the child, the beloved child, made but the least noise in the world, O, says the mother, the dear child crys, I must go and hush it: so time was, when many hearkened to the call of God, and could no more keep from the presence of God in secret, than a

fond

fond mother from the presence of her dear child. Now if your souls do prosper, this connection between you and God will be kept up; I don't say that you will always have the same fervour as when you first set out; I don't say you will always be carried up into the third heavens; the animal spirits possibly will not admit of such solace; but you should enquire with yourselves, whether you would be easy to be out of God's company? Steal from behind your counter, and go and converse with God. Sir Thomas Abney, who was observable for keeping up constant prayer in his family, being asked how he kept up prayer that night he was sworn in Lord-Mayor? Very well, says he, I got the company into my room, and entertained them, and when the time came, I told them I must leave them a little, while I went and prayed with my family, and returned again. God grant we may have many such Lord-Mayors. If our souls prosper, the same principle will reign in us, and make us conscientiously attend on the means of grace. It is a most dreadful mark of an enthusiastic turn of mind, when persons think they are so high in grace, that they thank God they have no need of ordinances.

nances. Our being the children of God, is so far from being the cause of our wanting no ordinances, that, properly speaking, the ordinances are intended for the nourishing of the children of God; not only for the awaking the soul at first, but for the feeding the soul afterwards. If the same nourishment the child receives before, feeds it after it is born; and as the manna never failed, but the children of Israel partook of it daily while in the wilderness, till they came to Canaan, so we shall want our daily bread, we shall want the God of grace and mercy to convey his divine life into our hearts, till we get into the heavenly Canaan. There faith will be turned into vision, and then we shall not want ordinances; and let people say what they will, if our souls prosper we shall be glad of ordinances, we shall love the place where God dwells; we shall not say, *such a one preaches and I will not go*, but if we are among them we shall be glad of a good plain country dish, as well as a fine garnished desert; and if our souls prosper, we shall be fond of the messengers as well as the message: we shall admire as much to hear a good ram's-horn, such as blowed down the walls of Jericho, as a fine silver trumpet. So in all the ordinances of the Lord, that of the Lord's-supper for example; if the soul does not attend thereon, it is an evidence that it does not prosper. It is a wonder if that soul has not done something to make it afraid to meet God at his table. *Adam, where art thou?* says the eternal Logos to his fallen creature; and every time we miss, whether we think of it or no, the Redeemer puts it down; but if our souls prosper, how shall we run to the table of the Lord, and be glad to come often to the commemoration of his death.

I will venture to affirm farther, that if your souls prosper, you will grow downwards. What is that? why you will grow in the knowledge of yourselves. I heard, when I was at Lisbon, that some people there began at the top of the house first. It is odd kind of preaching that will do for the Papists, resting merely in externals. The knowledge of ourselves is the first thing God implants. *Lord, let me know myself*, was a prayer that one of the Fathers put up for sixteen years together; and if you have high thoughts of yourselves, you may know you are light-headed, you forget what poor silly creatures you are. As our souls prosper we shall be more and more sensible,

ble, not only of the outside, but of the inside; we first battle with the outward man, but as we advance in the divine life, we have nearer views of the chambers of imagery that are in our hearts; and one day after another we shall find more and more abominations there, and consequently we shall see more of the glory of Jesus Christ, the wonders of that Immanuel, who daily delivers us from this body of sin and death; and I mention this, because there is nothing more common, especially with young Christians. I used formerly to have at least a hundred or two hundred in a day, who would come and say, O dear, I am so and so, I met with God; ah! that is quite well: a week after they would come and say, O, sir, it is all delusion, there was nothing in it; what is the matter? O never was such a wretch as I am, I never thought I had such a wicked heart. Oh! God cannot love me; now, sir, all my fervour, and all that I felt is gone; and what then? does a tree never grow but when it grows upward? some trees I fancy grow downward; and the deeper you grow in the knowledge of yourself, the deeper you grow in the knowledge of God and his grace, that discovers the corruptions of your hearts. Do
not

not you find that aged men look back upon some former states. I know some people can't look back to see how many sins they have been guilty of; but if grace helps us to a sight of our inherent corruptions, it will make us weary of it, and lead us to the blood of Christ to cleanse us from it; consequently, if your souls prosper, the more you will fall in love with the glorious Redeemer, and with his righteousness. I never knew a person in my life that diligently used the word, and other means, but as they improved in grace, saw more and more the necessity of depending upon a better righteousness than their own. Generally when we first set out, we have got better hearts than heads; but if we grow in the divine life, our heads will grow as well as our hearts, and the Spirit of God leads out of abominable self, and causes us to flee more and more to that glorious and compleat righteousness that Jesus Christ wrought out.

The more your souls prosper, the more you will see of the freeness and distinguishing nature of God's grace, that all is of grace. We are all naturally free-willers, and generally young ones say, O we have found the Messiah, of whom Moses and the prophets spoke;

which

which is right, except that word *we* have found; for the believer a little after learns, that the *Messiah* had found him. I mention this, because we ought not to make persons offenders for a word; we should bear with young Christians, and not knock a young child's brains out, because he cannot speak in blank verse.

Let it not be forgotten also, that the more your souls prosper, the more you will get above the world. You cannot think that I mean you should be negligent about the things of this life. Nothing tries my temper more, than to see any about me idle; an idle person tempts the devil to tempt him. In the state of paradise Adam and Eve were to dress the garden, and not to be idle there; after the fall they were to till the ground: but if any body says that the Methodists think to be idle, they injure them. We tell people to rise and be at their work early and late, that they may redeem time to attend the word. If all that speak against the Methodists were as diligent, it would be better for their wives and families. What do you think a true Methodist will be idle? no, he will be busy with his hands, he knows time is precious, and
there-

therefore he will work hard that he may have to give to them that need, and at the same time he will live above the world; and you know the earth is under your feet, so is the world. When he goes to sleep he will say, I care not whether I wake more. I can look back, and tell you of hundreds and hundreds that once seemed alive to God, and have been drawn away with a little filthy, nasty dirt. How many places are there empty here, that have been filled with persons that once were zealous in their attendance? As a person the other day, to whose having a place it was objected, that he was a Methodist; no, says he, I have not been a Methodist these two years. I do not, for my part, wish people joy when they get money; only take care it does not get into, and put your eyes out; if your money increases, let your zeal for good works increase. Perhaps some stranger will say, I thought you was against good works. I tell you the truth, I am against good works, don't run away before I have finished my sentence; we are against good works being put in the room of Christ, as the ground of our acceptance; but we look upon it, if we have a right faith, our faith will work by love.

Ever

Ever since I was a boy, I remember to have heard a story of a poor indigent beggar, who asked a clergyman to give him his alms, which being refused, he said, will you please, sir, to give me your blessing; says he, God bless you: O, replied the beggar, you would not give me that if it was worth any thing. There are many who will talk very friendly to you, but if they suppose you are come for any thing, they will run away as from a pick-pocket; whereas, if our souls prospered, we should *count it more blessed to give than to receive.* When we rise from our beds this would be our question to ourselves, what can I do for God to day? what can I do for the poor? have I two, or five, or ten talents? God help me to do for the poor as much as if I knew I was to live only this day.

In a word, if your souls prosper, my dear hearers, you will grow in love. There are some good souls, but very narrow souls; they are so afraid of loving people that differ from them, that it makes me uneasy to see it. Party spirits creep in among Christians, and whereas it was formerly said, *see how these Christians love one another!* now it may be said, *see how these Christians hate one another!*

I de-

I declare from the bottom of my heart, that I am more and more convinced that the principles I have preached are the word of God. Pray what do you do at Change; is there such a thing as a Presbyterian, or Independent, or Church-walk there? is there any chambers there for the Presbyterians, and Independents, and Churchmen to deal in? People may boast of their wildfire-zeal for God, till they can't bear the sight of a person that differs from them. The apostle commends Gaius for his catholic love, for his love to strangers. That was a glorious saying of a good woman in Scotland, *Come in*, says she, *ye blessed of the Lord*; I have a house that will hold a hundred, and a heart that will hold ten thousand. God give us such a heart; *he that dwelleth in love, dwelleth in God.* I could mention twenty marks, and so go on wire-drawing till nine or ten o'clock; but it is best to deal with our souls as with our bodies, to eat but little at a time. It is so with preaching; though I don't proceed any farther in my discourse, God bless what has been said.

But is there a child of God here that can go away without a drooping heart? I don't speak that you may think me humble: I love sincerity,

cerity, inward and outward, and hate guile. When I think what God has done to me, how often he has pruned me, and dug and dung'd about me, and when I think how little I have done for God, it makes me weep if possible tears of blood; it makes me cry, O *my leanness, my leanness*, as I expressed myself with my friend to day. This makes me long, if my strength of body would permit, to begin to be in earnest for my Lord. What say you, my dear friends, have all of you got the same temper? have you made the progress you ought to have done? O London! London! highly favoured London! what would some people give for thy privileges? what would the people I was called to preach to but this day se'ennight? A good, a right honourable lady, about three-and-twenty miles off, has brought the gospel there. The people that I preached to longed and thirsted after the same message; they said, they thought they never heard the truth before. You have the manna poured out round the camp, and I am afraid you are calling it *light bread*; at least, I am afraid you have had a bad digestion. Consider of it, and for Jesus Christ's sake tremble for fear *God should remove his candlestick from among*

among you. Labourers are sick; those that did once labour are almost worn out, and others they only bring themselves into a narrow sphere, and so confine their usefulness. There are few that like to go out in the fields; broken heads and dead cats are no more the ornaments of a Methodist, but silk scarves. Those honourable badges are now no more: the langour has got from the ministers to the people, and if you don't take care, we shall all fall dead together. The Lord Jesus rouse us, the Son of God rouse us all. Ye should show the world the way, and ye that have been Methodists of many years standing, show the young ones that have not the cross to bear as we once had, what ancient Methodism was.

As for you who are quite negligent about the prosperity of your souls, who only mind your bodies, who are more afraid of a pimple in your faces, than of the rottenness of your hearts; that will say, O give me a good bottle and a fowl, and keep the prosperity of your souls to yourselves. You had better take care what you say, for fear God should take you at your word. I knew some tradesmen and farmers, and one had got a wife perhaps with a fortune too, who prayed they might be excused,

excused, they never came to the supper, and God sent them to hell for it too; this may be your case. I was told to-day of a young woman, that was very well on Sunday when she left her friends, when she came home was racked with pain, had an inflammation in her bowels, and is now a breathless corpse. Another that I heard of, a Christless preacher, that always minded his body, when he was near death he said to his wife, I see hell opened for me, I see the damned tormented, I see such a one in hell that I debauched; in the midst of his agony he said, I am coming to thee, I am coming, I must be damned, God will damn my soul, and died. Take care of jesting with God; there is room enough in hell, and if you neglect the prosperity of your souls what will become of you? what will you give for a grain of hope when God requires your souls? *awake thou that sleepest*; hark! hark! hark! hear the word of the Lord, the living God. Help me, O ye children of God: I am come with a warrant from Jesus of Nazareth to night. Ye ministers of Christ that are here, help me with your prayers: ye servants of the living God, help me with your prayers. O with what success did I preach in Moorfields when I had

ten

ten thousand of God's people praying for me; pray to God to strengthen my body: don't be afraid I shall hurt myself to-night: I don't care what hurt I do myself if God may bless it; I can preach but little, but may God bless that little. I weep and cry and humble myself before God daily for being laid aside; I would not give others the trouble if I could preach myself. You have had the first of me, and you will have the last of me: the angels of God waited for your conversion, and are now ready to take care of the soul when it leaves the rotten carcase. The worst creature under heaven, that has not a penny in the world, may be welcome unto God. However it has been with us in times past, may our souls prosper in time to come; which God grant of his infinite mercy, Amen.

SERMON IV.

The Gospel a dying Saint's Triumph.

A FUNERAL SERMON.

MARK xvi. ver. 15, 16.

And he said unto them, Go ye into all the world, and preach the gospel to every creature. He that believeth and is baptized shall be saved, but he that believeth not shall be damned.

I AM persuaded I need not inform this auditory, that when ambassadors are sent to a prince, or when judges go their respective circuits, it is always customary for them to show their credentials, to open and read their commissions, by which they act in his Majesty's name. The same is absolutely necessary for those who are ambassadors of the Son of God, as they would be faithful to their Lord; since they are to sit with him on the throne,

throne, when he shall come the second time to judge both evil angels and men. If any should ask me, where is their commission? it has been just now read unto you. Here it is in my hand, it is written with the King's own hand, by the finger of the ever-blessed God, and sealed with the signet of his eternal Spirit, with his broad seal annexed to it. The commission is short, but very extensive; and it is remarkable, it was given out just before the Redeemer went to heaven; he reserved it in infinite wisdom for his last blessing, to appoint and employ vicegerents to carry on his work on earth. *He that hath an ear to hear, let him hear* what the Son of God says to a company of poor fishermen. There was not one scholar among them all. What does he say; *Go ye into all the world, and preach the gospel to every creature.* Let us pause a while, and before we go further let us see what mercy, what love, and yet withal, what equal majesty are blended in this expression or commission. *Go ye*, ye poor fishermen, ye that the letter-learned doctors will look upon as illiterate men; *Go ye*, that have hitherto been dreaming of temporal preferments, quarrelling *who should sit on my right hand and on my left hand*

hand in my kingdom; Go ye, not stay till the people come to you, but imitate the conduct of your Master; *Go ye,* remembring that the devil will not permit souls to be fond of hearing you: Go therefore; where? *into all the world;* there is a commission for you; there never was such a commission on the earth; there never was any like this; *Go into all the world,* that is, into the Gentile as well as the Jewish world. Hitherto my gospel has been confined to the Jews; I once told you, you must not go to the Gentiles; I once told a poor woman that came to me, *it is not meet to take the childrens bread, and give it unto dogs:* but the partition wall being now broke down, the veil of the temple being now rent in twain, he gave them a universal commission; *Go ye, therefore, into all the world;* how! what go into other ministers parishes? for there was not a district then but what was settled with shepherds, such as they were; yes, yes, *Go into all the world;* and though I will not pretend to say, that this enjoins ministers to go into every part of the world; yet I insist upon it, and by the grace of God, if I was to die for it, I will say, that no power on earth has power to restrain ministers from

preach-

preaching where a company of people are willing to hear; and if ministers were of a right temper, they would say as a minister did at Oxford, that used to visit the prisoners there; I remember once I went to ask him whether I might go and visit some of his parish, whether he was offended at our going to visit the prisoners? No, no, says he, I am glad I have any such young curates as you. And if ministers were of such a temper now, O dear the devil would fly before us. As good Mr. Philip Henry said to the minister of Broad Oaks, from whence he was ejected, but preached afterwards in a barn, and meeting the minister after sermon was over; *Sir*, says Mr. Henry, *I have been making bold to throw a handful of seed into your ground.* Thank you, sir, says he, God bless it, there is work enough for us both. We may talk of what we will, search into the bottom, it is not for want of light, but of more zeal and love to the Son of God: if we were as warm, and full of the love of God as we ought to be, these pretty excuses we urge to save our bones, would not be so much as mentioned; we should go out and leave these carcases to the grace of God. I don't see how we can act as priests of the church of England without doing it. Be so kind as read the Ordination Service as soon as you go home; for the office of ordination and consecration of bishops, priests, and deacons, is left out of most of the common prayer books, so that people are as ignorant of it as if it was not. The office of a priest is this: he is not to confine himself to his place, no; what then? why he is *to go forth, and seek after the children of God that are dispersed in this needy world*; these are the very words that the bishop speaks to us when we are ordained; but if we are confined to one particular place, and are to be shut up in one corner, pray how do we seek the children of God that are dispersed in this needy world? Parishes and settled ministers there must be, but we are not, I insist on it, to be hindered from preaching Christ any where, because he bids us *go into all the world*; here is our licence. I acknowledge the Chapel is licensed; here is my licence, and wherever I go I will produce my licence; where? why out of the 16th of Mark; *Go ye, and preach the gospel to all the world:* there is the licence, and the Spirit of Christ helping us to preach by that licence, will make all the devil's children cowards

cowards before us. We have tried them these thirty years, would to God we set about it now; if I had strength I would set about it to-morrow; I only grieve that my body will not hold out for field-preaching, else Kennington-Common should be my pulpit, for any place is consecrated where Christ is present. Well, what must we go forth to do? *Go ye into all the world, and preach;* preach! what is that? why the original word for preach is to speak out, as a crier does that cries goods that are lost; proclaim it. And Isaiah would be reckoned a dreadful enthusiast if now alive. How does he preach? he preaches in the King's chapels such language and eloquence as would carry all before it; and yet how does he preach? *Ho, every one that thirsteth.* O, *he lifts up his voice like a trumpet.* And the word preach signifies to proclaim; *to cry aloud, and spare not.* How do you like one that cries your lost goods if he only whispers? would you chuse to employ a man that you could not hear two yards? O, say you, I shall never find my goods: and if persons have what qualifications they may, if they cannot be heard at all; they need not preach at all. I know a prebend in the cathe-

dral

dral of York, who spoke so very low nobody heard him; somebody said, they never heard such a *moving* sermon in all their lives in that cathedral, for it made all the people *move out*, because they could not hear. The matter of the ministry of the gospel is of infinite importance: unless, my brethren, we could be heard, what do we preach for? It implies earnestness in the preaching, and the preacher. You expect a person, like one that is crying your goods, to be in earnest; and if we preach, and make the King's proclamation, we should be in earnest. It is said, *Christ opened his mouth and taught*. Now a modern critic would laugh at that; open his mouth, say they, how could he speak without opening his mouth? Would it not be better to say, *he taught them?* No, no, there is no idle word in God's book. It is said, *the Lord Jesus opened his mouth:* what for? why, to get in breath that he might speak loud to the people, when the heavens were his founding board; then did he open his mouth, and taught them in earnest, powerfully; and therefore the people make this observation when he had done speaking, *that he spoke as one having authority, and not as the Scribes.* There is no dispensation

tion from preaching, but sickness or want of abilities, to those that are ordained to preach; and therefore it was a proverb in the primitive church, *that it becomes a bishop to die preaching.* Bishop Jewell, that blessed minister of the church of England, gave that answer to a person that met his lordship walking on foot in the dirt, going to preach to a few people. Why does your lordship, weak as you are, expose yourself thus? says he, it becomes a bishop to die preaching. Lord send all the world that have bishops such jewels as he was! Pray what are they to preach? not themselves. What are they to preach? why they are to preach not morality: not morality! come, don't be frightened, any of you that are afraid of good works don't be frightened this morning: I say not morality; that is, morality is not to be the grand point of their preaching; they are not to preach as an heathen philosopher would. A late bishop of Lincoln, who has not been dead a long while, said to his chaplain, You are not a minister of Cicero, or any of the heathen philosophers; you are not to entertain your people with dry morality, but remember you are a minister of Christ; you are, therefore, to preach the gospel; and if

you

you will not preach the gospel in the church, you must not be angry for the poor people's going out into the fields where they hear the gospel; that is to be your grand theme, *Go into all the world and preach the gospel.*

Now the gospel signifies good news, glad tidings: *Behold I bring you,* said the angel, *glad tidings of great joy.* Mean and contemptible as the office of a preacher may be thought now, the angels were glad of the commission to preach this gospel: and Dr. Goodwin, that learned pious soul, says in his familiar way, and that is the best way of writing, God had but one Son, and he made a minister of him; and I add, he made an itinerant minister of him too. Well, and some say, you must not preach the law; you cannot preach the gospel without preaching the law; for you shall find by and by, we are to preach something that the people must be saved by: it is impossible to tell them how they are to be saved, unless we tell them what they are to be saved from. The way the Spirit of God takes, is like that we take in preparing the ground: do you think any farmer would have a crop of corn next year unless they plow now; and you may as well expect a crop of corn on
un-

unplowed ground, as a crop of grace, until the foul is convinced of its being undone without a Saviour. That is the reason we have so many mushroom converts, so many persons that are always happy! happy! happy! and never were miserable; why? because their stony ground is not plowed up; they have not got a conviction of the law; they are stony-ground hearers; *they hear the word with joy, and in a time of temptation*, which will soon come after a seeming or real conversion, *they fall away*, They serve Christ as the young man served the Jews that laid hold of him, who, when he found he was like to be a prisoner for following Christ, left his garments; and so some people leave their profession. That makes me so cautious now, which I was not thirty years ago, of dubbing people converts so soon. I love now to wait a little, and see if people bring forth fruit; for there are so many blossoms which March winds you know blow away, that I cannot believe they are converts till I see fruit brought forth. It will do converts no harm to keep them a little back; it will never do a sincere soul any harm.

We are to preach the gospel: to whom? *to every creature*: here is the commission, *every crea-*

creature. I suppose the apostles were not to see every creature; they did not go into all nations; they had particular districts; but wherever they did go, they preached. Did you ever hear Paul, or any of the apostles, sent away a congregation without a sermon? No, no: when turned out of the temple they preached in the highways, hedges, streets, and lanes of the city: they went to the water-side; there Lydia was catched. My brethren, we have got a commission here from Christ; and not only a commission, but we have a command *to preach to every creature*; all that are willing to hear. *He that hath an ear to hear, let him hear*; and if some shall say, they will not come if we do preach, would to God we tried them: *where the carcase is there will the eagles be gathered together*. We are to preach glad tidings of salvation; to tell a poor benighted world, lying in the wicked one the devil, their state and condition: we are to tell them, *God is love*; to tell them, that God loves them better than they do themselves. We must preach the law, but not leave the people there. We must tell them how Moses brings them to the borders of Canaan, and then tell them of a glorious Joshua that will carry them

them over Jordan; first, to shew them their wants; and then point out to them a Jesus that can supply, and more than supply, all their wants. This we are *to tell every creature*; and it is for this that people stone gospel preachers. I don't think the prisoners would be angry with us if we were to tell them, the king commissions us to declare to them that they might come out of their prison, that their chains may be knocked off. If you was to go to one of them and say, Here you have your chains; and he was to say, I have no chains on at all; you would think that man's brains turned; and so are every man's that does not see himself to be in the chains of sin and deceit. We are *to preach liberty to the captives, to proclaim the acceptable year of the Lord; sound the jubilee trumpet, and tell them the year of release is come*; that Jesus can make them happy.

But, pray, if we are to preach, what are the creatures to do that see their need of this salvation? I will tell you; they are to believe. *He that believeth, and is baptized*, &c. The grand topics Christ's ministers are to preach, are *repentance towards God, and faith in our Lord Jesus Christ*. The men of the world fancy

fancy they have believed already, and some of them lift up their heads and say, Thank God, we have believed ever since we were born; and in one sense many people believe, but in what sense? just as the devil believes; they believe, and still continue devils in their carnal state; that is, they assent to the gospel, they assent to it as a thing that is credible. This is our school definition of faith; and I believe there are thousands that call themselves Christians, that don't believe a thousandth part of what the devil does. The devil believes more than an Arian, for he does not believe Christ to be God; the devil says, *I know whom thou art, the Holy One of God.* The devil will rise up in judgment against him. He believes more than a Socinian, who believes Jesus Christ to be no more than an extraordinary man; and he believes more of Jesus Christ than thousands of professors do, who are neither Arians or Socinians. There are a thousand things in this book * that many people, if you come to close-quarters with them, will say they do not believe, though they are ashamed to own it. The furthest that they go, is to assent to the Creed, to the Lord's-prayer,

* Holding out his bible.

prayer, and Ten Commandments; and if a person can say these in their mother tongue, and have been baptized by the prieſt, and confirmed by the biſhop, and go to church once a week, and now and then on holidays, they think they are not only believers, but ſtrong believers. I am not againſt going to church, nor againſt the Creed, the Lord's-prayer, and the Commandments; I love and honour them, and I pray God we may always have them; and I would not have our liturgy or articles departed from for ten thouſand worlds. Many would have them altered, becauſe there are ſome faults in them; but if our modern people were to alter them, they would make them ten thouſand times worſe than they are. But believing is ſomething more; it is a coming to Jeſus Chriſt, receiving Jeſus, rolling ourſelves on Jeſus; it is a truſting in the Lord Jeſus. I do not know any one ſingle thing more variouſly expreſſed in the ſcriptures than believing; why? becauſe it is the marrow of the goſpel. Without faith we cannot be juſtified, either in our perſons or performances; and therefore the Holy Ghoſt has variouſly expreſſed it, to let us ſee the importance of the point. It is expreſſed by a coming, truſting, receiving, and relying, (all which amounts to the same thing) under a felt conviction that we are lost, undone, condemned without him: for, as a good old Puritan observes, Christ is beholden to none of us for our hearts; we never should come to Jesus Christ, the sinner's last shift, till we feel we cannot do without him. We are like the woman with the bloody issue; she spent a great deal of money upon physicians; if she had had the sum of one half-guinea more, till that was gone she never would have come to Christ; but having spent all, and then hearing that Jesus was to come that way, a sense of her need, a feeling sense of her impotence, and insufficiency of all other applications, made her come to Christ; saying in her heart, *If I could but touch the hem of his garment I should be whole; Jesus, the son of David, would have mercy on me;* or words to that purpose. She did not go about and say, pray lend me a common-prayer book; it was not in print then. Where must she borrow one? her heart, touched by God, was the best common-prayer; and a few words, uttered from a sense of her weakness and misery, was more rhetoric, was more music in the ears of God, than an extempore prayer

prayer by a gifted man, admiring himself for an hour and half. As a person told me but yesterday, of a poor outlandish Papist that was condemned to die, held out for a long while; he would not speak to a Protestant minister, but a night or two before he suffered, comes out to him, and says, *Me now see the necessity of a greater absolution than a priest can give me*; and then, in his broken language, cries out, *Dear Lord Jesus, show thy charity to thy poor sinner!* There is language! there is rhetoric for you! and we ourselves like such language. You don't like fawning people that come into your room, and by their very manner of coming prove they are not sincere; but a poor creature that comes to pour out two or three words you see is honest, you will not say to such a one, Why do you come to me, and not speak blank verse? why do you come to me, and not speak fine language? No; sincerity is the thing; sincerity is all in all. When we are once convinced of our need and helplessness, and of Jesus's being a Redeemer, that is mighty and willing to save, a poor soul then throws himself upon this Jesus, receives this Jesus, ventures upon this Jesus, believes the word, and by thus venturing on the promise,

mise, receives from Jesus the thing promised. *Faith comes by hearing, and hearing by the word of God.* But then where there is true faith, that will, my dear hearers, be attended with what? why, with salvation. *He that believeth, and is baptized,* saith our Lord, *shall be saved:* saved from what? why, from every thing that he wants to be saved from, and receives every thing that God can give to compleat his whole salvation. What is it a poor sinner wants to be saved from? O, sin, sin, the guilt of sin. The first conviction brings the creatures to God by force; there are very few that are drawn by love intirely: and I seldom find any of those that have been drawn by love, but have had dreadful conflicts afterwards: for either before or after conversion, our hearts must be plowed up, or we shall never be prepared for the kingdom of heaven.

Ye shall be saved from the painful guilt of sin: what is that? why, the common-prayer book will tell you, in the communion office; *the remembrance of our sins is grievous unto us, and the burden of them is intolerable.* There is methodistical language. Cranmer, Latimer, or Hooper, were, my brethren, what? why, they were Methodist preachers; and they used

to

to preach in Paul's-Cross, a pulpit said to be made in the shape of a cross, near St. Paul's church; and a salary given for that very purpose, I believe, to this day. No matter where we preach, so that sinners feel Christ's power in delivering them from this, which certainly implies a consciousness of pardon. I don't think the poor creature that was respited the other day, would have believed it, had he not seen the king's warrant just before the others were carried out. Why, say they, here is his majesty's pardon; he takes and receives it with joy, and is now freed from the gallows. And if persons can give this credence to an earthly king, why cannot a believer have a sense of the pardon of his sins from God? If a person's reading this to me, telling me the king has pardoned me, has such an effect, why may not God's word, backed by his Spirit, be brought home with such power on my heart, that I may be assured God has pardoned me, as well as a criminal that his king has saved? If this is gospel away with it, say some, who think we are not to be justified till we come to judgment. O blessed creatures! this is modern divinity! our reformers knew nothing about it. We are to be declared, if you please, justified,

in

in the day of Jesus Christ, who will pronounce it before all mankind. But, my brethren, we are to be married to Jesus Christ in this world, and the marriage is to be declared in another; and I will insist upon it, though I will not pretend to say that all that have not full assurance are not Christians, yet I will say, that assurance is necessary for the well-being of a Christian; the comfortable being, though not for his very existence: and I will venture to say, that a soul was never brought to Christ, but what had some ground of assurance of pardon; tho', for want of knowing better, he put it by, and did not know the gift of God when it came. But, my brethren, *we shall be saved from all our sins.* Here is *glad tidings of great joy* now come: satan may hear that; and any of you here that are coming into the Chapel as you pass along. I am glad to see poor creatures come, that I may tell them, *God is love.* Believers, you shall be saved from all your sins, every one of them; they shall all be blotted out. Generally, when persons are convinced, the devil preaches despair; some great sin lies upon them; and, says the poor sinner, I shall be saved from all but that; had I not been guilty of such a crime I might have hope, but

I am

I am guilty of such a sin, which is so awful, with such dreadful aggravations, I am afraid I shall never be pardoned. But, my dear souls, Christ is love; and when he loves to forgive, he forgives like a God; *I will blot out your iniquities, transgressions, and sins. Come now,* saith the Lord, *let us reason together; though your sins are as scarlet, yet they shall be as white as snow.* I am so far from being unwilling to save or pardon, that the angels, every time the gospel is preached, are ready to tune their harps, and long to sing an anthem to some poor sinner's conversion.

They shall be saved from the power of sin. Don't you remember that when Joshua was going on with his conquests, that there were some kings in a cave; and when he returned, he ordered them to bring the kings out for God's people to tread upon them. When I read that passage, I used to think these kings were like our corruptions hid in the cave of our hearts, and the stone of unbelief rolled to keep them in: but when we receive Christ by faith, and have pardon in him, our great Joshua takes away the stone, and says, *bring out these kings,* these corruptions, *that have reigned over my people, and by faith let them*

them tread on the necks of them. Our great Master, when he gave the command in the text, says, *these signs shall follow them that believe, in my name they shall cast out devils, they shall speak with new tongues, they shall take up serpents, and if they drink any deadly thing it shall not hurt them.* These were things peculiar, in one sense, to the apostles; but in the power of faith, and as brought home to every believer, he casts out devilish lusts; and if they had drank any deadly thing, as God knows we have, they may do by them as Paul did by the viper, through the power of faith cast them off, and by this means prove that Christ is God.

This is, my dear hearers, a present salvation. The wickedest wretch in the world will cry, I hope to be saved, though they have no notion of being saved but after their death; as a woman in Virginia told me once, when I said she must be born again; I believe you, sir, but that must be after I am dead. And by peoples living as they do, one would suppose that they think they are not to be saved till they die, because they live so. But as I have told you, I tell you again, Christ's salvation is a great salvation; and all that

Christ

Christ does for his people on earth, is but an earnest of good things to come, an anticipation of what he is to do for them in heaven. Our Lord says, *the kingdom of God is within you; the kingdom is come nigh unto you.* You must not only believe on Christ, but believe in him: we are not only to be baptized in the name of the Father, Son, and Holy Ghost, but we are to be baptized into the nature of the Father, Son, and Holy Ghost; this is the baptism of the Spirit, and this is that salvation which God grant we may all partake of.

We are to be saved, my brethren, from what? why, from the fear of death. *He came to deliver them who, through the fear of death, were all their life time subject to bondage.* What are there no children of God but those that have full assurance? you never heard me say so; yet I am apt to speak a little fast, but at the same time I would chuse not to speak so fast as to speak contrary to the word of God. There are a great many good souls, that at times may doubt of the reality of this work upon their souls: a relaxed habit of body, a nervous disorder, you may say what you please, will make a weak child of God doubt of what God has done in them, and that hurts the mind

mind as it has such a close connection with the body; but then a believer is low: God's people are low persons: as the greatest genuisses are most liable to lowness of spirit, for the scabbard is not strong enough for the sword, and persons that talk much must wear out in time; but this I stand to, it is our privilege to live above the fears of death. We do not live up to our dignity till every day we are waiting for the coming of our Lord from heaven; and I am persuaded of this, though I believe there may be some exceptions, that the reason why we do not live more above the fear of death is, because we keep in so much with these nasty earthly things. You may have the best eyes in the world, and only put your hands before them, you will find the sun hid from you; and so you may have a large fire, but throw some earth upon the fire that is in your parlour, or drawing rooms, and you will find the fire damped. And how can people have much of God or heaven, when they have so much of the earth in their hearts? It is our privilege to live above the fear of death, though we are not to be saved from dying; and I am sure a believer would not be saved from dying for a million of worlds; it would be death to him

him not to die; but a soul touched with the love of God, even in sickness, in the midst of a burning fever, in the midst of a fire that will burn a thousand bodies up, convulsed with tortures and pains in every limb; a believer is enabled sometimes to say, *O my God, O my God, thou art love; I am ready to come to thee in the midst of all.* Blessed be God, I need not go far for example; yonder, under the gallery, lies the remains, the carcase of a dear saint, who was for twenty-five days together burned with a fever, enough to scorch any creature up; yet, one filled with love and power divine, blessed the Lord Jesus; though she cried out, If I was not supported, the agony of my body would make me impatient; yet never said a murmuring word, but in the midst of all cried out to those about her, *God is love! O my joys! O the comforts that I feel!* and in her very last moments cried out, *I am a coming; dear Lord, I am a coming;* and so sweetly slept in Jesus. If this is enthusiasm, God give us a good share of it when we come to die! These are dying and yet living witnesses that *God is love!* She was in raptures when Mr. Sheppard went to visit her: she desired me to tell you, that *God is love*: desired fired me to tell you in the Chapel pulpit, that she was called about four years ago. I think Mr. Lee was the instrument of her conversion. Now her body is to be put to bed at noon; but her soul is crying, O the joys! the joys! the joys! of being saved by a blessed Emanuel! Now will any one dare to deny this evidence? Do you see worldly people work themselves up into that frame when they die? Visit them when they are near death: ah dear! they are in the vapours; they are so afraid of dying, that the doctor will not suffer us to come near them; no, not common clergymen, for fear we should damp their spirits: till they find they are just gone, and then they give us leave to say the farewel prayer to them: but they that are born from above, that are made new creatures in Christ, feel something that smiles upon them in death. She told them, *she believed God would let her go over Jordan dry shod*; that was her expression. If this is salvation on earth, what must it be in heaven? If in the midst of the tortures of a burning fever a raptured soul can cry, O the joys! O the comforts! Lord, I am coming! I am coming! what must that be when enclosed in a Redeemer's arms? in order to which, the glorious angels

angels stand at the top of the ladder to take a poor wearied pilgrim home. Lord, give us not only such a frame when we are dying, but while we are living; for if it is comfortable to die in such a frame, why not to live in it? to live in heaven on earth. O, say you, *I thank God I walk by faith;* I have got the promise. Well, thank God you have the promise; but with the promise, learn to walk by that *faith which is the evidence of things not seen,* which brings God down, brings heaven near, and gives the soul a heart-felt experience, that *God is love.* Here is a salvation worthy of a God! here is a salvation worthy of the Mediator's blood! for this he groaned, for this he bled, for this he died, for this he arose, for this he ascended, for this he sent the Holy Ghost, and for this purpose he now sends him into the hearts of his people.

My brethren, what say you to this? I hope it is enough to make you cry out, *Lord, let my latter end be like hers.* This may comfort you that are mourners about her corpse, this may comfort a fond husband, whose beloved is now taken away by a stroke. What a mercy is it, sir, that you was instrumental to bring her under the word? she was once averse

to

to coming here: *what, leave my parish church!* said she; *what, go to a conventicle, to a tabernacle of Methodists!* he advised her again and again to come: at last, one day as they were going to St. Giles's, she says, Well, come put up your walking-stick, if it falls towards St. Giles's I will go there; if to the Chapel, I will go there; the stick fell towards the Chapel, she came, and was converted to God. O with what joy must her husband meet her again in the kingdom of heaven! and O happy day, in which she was encouraged to seek after God. Last week, another was buried in the like circumstances; and, blessed be God, in yonder burying-ground are the remains of many precious souls, that in the day of judgment will let the world know whether this Chapel was built for God or not.

O what an awful word is that in the latter clause of the text, *he that believeth not shall be damned.* Pause,—I will give you time to think a little; if you would have Christ as good as his word of promise, remember he will be as good as his word of threatning. You hear the necessity of preaching the gospel, because upon believing or non-believing, our salvation or damnation will turn. What will you laugh at the minister that cries out, Lord help you

you to come; come, come, do you think that we have nothing else to say, and are at a loss for words, when we cry come, come, come, to fill up our sermons? no, it is part of our commission, it is one great part. And, my fellow-sinners, we are come to tell you, that our Master has a two-edged sword as well as a golden scepter; and if you will not come under the sound of the word, and do not feel the converting power of it, you must feel the confounding weight of it. I repeat it again to you, *he that believeth not shall be damned*; the very word is terrible, God grant you may never know how terrible it is. You are condemned already; he that believeth not is so, *John* iii. 18. why? *because he hath not believed on the name of the Son of God.* It is not his being a whore-monger or adulterer that will damn him, but his unbelief is the damning sin; for this he will be condemned; for ever banished from the presence of the ever-blessed God: and how will you rave, how will you tear, and how will you wring your hands, when you see your relations, your friends, those whom you despised, and were glad they were dead out of your way, *see them in Abraham's bosom, and yourselves lifting up your eyes in torment!* O

P   my

my dear hearers, do let me plead, let me intreat you; if that would do, I would down on my knees; if that would do, I would come down from the pulpit, I would hang on your necks, I would not let you go, I would offer myself to be trodden under your feet; I have known what it is to be trodden under the foot of men thirty years ago, and I am of the same temper still: use me as you will, I am a poor sinner; and if I was to be killed a thousand ways, I suffer no more than my reward as an unprofitable servant of God: but don't trample the dear Jesus under foot; what has he done to you? was it any harm to leave his father's bosom, come down and die, and plead for sinners? See him yonder hang on the tree! behold him with his arm stretched out! see him all of a bloody gore, and in his last agony preaching love! Would you give him a fresh stab? Are there any of you here that think the sword did not pierce him enough; that they did not knock the briers and thorns into his head deep enough? and will you give him the other flash, the other thorns? and will you pierce him afresh, and go away without believing he is love? I cannot help it; I am free from the blood of you all. Oh that you

may

may not damn your own souls! Don't be murderers; nor, like Esau, *sell your birth-right for a mess of pottage.* God convince you; God convert you; God help those that never believed to believe; God help those that have believed to believe more; that they may experience more and more this salvation, till faith is turned into vision, and hope into fruition; till we have all, with yonder saint, and all that have gone before us, experienced compleat salvation in the kingdom of heaven: even so, Lord Jesus. Amen and Amen.

SERMON V.

Repentance and Converſion.

Acts iii. ver. 19.

Repent ye therefore and be converted, that your ſins may be blotted out, when the times of refreſhing ſhall come from the preſence of the Lord.

WHAT a pity is it that modern preachers attend no more to the method thoſe took who were firſt inſpired by the Holy Ghoſt, in preaching Jeſus Chriſt! the ſucceſs they were honoured with, gave a ſanction to their manner of preaching, and the divine authority of their diſcourſes, and energy of their elocution, one would think, ſhould have more weight with thoſe that are called to diſpenſe the goſpel, than all modern ſchemes whatever. If this was the caſe, miniſters would then learn firſt to ſow, and then to reap; they would endeavour to plow up the fallow ground, and thereby prepare the people for God's raining down bleſſings upon them. Thus Peter preached when under a divine influence, as I mentioned laſt Wedneſday night: he charged the audience home, though many of them were learned and high and great, with having been the murderers of the Son of God. No doubt but the charge entered deep into their conſcience, and that faithful monitor beginning to give them a proper ſenſe of themſelves, the apoſtle lets them know that great as their ſin was, it was not unpardonable; that though they had been concerned in the horrid crime of murdering the Lord of Life, notwithſtanding they had thereby incurred the penalty of eternal death, yet there was a mercy for them, the way to which he points out in the text; *Repent ye therefore,* ſays he, *and be converted,* and adds, *that your ſins may be blotted out.* Though they are but few words, they are weighty; a ſhort ſentence this, but ſweet: may God make it a bleſſed ſweetneſs to every one of your hearts!

But muſt we preach converſion to a profeſſing people? Some of you, perhaps, are ready to ſay, go to America; go among the ſavages and preach repentance and converſion there;

or, if you must be a field-preacher, go to the highways and hedges; go to the colliers; go ramble up and down, as you used to do, preach conversion to the drunkards: would to God my commission might be renewed, that I might have strength and spirit to take the advice!

Possibly others will say, do not preach it to us; pray who are you? I answer, one sent to call you to repentance; and although I might, yet I will not come so close to you at present, as to inquire in my turn, who are you? yet permit me to pray, that while I am preaching God's Spirit may find you out; and not only let you know who you are, but what you are; and then you will not be easy with yourselves, nor angry with a minister of Jesus Christ for preaching conversion to your souls.

Repentance and conversion are nearly the same. The expression in the text is complex, and seems to include both what goes before and follows *turning to God:* and if the Lord is pleased to honour me so far to night to be useful to sinners, as well as saints, I will endeavour to shew you,

First, what it is not to be converted: secondly, what it is to be truly converted: thirdly, ly, offer some motives why you should repent and be converted: and, fourthly, answer some objections that have been made against persons repenting and being converted; and may God so bless my preaching, and your hearing, that every one may go away and say, Lord, convert me more and more.

First, I shall endeavour to show you what it is not to be converted; for I do verily believe there are thousands, and ten thousands, that think themselves converted, and yet at the same time, if you come and examine them, they know not so much as speculatively what real conversion is: the general notion many have of it is, a person's being a convert from the church of Rome to the church of England. There is a particular office in the large prayer book, to be used when any one publicly renounces popery in the great congregation. When this is done, that prayer read, and the person said Amen to the collects upon the occasion, every body wishes him joy, and thanks God he is converted; whereas, if this is all, he is as much unconverted to God as ever; he has in words renounced popery, but never took leave of the sins of his heart. Well, after this he looks into the church, and does

not

not like that white thing called a surplice; he looks, and thinks there are some rags of the whore of Babylon left still: now, says he, I will be converted; how? I will turn Dissenter: so after he is converted from the church of Rome to the church of England, he goes to the dissenting church: may be, curiosity may bring him to the Methodists, those monstrous troublesome creatures, and, perhaps, he may then be converted a third time, like their preaching, like their singing; O dear, I must have a Tabernacle-ticket, I must have a Psalm-book, I will come as often as there is preaching, or at least as often as I can; and there he sits down, and becomes an outside converted Methodist, as demure as possible.: this is going a prodigious way, and yet all this is conversion from one party only to another. If the minister gives a rub or two he will take miff perhaps, and be converted to some other persuasion, and all the while Jesus Christ is left unthought of; but this is conversion only from party to party, not real, and that which will bring a soul to heaven. Possibly, a person may go further, and be converted from one set of principles to another; he may, for instance, be born an Arminian, which all men

naturally

naturally are; and one reason why I think Calvinism right is, because proud nature will not stoop to be saved by grace. You that are brought up in an orthodox belief, under an orthodox ministry, cannot easily make an allowance for thousands that have nothing ringing in their ears but Arminianism; you have suck'd in orthodoxy with your mother's milk, and that makes so many sour and severe professors. I knew a rigid man that would beat Christianity into his wife; and so many beat people with their bibles, that they are likely, by their bitter proceeding, to hinder them from attending to the means God has designed for conversion. What is this but being converted from one set of principles to another? and I may be very zealous for them, without being transformed by them into the image of God. But some go further, they think they are converted because they are reformed: they say, *a reformed rake makes a good husband*, but I think a renewed rake will make a better. Reformation is not renovation: I may have the outside of the platter washed; I may be turned from prophaneness to a regard for morality; and because I do not swear, nor go to the play as I used to do; have left off cards;

and perhaps put on a plain dress; and so believe, or rather fancy, that I am converted; yet the old man remains unmortified, and the heart is unrenewed still. Comparing myself with what I once was, and looking on my companions with disdain, I may there stick faster in self, and get into a worse and more dangerous state than I was before. If any of you think me too severe, remember you are the person I mean; for you think me so only because I touch your case. The drunkards and sabbath-breakers, cursers and swearers, say to us, you can never preach but you preach against us: as a good man once replied to a person, who complained against us ministers for this preaching; I will put you in a way, said he, that we shall never preach against you; how is that? why, leave off cursing and swearing, &c. then your consciences will be clear, and the minister will look over your heads: happy they that are convinced of it! You have not heard me, I hope, speak a word against reformation; you have not heard me speak a word against being converted from the church of Rome; against being converted to the church of England; or, against being good: no; all these are right in their place; but all

these

these conversions you may have, and yet never be truly converted at all. What is conversion then? I will not keep you longer in suspense, my brethren: man must be a new creature, and converted from his own righteousness to the righteousness of the Lord Jesus Christ; conviction will always preceed spiritual conversion; and therefore the Protestant divines make this distinction, you may be convinced and not converted, but you cannot be converted without being convinced; and if we are truly converted, we shall not only be turned and converted from sinful self, but we shall be converted from righteous self; that is the devil of devils: for righteous self can run and hide itself in its own doings, which is the reason self-righteous people are so angry with gospel preachers; there are no such enemies to the gospel as these: *there were Jews who trusted in themselves that they were righteous*, that set all in an uproar, and raised the mob on the apostles. Our Lord denounced dreadful woes against the self-righteous Pharisees: so ministers must cut and hack them, and not spare; but say wo, wo, wo to all those that will not submit to the righteousness of Jesus Christ! I could almost say, this is the last stroke the

Lord Jesus gave Paul, I mean in turning him to real Christianity; for having given him a blow as a persecutor and injurious, he then brought him out of himself by revealing his person and office as a Saviour. *I am Jesus.*—Hence says the apostle, *I count all things but loss—that I may win Christ, and be found in him; not having my own righteousness, which is of the law, but that which is through the faith of Christ; the righteousness which is of God by faith.* You hear him not only speak of himself as injurious, as a blasphemer, but also as a Pharisee; and in vain we may talk of being converted till we are brought out of ourselves; to come as poor lost, undone sinners, to the Lord Jesus Christ; to be washed in his blood; to be cloathed in his glorious imputed righteousness: the consequence of this imputation, or application of a Mediator's righteousness to the soul, will be a conversion from sin to holiness. I am almost tempted to say, it is perverseness in people to preach against the doctrine of imputed righteousness, because they love holiness, and charge the Calvinists with being enemies to it: how can they be charged with being enemies to Sanctification, who so strenuously insist on its being the genuine

nuine fruit, and unquestionable proof of the imputation of the righteousness of Christ, and application of it by the Spirit of grace? They that are truly converted to Jesus, and are justified by faith in the Son of God, will take care to evidence their conversion, not only by the having grace implanted in their hearts, but by that grace diffusing itself through every faculty of the soul, and making a universal change in the whole man. I am preaching from a bible that saith, *He that is in Christ is a new creature, old things,* not *will* be but, *are passed away, all things,* not only *will* but, *are become new.* As a child when born has all the several parts of a man, it will have no more limbs than it has now, if it lives to fourscore years and ten; so when a person is converted to God, there are all the features of the new creature and growth, till he becomes a young man and a father in Christ; till he becomes ripe in grace, and God translates him to glory. Any thing short of this is but the shadow instead of the substance; and however persons may charge us with being enthusiasts, yet we need not be moved either to anger or sorrow, since St. Paul says, *I travel in birth till Christ be formed in your hearts.*

The

The author of this conversion is the Holy Ghost: it is not their own free will; it is not moral swasion; nothing short of the influence of the Spirit of the living God can effect this change in our hearts; therefore we are said to *be born again, born of God, of the Spirit, not of water only, but of the Holy Ghost; that which is born of the flesh is flesh, but that which is born of the Spirit is spirit:* and tho' there is and will be a contest between these two opposites, flesh and spirit, yet if we are truly converted, the spirit will get the ascendency; and though for a while nature and grace may struggle in the womb of a converted soul, like Jacob and Esau, yet the elder shall serve the younger, Jacob shall supplant and turn out Esau, or at least keep him under: God grant we may all thus prove that we are converted. This conversion, however it begins at home, will soon walk abroad; as the Virgin Mary was soon found out to be with child, so it will be soon found out whether Christ is formed in the heart. There will be new principles, new ways, new company, new works; there will be a thorough change in the heart and life; this is conversion: at first it begins with terror and legal sorrow, afterwards it leads to joyfulness;

ness; first we work for spiritual life, afterwards from it: first we are in bondage, afterwards we receive the Spirit of adoption to long and thirst for God, because he has been pleased to let us know that he will take us to heaven. Conversion means a being turned from hell to heaven, from the world to God. We have not so much as asked a person to sell his all, to leave his shop, to lay any thing at our feet: when we talk of being converted from the world, we mean being converted from the love of it: the heart once touched with the magnet of divine love, ever after turns to the pole. I think it is said of a sun-flower, though I question whether it will always hold true, that it turns to the sun; I am sure it is true of the Redeemer's flowers that grow in his garden, they not only look to the sun, but they find fresh life, warmth, and transforming influence from him who is their all in all. Here Christianity appears in its glory; here the work done is worthy the Son of God. To be converted only to a party, is that worth Christ's coming from heaven to earth for; that we might have a set of principles without having them affect the heart? for to be baptized when young, or as some to come out of the water at age,

age, and turn out as bad as ever, is a plain proof of the necessity of being baptized by the Holy Ghost.

What say you to this change, my dear souls? is it not god-like, is it not divine, is it not heaven brought down to the soul; have you felt it, have you experienced it? I begin to catechize you already, for I could spend a whole sermon in speaking of conversion; but I am afraid those that sit under the gospel have more need of heat than light: would to God we had as much warmth in our hearts, as light in our understandings! But if there be any of you here that are not yet converted, upon what grounds do you hope for conversion? give me leave to say, that you ought to repent and be converted, for till then you never can, never will, never shall find true rest for your souls. What wrong notions have people got of conversion! they think it is a wretched thing, and dread being converted; not knowing what it is, they think it is a frightful thing. I knew one sometime ago that came to some Methodists; dear, says the person, you are chearful, I could be glad if I was a Methodist too, if there was a majority of them in the land: but God help us to go to heaven with the minority,

if

if the majority will not follow. But, my dear hearers, there is not a single soul of you all that are satisfied in your stations: is not the language of your hearts when apprentices, we think we shall do very well when journeymen; when journeymen, that we should do very well when masters: when single, that we shall do well when married; and to be sure you think you shall do well when you keep a carriage. I have heard of one who began low; he first wanted a house, then, says he, I want two, then four, then six; and when he had them, he said, I think I want nothing else; yes, says his friend, you will soon want another thing, that is, a hearse and six to carry you to your grave; and that made him tremble. O if you are Christians, if the Lord loves you, he will put a thorn in your flesh. I have often thought of what a good man says in his Diary, the Lord put a thorn in my flesh. Among politicians, when they find a man ambitious, they say, kick him up, that he may fall and break his neck: so it is in every condition; there is not one of you fifty years old, but have had many changes: have not you found thorns even on the rose that smelt so sweet, and thorns perhaps that pricked you so closely, that you have forgot the scent of the rose by it? and what is all this for, but to teach you that happiness is only to be found in the Lord. If a soul is truly converted, there will be a battle, and an awful chasm that will never be filled up but with the love of God; and therefore when we say, Repent and be converted, it is no more than saying, repent and be happy. Indeed we shall never be compleatly happy till we get to heaven. O that every man could see the good of every thing of a sublunary nature drop off like leaves in autumn: God grant this may be known by every one of you.

If it is asked, why you should repent and be converted? I answer, because else you can never be happy hereafter. What do you think heaven is? why, says the covetous man, I think it is a place full of gold; so you think to steal some of the gold, do you? Others would like heaven very well if there was a good gaming-table in heaven; if there was card-playing in heaven. I have heard of a lady that was so fond of gaming, that though she had the pangs of death upon her, yet when in the midst of her fits, or just coming out of one, instead of asking after Jesus, where he

was

was to be found, she asked, what is trumps? So the gamester will ask, where is the backgammon table? where is the box? he will want to shake his ungodly hand in heaven; he will say, let us have a gaming-table in heaven, where, as he will find, he has lost the game; that God has damned him without an interest in Christ. *Can two walk together unless they are agreed?* If you die and do not love God here, if you cannot love praying to God here, and cannot watch one hour, suppose you was to be struck by death and be taken to heaven, there is no such language and amusement there, what would you do? Why, say you, these Methodists are presumptuous people, they can tell us whether we are to go to heaven or no. Good Mr. Rogers, a Welsh Boanerges, preaching in the mountains, said, Christ is heaven, if I worship God here, and do all to God, and for God, without any hopes of reward upon the earth. My dear brethren, the devils would never be troubled with such a wretch in hell, he would set all hell in an uproar; if a true Methodist was to go to hell, the devil would say, turn that Methodist out, he is come to torment us: therefore, you must be converted if you will go to heaven. Dr. Scott says,

says, if a natural man was to be put into heaven, it would be such a hell to him, that he would be glad to go to hell for shelter: angels they hate, God they hate; and as Adam was afraid to meet with God when he first fell from him, so his sons hate God and flee away.

I mention one thing more, which is, that you must be converted, or be damned, and that is plain English, but not plainer than my Master made use of, *He that believeth not shall be damned.* I did not speak that word strong enough that says, *He that believeth not shall be damned*; that is the language of our Lord; and it is said of one of the primitive preachers, that used to speak the word damned so that it struck all his auditory. We are afraid of speaking the word damned for fear of offending such and such a one; at the same time they despise the minister for not being honest to his master. Some have said, and stand to it, that hell is only a temporary punishment: Who told them so? A temporary punishment! nothing but a guilty conscience. O go to Bedlam! Do ask a child of God what he feels when his Lord is absent? Ask the spouse what she felt when she cries, *Saw ye him whom my soul loveth?* Ask a child of God when he is using this plaintive language,

language, *Why standest thou afar off, O Lord?* and he will tell you, it is hell to my soul to be but one moment without the presence of my beloved. And if his absence for a quarter of an hour can scarce be bore by a child of God, what must that soul undergo that is commanded to depart from him for ever? and yet these very words were said to those that thought they bid fair for heaven; to these Jesus says, *I know ye not.* God grant you may never know the meaning of these words by awful experience! Now, what say you? I could make a hundred heads more, but I chuse to make as few as possible, that you may remember them. I say, conversion makes you happy hereafter, and without it you are damned for ever.

Are these things so? why then, my dear hearers, do you think there can be any objection raised against conversion, do you think there can be any argument raised against turning to God directly? is there any person here that will give himself time to consider a moment that will not say, though you speak in a rough, incoherent manner, yet there is some truth in what you say; I believe men ought to be converted, but the common saying is, I
don't

don't care to be converted yet; we think it is time enough to be converted. Is not this acting like the cardinal, when told he was elected pope, and desired to come that night and have the honour of pope conferred on him; because it was pretty late said, it is not a work of darkness, I will put it off till the morning; before which they chose another pope, and he lost his triple crown. You may think to put it off till the morning, though before the morning you may be damned. Pray why will you not be converted now? if you was in prison, and a person would take you out, you would chuse to be let out to-night before morning, that you might sleep the better; why will you not do that for your soul you would for your body? Well, I would be converted but I shall be laughed at: suppose you was to have it promised, you should have a ten thousand pound lottery ticket, but you must be laughed at all your life-time; there is none but would say, give me the ten thousand pounds, and call me Methodist as long as I live: so if you loved God and your souls, you would say, give me God and call me what you will. You are afraid of being laughed at and nick-named, and skulk into this and that place, because it does not stink so much of Methodism as this. Put your cockades in your hats, and let the world see that you are not ashamed of God's badge: let the devil and his agents preach to you; they can proclaim their sin like Sodom; they are not ashamed of going to balls and assemblies, to parties of pleasure, and subscribing to horse-races. Is the gospel the glory of the land, and are you ashamed of the gospel? What think you, if you had given an hundred pounds to learn such a trade, would you say, I shall never attain it! no, you will persevere, and by giving diligence make an excellent mechanic, an admirable tradesman; and do you think to go to heaven without some trouble? do you think the leopard can change his spots, the Ethiopian put his skin intirely off? can we have any thing to nourish our bodies without the labour of particular persons? and therefore we are commanded *to work out our salvation with fear and trembling*. Remember our Redeemer *will not quench the smoaking flax, nor break the bruised reed; he will gently lead those that are with young*. We are like poor swimmers; some people will put one foot in and cry oh! and then another, but a good swimmer plunges in at once, and

comes

comes out braced up: would to God we could do so, plunge into God at once, and God will bear up our souls indeed.

But say you, all in good time, I do not chuse to be converted yet; why, what age are you now? I will come down to a pretty moderate age; suppose you are fourteen: and do not you think it time to be converted? and yet there are a great many here, I dare say, twenty years old, and not converted. Some are of opinion, that most people that are converted, are so before thirty. There was a young man buried last night at Tottenham Court but seventeen, an early monument of free grace! Are you forty, or fifty, is not that time? Is it time for the poor prisoners to be converted that are to be hanged to-morrow morning? if it is time for them, it is time for you, for you may be dead before them. There was a poor woman, but two or three days ago, that was damning and cursing most shockingly, now she is a dead corpse, was taken suddenly, and died away. God grant, that may not be the case with any of you; the only way to prevent it is, to be enabled to think that *now is an accepted time, that now is the day of salvation.* Let me look round,

round, and what do you suppose I was thinking? why, that it is a mercy we have not been in hell a thousand times. How many are there in hell that used to say, Lord convert me, but not now? One of the good old Puritans says, Hell is paved with good intentions. Now can you blame me, can you blame the ministers of Christ if this is the case, can you blame us for calling after you, for spending and being spent for your souls? it is easy for you to come to hear the gospel, but you do not know what nights and days we have; what pangs we have in our hearts, and *how we travel in birth till Jesus Christ be formed in your souls.* Men, brethren, and fathers, hearken, God help you, save, save, save *yourselves from an untoward generation.* To-night somebody sits up with the prisoners; if they find any of them asleep, or no sign of their being awake, they knock and call, and the keepers cry, awake! and I have heard that the present ordinary sits up with them all the night before their execution: therefore, don't be angry with me if I knock at your doors, and cry, poor sinners, awake! awake! and God help thee to take care thou dost not sleep in an unconverted state to-night. The court is just sitting, the executioner stands ready, and before to-morrow, long before to-morrow, Jesus may say of some of you, *Bind them hand and foot.* The prisoners to-morrow will have their hands tied behind them, their thumb-strings must be put on, and their fetters knocked off; they must be tied fast to the cart, the cap put over their faces, and the dreadful signal given; if you were their relations would not you weep? don't be angry then with a poor minister for weeping over them that will not weep for themselves. If you laugh at me, I know Jesus smiles. I cannot force a cry when I will; the Lord Jesus Christ be praised, *I am free from the blood of you all:* if you are damned for want of conversion, remember you are not damned for want of warning. Thousands that have no gospel preached to them, may say, Lord, we never heard what conversion is; but you are gospel-proof; and if there is any deeper place in hell than other, God will order a gospel despising-Methodist to be put in there. You will have dreadful torments; to whom so much is given, much will be required. How dreadful to have minister after minister, preacher after preacher, say, Lord God, *I preached but they would not hear.* Think of this, professors, and God make you possessors!

You that do possess a little, and are really converted, God convert you and me every hour in the day; for there is not a believer in the world, but has got something in him that he should be converted from; the pulling down of the old house, and building up the new one, will be a work till death. Do not think I am speaking to the unconverted only, but to you that are converted. God convert you from lying a-bed in the morning; God convert you from your conformity to the world; God convert you from lukewarmness; God convert us from ten thousand things which our own hearts must say we want to be converted from; then you will have the Spirit of the living God. Do not get into a cursed Antinomian way of thinking, and say, I thank God, I have the root of the matter in me: I thank God, that I was converted twenty or thirty years ago; and once in Christ always in Christ; and though I can go to a public-house and play at cards, or the like, yet, I bless God, I am converted. Whether you was converted formerly or not, you are perverted now; and may God convert you all to close Christianity with God!

You that are old professors, don't draw young ones back from God, by saying, ah! you will come down from the mount by and by; you will not always be so hot; and instead of encouraging poor souls, you will pull them down, because you have left your first love: would you have Jesus Christ catch you napping, with your lamps untrimmed?

O ye servants of the most high God, if any of you are here to-night, though I am the chief of sinners, and the least of all saints, suffer the word of exhortation. I am sure I preach feelingly now; God knows I seldom sleep after three in the morning; I pray every morning, Lord, convert me, and make me more a new creature to day. I know I want to be converted from a thousand things, and from ten thousand more: Lord God, confirm me; Lord God, revive his work.

You young people, I charge you to consider; God help you to repent and be converted, who woo's and invites you. You middle-aged people, O that you would repent and be converted. You old grey-headed people, Lord make you repent and be converted, that you may thereby prove that your sins are blotted out. O I could preach till I

preached

preached myself dead; I could be glad to preach myself dead, if God would convert you! O God bless his work on you, that you may blossom and bring forth fruits unto God. Amen and Amen.

SERMON

SERMON VI.

Glorifying God in the Fire; or, the right Improvement of Affliction.

ISAIAH xxiv. ver. 15.

Wherefore glorify ye the Lord in the fires.

YOU have oft, my dear hearers, let me tell you, met with affliction; and I believe you may perſuade yourſelves affliction is at hand, which makes ſuch deep impreſſions, when ſent and bleſſed by heaven, as to thaw the very heart. Faith, like ſome glaſſes to view objects near us, ſets them in ſo ſtrong a light, that we cannot help being affected with the weight of the impreſſion; hence the prophets, when under a divine impulſe, foreſaw things at a diſtance; ſpoke and wrote of them as though actually preſent. *They ſung both of judgment and mercy*, in ſuch ſtrong and perſuaſive ſtrains, as to convince of the reality of their exiſtence. Iſaiah, who had a

courtly

courtly education, being probably brother to a king, seems to excel in this kind of speaking; a person of good natural, as well as acquired abilities, which being tempered by the Holy Ghost, made him a kind of an angel of an orator, of a writer, and a prophet. When he penned this chapter, he probably foresaw the dreadful calamities coming on the land; and so strong was his persuasion, that he writes as though he saw the things taking place. *Behold*, says he, *the Lord maketh the earth empty, maketh it waste, and turneth it upside down, and scattereth abroad the inhabitants thereof.* How much is expressed in a few words! *As with the people so with the priests*, who perhaps, on account of their situation in the church, might think they should be exempted; but if the priests sin with the people, they shall be punished with the people. *As with the servant, so with his master; as with the maid, so with her mistress; as with the buyer, so with the seller; as with the lender, so with the borrower; as with the taker of usury, so with the giver of usury to him.* So you see that the visitation would be universal; that it should fall on all sorts of people. Ver. 3. *The land shall be utterly emptied and utterly spoiled;*

spoiled; probably, by a foreign foe taking advantage of the domestic confusions, who shall destroy the fruits of the earth. Some may think, perhaps, that this will never come to pass; but, saith Isaiah, *the Lord hath spoken it.* It pleased God the nation should be devoted to a dreadful stroke: *The earth mourneth and fadeth away, the world languisheth and fadeth away, the haughty people of the earth do languish,* whose crimes, one would think, would never be brought to punishment, on account of the eminence of their stations; they thought themselves out of danger, but they shall feel the common scourge: *For the earth also,* as in the fifth verse, *is defiled under the inhabitants thereof; because they have transgressed the laws, changed the ordinances, broken the everlasting covenant.* God did not strike without a cause; for the earth groaned, as it were, under the sins of the inhabitants for their neglect of religion, for disowning God, for turning their back on the Most High. *Therefore hath the curse devoured the earth,* (ver. 6.) *and they that dwell therein are desolate.* He does not say it shall be, but it is done. *The inhabitants of the earth are burned,* with dreadful fire of consuming vengeance, *and few men left.*

All the merry hearted, that minded nothing but jollity and mirth, even *they do sigh. The joy of the harp ceaseth; they shall not drink wine with a song, strong drink shall be bitter to them that drink it. The* very great *city*, the metropolis, *is broken down; every house is shut up, because desolation is left in it.* The inhabitants forsake it, their houses are left, shut up, because they are afraid some foreign power should come to their destruction. *There is a crying for wine in the streets, all joy is darkened, the mirth of the land is gone:* no plays, no routs, no assemblies now; *the city is left desolate;* the court not excepted; desolation herself takes her seat and ravages there. *The earth shall reel to and fro like a drunkard, and shall be removed like a cottage; and the transgressions thereof shall be heavy upon it, and it shall fall, and not rise again.* What an amazing scene is this! enough to fill us with horror even at this distance of time and place! But is there no way for escape? is there no light breaking through this dark shade? blessed be God, there is; look at ver. 13, you will find in the midst of dangers, God shall lend his presence. *When thus it shall be*, pray mind that, *in the midst of the land among the people,* what follows? *there shall be as the shaking of an olive tree, and as the gleaning grapes when the vintage is done*; there shall be a few godly people left, let the devil do what he will; but there will be but few. You know, after the people have gathered the fruits from the tree, they shake it to bring down the remainder; and after reaping of corn there are a few gleanings, so the Lord says, it shall destroy most people, yet in so discriminating a way, that God's people should be safe.

I cannot well recollect how archbishop Usher applies this; but this I am sure he says, there will certainly come a time when the world will undergo the greatest scourge that ever it felt, which shall chiefly fall on the outward-court worshippers, upon those that know not God; God will take particular care of securing his own; and when the wicked are all destroyed, the Christians shall go to a little city, and there shall dwell in Goshen, till God shall call home his ancient people the Jews. So God will take care of his people, that they shall be safe: pray look to ver. 14, *they shall lift up their voice*; what, to cry? no, they have done with prayers, they have done with fasting; they have lifted up their voice,

voice, and often exhorted their neighbours to *flee from the wrath to come*; but now they shall sing for the majesty of God; when all people are mourning, they shall rejoice. And at the great day, when Jesus Christ pronounces the wicked damned, *depart ye curfed*, God's people will then lift up their voices with majesty and triumph; which made a good man say to his son, just before he died, I am afraid I shall never see thee any more till I hear Jesus Christ say unto thee, *depart thou curfed!* Some years ago, being present at the trial of a very vile person at the Old-Bailey, and being in suspense whether he would be brought in guilty or no, when the word *guilty* came, and the people heard of it, they did in effect give an eclat to it; whether just or unjust, I thought it was an emblem of that awful day, when all the angels of God, and his saints, shall say Amen; when God consigns the wicked to hell: God grant this may not be any of your case. Says the prophet, *they shall cry aloud from the sea*; some of them may be on the other side of the water, gone abroad while others stay at home; but whether at home or abroad, though they have been banished by persecution, though they have been driven to

the

the other side of the water, which has been the case of many persons before now, *yet they shall cry aloud*; they shall find the same God abroad as they did at home. A judge said to a good old Christian that was persecuted in Charles II.'s time, I will banish you to America; says she, Very well, you cannot send me out of my Father's country. They shall cry aloud from the sea, *wherefore glorify ye the Lord in the fires*; if this is the case, the prophet draws the inference; what must they do under these circumstances; why, they must study how to glorify God in the fires, not how to escape or run away from him, but how to glorify him; *wherefore*, saith he, *glorify me*, glorify me the Lord, *in the fires*; not the fire, in the singular number, but in the plural number, fires. We are, my brethren, very much mistaken, if we think we have but one fire to go through.

The words imply, in order to bring them home to ourselves, that all God's people must be put into the fires. Fire sometimes denotes the love of God, sometimes the work of the Holy Ghost, and very often it denotes affliction; therefore, the apostle talks of a *fiery trial*; and let it be of whatever kind it will,

let

let it be upon mind, body, or estate; whether it comes from friend or foe, or whether it comes immediately from the hand of God himself upon the soul, it may well be compared to fire, for you all know that fire scorches; God expects when he strikes, that we should feel. Of all things in the world to be avoided, a stony heart, or a stupidity under God's afflicting hand, is most to be deprecated. I suppose you have heard of the Stoics*, with whom the apostle Paul disputed in the place of public traffic in Athens. Paul did not take a walk to Change to talk on trade, he went to talk about Jesus Christ, if he could meet with one to talk with: I wish the clergy took no other walks but these. Every thing is to be tried by fire; we may talk what we please, but we shall never know what metal we are made of, till God puts us into the fire. It is very easy talking what we can bear, and what we can do, but let God lay his hand on us, and we shall see what we are. We are apt to find fault, and be peevish with our friends and relations under such circumstances; they are apt to say,

you

---

* They taught that a wise man should be free from all affections and passions whatsoever.

you should be patient, and patient, and patient; ah! put these reprovers into the same furnace, and see how patient they will be: they say, there is no putting old mens heads upon young mens shoulders; and there is no putting old heads upon souls young in experience. The devil knew very well how it was when he said, *Hast thou not made an hedge about Job, and about his house, and about all that he hath on every side; thou hast blessed the work of his hands, and his substance is increased in the land; but put forth thy hand now, and touch all that he hath, and he will curse thee to thy face*; so we should all do if God was to leave us to ourselves, and our faith is not of the right sort.

How shall we know if our faith is good? we often pray, Lord, give us Abraham's faith, but never pray, give us Abraham's trial at the same time. I was once in Scotland, at a great man's house, where several rich people were that knew Jesus Christ; God having blessed my labours at a former visit, I was desired by the nobleman to pray; and I remember I prayed the Lord to give us great faith and patience; —O said Satan, as strong as if he had spoke to me, don't pray for that, for thou shalt have

great

great trials. O, said I, if that be the case, I will turn the devil's prayer against himself; and I prayed, *O Lord, give us great grace, and never mind what trials.* Often when we are under temptations, God takes us at our words: O, says one, what a prayer I had, I prayed for faith and patience; I was upon the mount, and never thought of coming down, and feeling a storm again.

Fire, my brethren, not only burns and purges, but you know it separates one thing from another, and is made use of in chymistry and mechanical businesses. What could we do without fire? it tries metal to purge it: God Almighty knows, we are often purged more in one hour by a good sound trial, than by a thousand manifestations of his love. It is a fine thing to come purified, to come pardoned out of the furnace of affliction; it is intended to purge us, *to separate the precious from the vile, the chaff from the wheat;* and God, in order to do this, is pleased to put us into one fire after another, which makes me love to see a good man under afflictions, because it teaches something of the work of God in the heart. I remember some years ago, when I first preached in the north of England, at Shields near Newcastle, I went into a glass-house, and standing very attentive, I saw several masses of burning glass of various forms: the workman took one piece of glass and put it into one furnace, then he put it into a second, and then into a third: when I asked him, why do you put this into so many fires? he answered, O, sir, the first was not hot enough, nor the second, and therefore we put it into the third, and that will make it transparent. Taking leave of him in a proper manner, it occurred to me, this would make a good sermon: O, thought I, does this man put this glass into one furnace after another, that we may see through it; O may God put me into one furnace after another, that my soul may be transparent; that I may see God as he is. My brethren, we need to be purged; how apt are we to want to go to heaven upon a feather-bed; many go lying upon beds of pain and languishing, which is the King's highway thither. You know there are some ways in London called the king's road, and they are finely gravelled, but the King's road to heaven is strowed with crosses and afflictions. We are all apt to think well of being Christians; it is very pretty talking of being Christians,

tians, till we are put into one furnace after another; *think it not strange,* saith the apostle, *concerning the fiery trial which is to try you.* What must I do? why, since I must be in the fire, I must thank my corruptions for it; God will not put you or me into the fire if there was not something to be purged away; the grand thing is to learn to glorify God in the fire. *Wherefore glorify ye the Lord in the fires.*

When do we glorify him? when we endeavour to get such grace from the Lord, that we may not dishonour him when we are under the cross, and therefore we glorify God in the fire when we quietly endure it as a chastisement for our sins: if you keep watch now, and live near to God, you will never find that you are put into a fire, but you first brought yourselves into it; and I do verily believe from my heart, that our sin is always to be seen in our punishment. If any of you part from a child that he loves dearly, upon examination he will say, I find now the creature's gone, that the ivy twined too much about the oak; and then he turns off; ah! says he, God has met with me now. And you will find in all the Old and New Testament, that the afflictions of God's people were suitable to their faults: Jacob

cob was over-perſuaded by his mother to get the bleſſing by a lie; but he was a ſimple-hearted poor creature. Some perſons think nothing of a lie; if they can but get by it, they do not mind it; but an honeſt man will ſhun it. Jacob argues with his mother againſt it; O, ſays ſhe, *the curſe be on me, my ſon!* O dreadful! for a good woman to ſay ſo. Doubtleſs, ſhe was perſuaded God would give Jacob the bleſſing, but ſhe took a wrong way to obtain it; ſhe might have waited for the bleſſing to come with a bleſſing. How did God puniſh Jacob? why, in a night afterwards poor Jacob was impoſed upon by a wrong wife, he got a Leah inſtead of a Rachel; the poor creature was impoſed upon there, and ſo all along almoſt to the end of his life; he had a furnace of affliction. Happy they who pray in the furnace, Lord, let me know why thou doſt contend with me. Therefore God ſends this meſſage to Ely by Samuel, *the thing that thou knoweſt*, ſeems to me to refer to his too great lenity to his ſons; *the thing that thou knoweſt*; thou doſt not act like a magiſtrate. Theſe ſons were the means of bringing a judgment on his houſe, and breaking their father's neck: God Almighty keep us from bringing a rod upon ourſelves.

We

Ser. VI. *Improvement of Afflictions.*

We glorify God in the fire when we bear it patiently. It is a dreadful thing when we are saying with Cain, *My punishment is greater than I can bear*; but the language of a soul that glorifies God in the fire is this, shall I, Lord, shall I a sinful man, complain for the punishment of my sins? It is a glorious thing when we can say with a good man, one of whose particular friends told me more than once, that when he was racked with pain, and groaning all night with trouble, he would often say, Lord, I groan; Lord, I groan; Lord, I groan; but, Lord Jesus, I appeal to thee, thou knowest I do not grumble. Then we glorify God in the fire, when, though we feel pain and anguish, we at the same time say, Lord, we deserve this and ten thousand times more.

We glorify God in the fire also, when we are really and fully persuaded, God will not put us in the fire but for our good, and his own glory. I am afraid some people think God does as some cheating apothecaries, that bring five things when they need not bring but one, especially when they have some silly patients that love to be taking physic; they send one after another, when, perhaps, the best thing would be to throw them all away; so we think of God, but it is a mistake; he never sends one but what is necessary, and something to be purged away.

We glorify God in the fire when we say, Lord, don't let the fire go out till it has purged away all my dross. Then we glorify God when we wish for the good of the fire, and not to have it extinguished; when the soul can say, *Here I am, my God, do with me as seemeth good in thy sight*; I know I shall not have one stroke but thou will give me a plaister, and let me know wherefore thou contendest with me.

We glorify God in the fire when we are content to say, *I know not what God does with me now, but I shall know hereafter*. Do you tell your children that are five years old the reason of things, no; and do you think God will tell us? *What shall this man do?* saith the disciples; *what is that to thee?* saith Christ, *follow thou me*. You glorify God in the fire, when you are content to walk by faith and not by sight.

You glorify God in the fire when you are not grumbling, but humbly submitting to his will; a humble spirit walks not in sulkiness

and

and stubbornness: there are some spirits too stout, they will not speak. When that awful message was brought to Ely, what does he say? *It is the Lord, let him do what seemeth him good;* let my children be killed, whatever be done it is the Lord's doing; only, Lord, save my soul at last.

We glorify God in the fire, when in the midst of the fire we can sing God's high praises. Thus the children of Israel glorified the Lord; the song of the three children in the fiery furnace is a sweet song; as are all that are made in the fire. *O all the works of the Lord, praise and magnify him for ever!* Then we glorify God in the fire when we rejoice in him, when we not only think, but know it best, and can thank God for striking us; can thank God for whipping us; can bless God for not letting us alone; thank God for not saying, *let him alone:* this is to glorify God in the fire. *Not only so,* faith the apostle, *but we glory in tribulation, knowing that tribulation worketh patience.*

In a word, we glorify the Lord in the fire when we have in exercise, patience, meekness, humility; learning more to distrust ourselves, having a deeper knowledge of our own weak-

weakness, and of God's omnipotence and grace. Happy when we can look back and say, thus have I been enabled to glorify God in the fire. Who can put his hand to his heart and say, I have glorified God in the fire as I ought? instead of that I am afraid the soul must say, that instead of being thankful and resigned, I have been fretful; and because I will not find fault with myself, nor let the world know I find fault with God, I find fault with all about me. Did you never find yourself in such a humour when your spirits were low? I heard a good man once speak on those words, *they shall bring forth fruit in old age:* O the fruit, said he, is pevishness; I thought it was the infirmity of old age, the fruit of which ought to be heavenly-mindedness, deadness to the world, and a liveliness to God.

My brethren, let us humble ourselves to-night, and let us be ashamed and abashed before God, and wonder he hath not struck us into hell when we have been complaining the fire was too hot, that God sent us not to the devil. Let us weep, let us weep, let us weep for our stubbornness. Happy they who are used to be put into the fire betimes! *It is good for a man to bear the yoke in his youth.* Some years

years ago, when I was at the Orphan-house, they told me they were going to yoke two steers together, one sturdy and old, the other a little one, on which they no sooner put the yoke, but he kicked once or twice, and then bore it very well: O, thought I, it is a good thing to have the yoke betimes.

Are any of you now in the furnace, are any of you troubled, or can any of you say, I have no trouble; a calm is sometimes the fore-runner of a storm; thank God, you are not in the fire; surely you have been in the fire. There is the devil's fire; the fires of *the lust of the flesh, the lust of the eye, and the pride of life:* God help you to come out of these fires, left they damn your souls for ever. You must be put either in the devil's fire or God's fire, and the devil's fires are hottest, because there is no God to support under the trouble they bring upon the soul. O what a dreadful thing it is to be in the devil's fire continually, and to go out of the fire of the devil here to burn with the devil in hell hereafter! If there are any of you in this case, Lord Jesus Christ shorten them, Lord Jesus Christ sanctify his afflictions to his people, as he did to one of the prisoners last Wednesday: how sweetly he behaved!

while

while the others were cursing and swearing, tossing up who should sit on the right hand in the cart, he was glorifying God, thanking God he was sent there, and going to be executed: God, saith he, hath stopt me, I might have gone on in sin to ruin. O send to my father, go to him, warn him to *flee from the wrath to come:* somebody went to his parent, and the father sent back this *loving* message; tell him to mind his own soul, and be damn'd! O, dear Lord, what lengths has man gone! never was such a message sent to a son before; he bid him mind his own soul and be damn'd! God grant none of you may ever have such a frame of mind as that! O remember fire hardens as well as softens; and if you are not better by afflictions you will be worse: and indeed you will know you cannot come out of the furnace as you went in, you will either be hardened or else be purified; and if this be the case, the Lord Jesus Christ help you to bear the fire now, that you may never be cast into the fire of hell. God haste you, hasten you that are out of the devil's fire to flee, flee, ye weary souls, to Jesus Christ; fly to the Lamb of God, from hell to heaven, as far as you can from these hellish fires, to the fire of his blessed merit and love.

Happy

Happy you that have got into Chrift's fire! happy you that have found his fires in your fouls! I believe many fouls have: O Lord Jefus Chrift help you to glorify him in whatever fires he fhall be pleafed to fend you, and into whatever furnaces he fhall be pleafed to put you: we fhall then fing "*the church triumphant*," much better than we fing to-night; we fhall fee Jefus Chrift ready to help us when we are in the furnace: O that this thought may make every poor finner fay, by the help of God I will be a Chriftian; by the help of God, if I muft burn, it fhall be burning with the love of Chrift. I will fay then, O Lord, glorify thyfelf by fnatching me as a brand from the devil's fire. O that this might be the cry of every heart!

I am going to afk a favour of you to-night which I never did before, and, perhaps, may not again for fome time: I have had complaints made to me by the perfons that take care of the poor, that the poor's ftock is very low; though I cannot fpeak on Sunday night, yet I will fpeak a word to the poor on Wednefday evening. There are numbers of poor that are ready to perifh, and if you drop fomething to them in love, God will take care to repay you when you come to judgment. We shall not only glorify God by a submission to his will, when he is putting us in the fire, but in doing any good, when we lay all the glory at the foot of Jesus; which God grant for Christ's sake. Amen.

SERMON VII.

The Beloved of God.

DEUT. xxxiii. ver. 12.

And of Benjamin, he said, The beloved of the Lord shall dwell in safety, by him; and the Lord shall cover him all the day long, and he shall dwell between his shoulders.

OH! what a dismal sight is it, to see an old man with his hoary head grown grey in sin, and hardened in iniquity. On the other hand, I believe to all that consider rightly, there is no grander sight almost under the sun, than to see an old grey-headed man keeping up a consistent character; and proving, by his conduct, that *his path*, like that of the just, *is as the shining light, that shineth more and more to the perfect day;* especially when persons have been called to act in a public character; when they have been eminent either for the highness of their station,

or for the largeness of their income. It is on this account that I admire old Jacob; how grand he looked when leaning on his staff, with all the composure in the world, under a divine influence, blessing his children standing round him. But, methinks, there is one who was called to act a more public part, namely, Moses, who was honoured of God to be a great legislator, king in Jeshurun, a lawgiver between Judah's feet, as pupils used to be at the feet of their teachers, to receive their instruction; if you have a mind to see how bright he shines, you must read Deut. xxxii. indeed you must read all Deuteronomy, which is nothing but a sermon that Moses, at various times, preached to the children of Israel; and having done preaching, he sang a hymn of his own composing, and that too at a time when he knew, at the very finishing the song, he should immediately have his soul kissed away, and be called to sing a better song in the kingdom of heaven. A person would need a good deal of composure, a good deal of the Spirit's influences, a large measure of it, chearfully thus to stand in view of death, just on the very borders of the grave; you see this in chap. xxxii. and here in chap. xxxiii. One would have
thought

thought he had said enough, yet he seems as it were not to know how to leave off; he parted from the people blessing them; they had used him ill, they provoked him in the wilderness; he had bore with them many, many long years; sure you would have thought he would have went away in a huff; no, that eminent sun by no means goes down in wrath; his eyes did not so much as wax dim, nor his intellectual powers impair in all that time: he sweetly gives them all a blessing before he goes. If you read this chap. xxxiii. you will find how various, yet special, are the blessings which, in a prophetic strain, he foretels should attend particular persons, or tribes. I have been reading them over, and though I admire them all, I was at a loss which to speak from, till the blessing of Benjamin fixed my attention, not only as sweet, but instructing. *The beloved of the Lord shall dwell in safety, by him; and the Lord shall cover him all the day long, he shall dwell between his shoulders.* This is a blessing indeed, if we look only to the literal interpretation of the words, and a literal commentator can go no further; he must confine them to Benjamin; and will tell us, that this scripture was fulfilled at the building of the

Temple,

Temple. The Temple was built upon two hills, one in the tribe of Benjamin, the other in the tribe of Judah; the Temple being built there, and Benjamin being placed near it, then Benjamin dwells in safety by the Lord, by having his lot cast near the Temple. How often, alas! is it the case, I am sure it is very often the case in London, the nearer the church the further from God; but some make good use of it, and are glad to get near the church that they may be nearer God. The Temple being placed between two hills, so Benjamin as it were dwells between God's shoulders; so far a literal commentator can go, here he stops; a spiritual commentator, and a spiritual reader, go further; O, says he, this is true, but at the same time this is not the whole truth; and I am persuaded, when a person is helped by the Spirit to read the scriptures, the declarations that are made, and those particular promises, the true believer applies with great propriety to himself; and therefore I think I may venture to aver, that the blessing which Moses here pronounces upon him in the name of the Lord, belongs to God's people in all ages whatever; God, in his infinite mercy, grant that this blessing may descend upon us and

ours,

ours, that it may descend to your latest posterity.

Observe how wonderfully the persons, to whom the blessing is given, are characterized: of Benjamin it is said, *the beloved of the Lord*; the beloved of the Lord, pray who are they? why, the men that the scriptures always speak of, whose constant uniform character is, they love God in all ages. It is not said, the Presbyterians shall dwell in safety; Moses never heard of a Presbyterian in his life; he never heard of the name; nor it is said the Independents shall dwell in safety; he never heard of that word; nor is it said the Papists shall dwell in safety; he never heard of Papists, nor of the pope; nor is it said that the Church of England shall dwell in safety, no; neither is it said that the Methodists shall dwell in safety, though I trust there are a great many good people among these mongrels of the church; but it is spoken of all the people of God; God help us all to apply it to ourselves.

Here is a dispute between the Arminians and the Calvinists: ask an Arminian what is meant by *the beloved of the Lord*; O, say they that are for general redemption, the beloved of the Lord signifies, all the men that were ever born

born into the world; that is a good broad bridge to take them in; but broad bridges are not always the strongest bridges in the world. The Arminians will assert it, that Judas was as much beloved of God as Peter, or any other of the apostles; and those that are not Arminians, but are what you call Quakers, and there are a good many, I believe, among them, that have better hearts than heads, they say, that we are all alike, that we all come into the world with a seed of grace, and shall be happy according to the improvement of that grace; hence they talk nothing of a Christ *without* but *within*; happy they that experience a Christ within! God's mercy is sure, and over all his works; and in one sense, our Lord Jesus Christ is the Saviour of all men, that is, of all sorts of men; even the wicked are beholden to Jesus Christ, whom they despise, for every worldly comfort they enjoy; in this sense we should learn to love as our Lord, we are told, loved the young man when he saw he had been a harmless and good liver: but we must go more to what we call Calvinism, what I call scriptural truth. The love which Jesus Christ bore for the young man, quite differed from that love with which he loved Martha, Mary,

Mary, and their brother; there was a cargo for you! three in one family; God grant it may be your happy lot and mine! two sisters and one brother, three to entertain Jesus Christ, all in a peculiar manner beloved of the Lord. It is not said of Benjamin, they shall, that is, they that love the Lord, they shall dwell in safety, no; it would not be so strong to them, as to say *the beloved of the Lord*; for God knows our love is not worth a shilling; all the faith of God's people, says bishop Hall, is but meer infidelity; and all the love of the people of God is but meer hatred, compared with God's love, or that which his law justly requires; therefore it is said, *beloved of the Lord*, and that because if ever we love God, he first loved us, which is what Moses's very expression means; as streams flow from the fountain, so they shall return to it. Hence the apostle says, *Knowing your election, brethren, beloved of God.* I know very well the Mysticks talk of loving God with a love for himself only, without any respect to the creature at all; that is, we must love God without any regard at all for what God has done for us; nay, some go so far as to say, that if we do not so love God, we are not converted, though

though we have as much grace as we can have; that we do not love God properly till we love him for what he is, not what he has done for us: I verily believe, the angels do not love God in that manner; and we cannot love God till we are made partakers of a divine nature, and have eyes given us to see his glory.

The grand enquiry is then, how shall I know that I am one of the beloved of the Lord? The natural man never minds the love of God; he flatters himself he loves God naturally, that the love of God is a plant that grows in nature's garden; but a spiritual person does not so. What does the king take notice of me? does the king look pleasant upon me in a drawing-room? am I called to wait upon him? am I beloved of this, and that, and the other person? if I am, let God go, I care not; if I have but the love of this and that courtier, I care not whether God loves me or no; this will not do for an awakened soul; and therefore the grand enquiry, and one proof of a person's being awakened is, how shall I know whether God loves me or not? why try; I am persuaded of it, that we may as well know that God loves us, and we love God, as we may know that the sun shines at noon-

noon-day; how shall I know it but by the effects of this love, by the fruits of it? That great man, Dr. Watts, who was called the sweet singer of Israel, says, " we should go first to the grammar-school of faith and repentance, before we go to the university of predestination:" whereas, the devil would have them go first to the university, to examine whether they were elected or rejected, or no: they should do as a good woman once did, when satan tempted her, and wanted to distress her, that there were but few to be saved; she said, if there were but two to be saved, she would strive to be one of them. Surely I am beloved of the Lord, if my natural enmity against the Lord is slain. How do I know I love a person? how can you prove that you love me? why, say you, I hated you the other day: how many people met I with the other day, that could a few weeks ago have pulled me out of Tottenham-court, but God has overcome their hearts. The person now confesses his former enmity, and when that enmity is removed, and you are reconciled to them, cannot you know that you love them? and if God has removed that enmity to Christ out of your hearts, surely you are one of the beloved of the Lord.

We are the beloved of the Lord, if we are brought to abhor and renounce that which stands between us and the Lord; I mean, our cursed self-righteousness. Can I prove that I have renounced my own duties, that I am sick of my duties as well as my sins; none but the beloved of the Lord see this: an enemy to the Lord may have this in his head, but it is only a friend of the Lord that has this in his heart: a talkative professor can speak of it; you may teach, perhaps, a parrot to pray, but it is odds to talk like a parrot, and experience like a Christian. Now if I have renounced my own righteousness, and been helped to trust to Christ's, to believe on the Son of God, let satan say what he will, I am sure I am the beloved of the Lord, for none but those that are beloved by him with an everlasting love, are brought to believe on him.

I may know I am beloved of the Lord, from what? why, experiencing *his love shed abroad in my heart by the Holy Ghost*. Jonathan loved David as his own soul. Most of you know what love is in a carnal sense; and if there be a union of souls between creature and creature, surely there must be a union of souls between the Creator and the creature beloved

beloved of God; it cannot be otherwife; this love will have its effects.

If I am beloved of the Lord, if having his love in my heart, I fhow it by loving thofe he has loved. Some people may fay, I love you, but I do not love thofe about you, your friends; why you are not bound to love all alike, but it may teach you to be civil to that perfon's beloved. As foon as ever we hear of a Chriftian, as foon as ever we hear of a believer, as foon as ever we hear of a finner turning to God, O it will rejoice us; and we fhall be like the angels in heaven, who *rejoice over one finner's repentance, more than over ninety-nine juft perfons that need no repentance.* Some people may fay, I love dearly to hear of a perfon's being converted by fuch a minifter; I love dearly to hear of perfons converted by a diffenter; I love dearly to hear of perfons converted by a churchman, but I do not like people fhould be converted by this and that perfon; why I believe there are a great many people whofe hearts are thus narrow, but this mixture is not of God; and I pray God they may know it by experience; that they may know they are beloved of God, then they will rejoice when other people are brought to believe on him,

him, whoever is made the instrument. *Grace and mercy be with all them that love the Lord Jesus Christ in sincerity.* What would have become of poor Paul if he had only loved his own followers: the Romans he never saw till he was taken there a prisoner, but he loved all the rest of the apostles, writ letters to all sorts, not to their particular parties or churches, but to all those *that loved the Lord Jesus in sincerity;* and if we do love in this manner, we may be assured we are beloved of the Lord, for none but the Lord could beget such love in us.

If we are beloved of the Lord, we shall be hated by the world. *If you were of the world, the world would love you, but because you are not of the world, but I have chosen you out of the world, therefore the world hateth you.* Will you make me believe that any of you are beloved of the Lord, that never lost your good character by it; why you may as well make me believe that you are emperors of the world: where is the blessing the sermon on the mount speaks of; where is the blessing of persecution; where is the blessing of being hated of all men; where is the blessing of being hated for the cross? you love the Lord,

and

and not carry the cross after you; you love the Lord, and not be hated as your Lord was? I don't say all are hated alike; poor ministers are set in the front of the battle; in proportion to our successes we shall be hated. There are numbers of ministers now sleep in whole skins, that were formerly in a worse plight; the devil disturbs them not because they are quite civil, and do not trouble and contradict him; but if you oppose the world and the devil, the world will hate you; and no greater proof of being beloved of the Lord, than the world hating you, but it must be for Christ's sake. So Ahab said of the prophet, *all his prophesying is against me*; I hate him; the world hated him; *the world hated me,* says our Lord, *before it hated you*; and the apostles, when they began to speak for God too, they were hated like their Lord; and glory to God for it, for it is a blessed mark of their belonging to God, when they are honoured to suffer for him, and we are never right till we are bearing the cross: to see men or women sleeping under the cross, sculking and hiding from it, is this love? give me a professor that will wear a cockade in his hat, and is never easier than when he is combating the enemies of his King.

If I am the beloved of the Lord, I really shall live above the world. You may say what you will, and you may bring the scriptures as low as you think proper, *but the friendship of the world is hatred to God; and if any man love the world, the love of the Father is not in him.* Now by not loving the world, I don't mean that you should shut up your shops, and run into a convent: how idle for persons to say they love God, and hide themselves from the world; that is no religion at all. But the greatest proof of a Christian's loving God is, I am in the world, but not of it; I work with my hands all the day, but my heart is from it. I remember a dear friend once sent me word, many years ago, how busy he was morning and night, up early and late; perhaps, says he, you will think by this account, I am worldly; he said, no, sir, I thank God that my heart is above the world: God grant we may thus prove we love God! I don't say, but many that love the Lord may be in another situation; but when persons are enabled to leave all for Christ, it is a great mercy: God be praised, we have some such; God add to their happiness.

They

They that love the Lord, will study to keep from offending God, not for fear of being damned, but because sin murdered his dear Son; there are a great many people abstain from sin for fear of punishment; but hear what Joseph said, *My master has done thus and thus by me, how can I therefore do this great wickedness and sin against God?* my God that loves me; so they would not stab him, because he has been wounded enough already.

If we are the beloved of the Lord, we shall be willing to work for the Lord; faith without works is the religion of every carnal man; make an end of one good work and then begin another, and lay it down and wonder that Jesus Christ should accept any thing at your hands. I knew a lady sometime ago, that wanted still more to be employed for God; says she, if Jesus Christ would but help me to do such and such a thing I have in view, O I would kiss his feet, and dedicate myself more and more to his honour: a true Christian loves to be thus employed, but above all he is glad he has the blood of Christ to wash his duties in.

I shall mention but one thing more, though I might mention twenty; if we have the love of God in our hearts, though we cannot get over the fears of death at all times, yet I think the bent of the mind of such a person will be, when shall I see the object of my love, *him whom my soul loves?* they sit at ordinances, and long to be led to the fountain head. *I am in a strait between two*, says Paul; the word signifies a strong, an intense desire to be with Christ: he does not say to be in heaven, but *to be with Christ, which is far better*; but to stay here is better for you, therefore you should be content to stay, not because you love the world, but as willing to wait your Master's call. I could not help admiring while I was reading it, that when Christ ascended to heaven, one angel, one particular angel, it must have been a blessed one, left those that were attending Christ into glory, stopped in the way, for what? why, to preach to the apostles: *Why stand ye thus gazing into heaven?* I am ashamed of you, says he; here is an angel, one of the convoy, waiting upon them: he does not say, let me go to heaven with thee, and let me come down again and preach, no; he stays down thus to preach to a few poor fishermen. Lord search us, Lord try us, Lord God Almighty help us to examine ourselves, that we may know whether we are beloved of the Lord or not. So

So that some may say, I think I can apply all the marks, though I don't depend upon marks. I have a number of bills here to-night; one says, if I am beloved of the Lord, why am I so poor? another says, if I am beloved of the Lord, why am I so afflicted? says another, if I am beloved of the Lord, why am I left to starve; can I think God loves me, when I see thousands and thousands squandered away every day, and yet my poor babes groaning, my poor children quite emaciated, for want only of a little bread that I see in the baker's shop as I go along; if I am beloved of the Lord, how is it that my poor children are ready to cry for bread, and I have none to give them; that others are adorned with diamonds, but I have not so much as a rag to put on my little one's back. If I am beloved of the Lord, how is it that my friends are against me; my children, instead of being a blessing, are a curse, and break my heart. If I am beloved of the Lord, how is it that I have so many domestic trials that cause me to cry out, *Wo is me that I sojourn in Mesheck, and dwell in the tents of Kedar.* If I am beloved of the Lord, how is it that I am harrassed with blasphemous thoughts thus; the trials I meet with in bringing down the outward man. If I am beloved of the Lord, how is it that instead of living in plenty, I now want bread to eat, and should be glad to have it from those *I once scorned to set with the dogs of my flock? Whom the Lord loveth he chasteneth, and scourgeth every son whom he receiveth.* Our dear Jesus was never more beloved of his father than when he cried out, *My God! my God! why hast thou forsaken me?* never more beloved of his father than when he was sweating great drops of blood, when he cried, *Father, if it be possible let this cup pass from me.* I remember a dear minister of Christ, now in Suffolk, told me, when he was in Scotland, going to receive the sacrament, he was so dry and dark, and benumbed and tempted, that he thought he would go away; as he was going this word came to his mind, when was Jesus Christ most acceptable to his Father? when did he give the greatest trial of his love? when he cried out, *My God! my God! why hast thou forsaken me?* Why then, says he, upon this I will venture; if I perish, I perish at Christ's feet; and he came away filled with comfort from his blessed God and Father in Christ.

Well

Well then, what is to be done to those that are beloved of the Lord? here's for you, *they shall dwell in safety*; why? *they shall dwell between his shoulders*; observe the expression, the prophet says *they shall dwell in love*. *Will God indeed dwell on earth?* says Solomon; yes, God, says he, dwells in my earthly heart, made heavenly by the grace of God. Did ever any hear such an expression from the mouth of God, *I will be thy God*; *I am thy shield, and thy exceeding great reward?* He does not say an angel shall go; if God had only said in his word, that I was to be kept by angels, I am sure my wicked heart would despair, because it would deceive all the angels in heaven: but God saith, *I will be thy keeper*; so they that would hurt his people, must go through God himself. *They shall dwell on high*; *bread shall be given to them, and their waters shall be sure. They are kept by the mighty power of God through faith, to everlasting salvation.* It is said, *they shall dwell between his shoulders:* the government of the church, and the world, and all, are upon the Redeemer's shoulders, and the Lord's everlasting arms are under his people. Observe it is said, *they dwell in safety*; and very often we are safest when we think we are most in danger.

They

They shall dwell in safety; those that are lovers of the Lord Jesus shall dwell safely with God on earth, and eternally with him in heaven. O may God bless this foolishness of preaching to some of God's poor, and, perhaps, doubting beloved ones. Come you poor souls, I often think that this *field* preaching is particularly comfortable to the poor; whenever *field* preaching is stopped, farewel to the power of religion. When poor people have been working hard all day, how sweet must it be for them to come to a place of worship, and get a lift for to-morrow: may the Lord God bless this barley-bread! If you can wrap yourselves in God, let the world hate you; God's children are the greatest plagues and trials one to another, but God loves them, God smiles upon them, and therefore they shall dwell in safety. The devil told me I should not dwell in safety, but I bid him defiance, and turned him to Deut. xxxiii. and told him Benjamin's lot was mine; *the beloved of the Lord shall dwell in safety by him.*

Wo, wo, wo be to you that have no marks of being beloved of the Lord. Have we any prophane Esaus here to-night, that are saying, do not tell me of your being beloved of the Lord;

Lord; if I can have the love of such a person, I don't care whether God loves me or not; you may tell me God loves people when they are afflicted, I want none of these marks, I think God loves me because I am in a good frame; I think God loves me because I prosper; I think God loves me because I am very healthy and strong; I do not care whether I wait upon God or not, or give to the poor or not. I will not soften the matter, there is no going to heaven without wearing a fool's coat. O, you may say, that is owing to your imprudence; you make people uneasy, and set them upon a false scent, and make them their own persecutors; thank God, I can go into a hundred companies, and not give them reason to say I am a Methodist: I can go into company and sing an innocent song, I don't tell them I have a Tabernacle hymn-book in my pocket. There are few have the courage that the gentleman had who loved God, and went to see some carnal relations after he became a fool for Christ's sake: says one of the relations, it is always our custom after dinner to sing a song, and asked him to sing; he said, he would in his turn; two of them sung; his relation said to him, come, cousin, sing; says he, I have

not

not sung a song a good while, but, if you please, I will sing a hymn: he sung it out, but they never asked him to sing again, nor did they sing afterwards. How sweet it is to go through boldly with a thing for Christ! Do not you think you are a coward? are you not ashamed? are any of you such cowards as to plead your prudence: God help you to be unmasked to-night. I do not know whether you go to a masquerade, but you have a dreadful masque upon your souls, a dreadful religious visage. I heard somebody appeared the other night, in order to bring contempt upon us, in a Methodist dress, that was one of the dresses. O how can they do so? say you; how canst thou do so? pretend to be a Methodist among God's people, and behave light and foolish among the children of the devil; for shame unmask yourselves, for God will, by death, unmask your soul, and show your hypocrisy. The word hypocrite is taken from a stage-player, who acts that part he is not: God, of his infinite mercy, keep all here from stopping short.

If any of you are awakened and convinced, the Lord grant you may never rest till you know you are the beloved of the Lord. Ah! says say you, I shall never know that, that I am the beloved of the Lord: I am that old grey-headed wretch you mentioned at the beginning of your sermon; can God love me a drunkard, sabbath-breaker, a whoremonger, an adulterer, an unclean wretch as ever trod on the ground! Pray what was Paul? what was the jailor? what were all the three thousand that were converted at once; what was their case? nay, what was Adam the first sinner? and yet Adam and Eve both, I believe, received mercy of God; she is therefore called *the mother of all living*, because she is the mother of all believers. Come then at a venture, come then, throw thyself upon Christ; do not say, Pardon my iniquities because they are small, but say, *Lord, pardon my iniquities for they are great*. One that was executed to-day for forging something to rob his father; what a father deal thus with his son? well, said I, it is so with a man, but our heavenly father will pardon; and though the law is called a fiery law, yet there is, blessed be God, a new and living way. Oh sinners! oh sinners! God help you to come and venture, and strive, though you have none of the marks that have been mentioned, yet say, God can put these marks

A a   upon

upon me. I have been courting this and that person's love; nay, I made no other use of coming to worship, but to look out for something to advance myself. I have been looking out for nothing but beauty; I have been looking out for nothing but money, or something or other to make my fortune; but now begone, vain world; now, Lord, I would look after thee. That you may know you are the beloved of the Lord, dwell in safety on earth, and after death be conveyed to dwell with, and love him to all eternity, God grant for Christ's sake. Amen.

SERMON

SERMON VIII.

The Furnace of Affliction.

ISAIAH xlviii. ver. 10.

I have chosen thee in the furnace of affliction.

GRACIOUS words indeed! words worthy of a God! who has promised that *he will not always chastise, that he will not keep his anger for ever*; but, on the contrary, will take care in the midst of judgment to remember mercy; and if he strikes with one hand, will uphold with the other.

I hope I need not tell you, my dear hearers, that these words were spoken to comfort the captives in Babylon, who, for their various sins and great backslidings, constrained the God of love, the God of mercy, their covenant God, to send them captives into a foreign soil; upon this their enemies take occasion to insult them, *where are now your songs?* say they; give us one of your Temple songs, with which you used to pour out your allelujahs; let us see now whether you can praise him in a strange land. The enemy of souls joining inwardly with them without, makes some that can sing, even afraid *that God hath forgotten to be gracious, that he hath shut up his loving kindness in displeasure*, that the darkness in which they were now involved would not be a temporary, but a perpetual one; and notwithstanding the prophets were sent in mercy of God to comfort them in their trouble, yet many of them were tempted to say, *all men,* yea the prophets, *were liars*; it is very well if they stopped there, and did not say, God is a liar too. The enemy being thus suffered to break in upon them like a flood, it was high time for the blessed God to lift up a standard against him; and therefore the great Redeemer, the angel of the everlasting covenant, lets them know that he would some time or other, nay, very speedily, appear to relieve his afflicted people: he assures them, that however for a while he might suffer them to be tried, he would cause a speedy deliverance, that should make them look upon him as their God; and this not for any merit found in this people, not for any good foreseen, but he says,

for

for my own name's sake; that the heathen might not say God had utterly forsaken them, he will appear for their relief, and *make them more than conquerors through him that loved them*; that however dark the season of affliction might be, yet he would let his own people know that all that happened, happened out of love; that it was so far from being true, that they were really cast off from God, that, on the contrary, he intended to over-rule these troubles, both foreign and domestic, to bring them nearer to, and at last to lodge them safe in the world above: well therefore for their comfort might it be ushered in thus, *for my name's sake will I defer my anger, and for my praise will I refrain for thee, that I cut thee not off*. And to fix their attention and gratitude, 'tis added, *behold I have refined thee, but not with silver*; for this is so far from being contrary to the everlasting decree, or purpose, hid in my bosom, that, on the contrary, it is the fulfilling it; for, saith God in the words of our text, *I have chosen thee in the furnace of affliction.*

Though the words are spoken in the singular number, yet they are of a complex and large import; the great God not only speaks

to

to them as a people collectively considered, but particularizes them in this manner; not *I have chosen you, but I have chosen thee*; for the word of God itself will never, never, never do us good, if it is not applied by the blessed Spirit of God to you and I. The wisdom and kindness of the Holy Ghost deserves our notice; had the prophet gone on and said, *I have chosen you*, unbelief might have said, ah, this prophesy belongs only to the people of Israel, the words were addressed to those who were under the Jewish dispensation, what have I to do with them? or unbelief would persuade us to say so of such a general promise as this; but when it is said I have chosen *thee*, and we know that no scripture is of private interpretation, but, like its blessed author, is *the same yesterday, to-day, and for ever*, there is no loop-hole, as it were, for unbelief to creep out at; but every believer may, in all ages, in the words of the text, say to himself, *God has chosen me in the furnace of affliction*. Perhaps, there is not a more comfortable passage in the whole book of God; I do not know of one that has a greater tendency to silence a complaining child of God, or to make a poor suffering believer happy, and to rest under

the

the promise, to kiss the rod of God that strikes the blow.

Where shall I begin, where shall I end? the very first words open such a field, that eternity itself will be but just long enough for us to take a view of it; the time is come that even some good people that have the grace of God in their hearts, have such muddy heads as to kick at the doctrine of election, and look upon it as having a tendency to make us bad in our heads, or Antinomians in our hearts; but if we have eyes to see, and ears to hear, and if our hearts are really informed by the Spirit; if we have been anointed with his eye-salve, O then electing, sovereign, distinguishing love flows in such a scene, such a transporting scene, as will make a believer's heart leap for joy. For my own part, I know no other doctrine that can truly humble the man; for either God must chuse us, or we must chuse God; either God must be the first mover, or man must be the first mover; either God must chuse them on account of some goodness, on account of some purity, or acts of piety, or God must chuse them merely of his grace, for his own name's sake, and to let us know that we have not chosen him, but he has chosen us. I verily believe,

believe, that the grand reason why such doctrine is so spurned at, and hated by carnal people, is, that it strikes at the very root of human pride, cuts the sinews of free-will all to pieces, and brings the poor sinner to lie down at the foot of sovereign grace; and, let his attainments in the school of Christ be ever so great, it constrains him to cry out, Lord, why me! why me! Our Master, and I think we should not attempt to be wiser than our Master was, speaks particularly of and to his own school, his little college of apostles: *Thine they were, and thou gavest them me; I have chosen you, but ye have not chosen me.—Because I have chosen you out of the world, therefore the world hateth you.* Before they were fully enlightened, though they were afterwards brought more to the light, two of them at first said, *we have found the Messiah*; yet when they were sunk deeper in the knowledge of themselves, they changed their note, and said, the Messiah has found us. Observe the manner of the Redeemer's addressing our first parent, when their guilt had caused them to hide themselves, *Adam, where art thou?* Pray who called first, did Adam call after Christ, or did Christ call after him; or do you think there is

any

Ser. VIII. *The Furnace of Affliction.* 185

any difference between us and Adam, or that we have got better hearts than Adam had; do you think we are wifer and better now? Adam run away from God, and so should we to this very day, unless Jesus Christ had called us to himself.

Some persons, perhaps, may say, Well, I like your doctrine very well; God chuses us, you say, when we have no regard to any good works at all, therefore I will go on sinning, because the fitter I shall be for God's grace; and the fitter thou mayst be for hell.—Grace does not destroy the use of the law; an honest heart will draw that inference from it, as a good woman once did when the devil told her, that either God had chosen her and she should be saved, or if she was rejected she should be damned, so, said he, you need not strive; she answered, if there were but two to be saved, I would strive to be one of them: God help us to draw that inference.

Now this word *chosen,* refers us to God's eternal election; it comprehends, and is the source of all that God has done for believers, for every individual believer in particular when Jesus bowed his head and gave up the ghost. Hence the apostle, in the eighth of the Ro-

B b mans,

mans, mentioning this doctrine in the clearest manner, triumphs over the accuser by asking, *Who shall lay any thing to the charge of God's elect?* and in the same chapter declares, *that it is God that glorifies:* for though glorification is the last thing done to us, yet it is the first thing God designs for us. What is the great thing for a natural man to hear? what is it? why, not only that God has chosen us, but *chosen us in the furnace of affliction:* O that the Spirit of God may vouchsafe to transcribe these words into our hearts! God help thee to take it to thyself, O man; to take it to thyself, O woman; to take it to thyself whoever thou art that art either a Christian now, or desires or hopes to be a Christian before thou diest, *I have chosen thee in the furnace of affliction.*

What can be the meaning of the words? why, 'tis very plain that the import of them must be this; I have chosen thee, and it is my determination from everlasting to the end of time, and for ever. I have chosen thee with this determination, that the way to heaven should be through the road of affliction: this is the believer's way, especially the ministers of Christ. When Paul was converted,

pray

pray what preferment did God promife him? was it to be a great dignitary in the church? no, nothing about the church? was it any more eafe, was it to wear a triple crown, were perfons to come and kifs his toe, what preferment did God chufe him to? what? fays God, *I will fhow him what great things he muft fuffer for my name's fake.* I verily believe, that if we were to have no other preferment than this of Paul, there is not one in a thoufand of the minifters that would afk for a living, if they knew they were to have fuch poor wages as Paul had. Minifters that hold the ftandard up, muft expect the enemy will fire on them from every quarter; and if they happen to be inftrumental in comforting others, *with the fame comforts wherewith they themfelves are comforted of God,* they muft expect to bear their part, not only for their own purification, but for the benefit of thofe to whom they minifter; and I believe audiences find that minifters minifter beft, and the bread comes beft, when it comes out of the furnace of a minifter's affliction.

The word affliction is of a very complex kind; it is like the word tribulation, which comes from the latin *tribulus,* fignifying a

pricking

pricking thorn, a scratching briar, or wounding spikes concealed in the way; and the word affliction arises from a word that signifies something that beats down, presses sore, and is very grievous and tormenting; it is a word of so general import, that it takes in all the trouble we meet with from men, all the wounds we receive from enemies, as well as in the house of our friends; it takes in all our domestic trials, all our inward struggles and dreadful temptations occasioned by the fiery darts of a watchful devil; and if I am not mistaken, when the great God said, *I have chosen thee in the furnace of affliction*, it implys, that this is really to continue with us even to the very end of our days: this is what young converts, in the time of their first love, do not see; that is, do not wholly see it; for if young Christians were to know all they have to suffer, it would dreadfully discourage them. God says, his people shall not do so and so, because at their first setting out they would be disheartned, and think of going back. It is our happiness God lets us know our trials but very little before-hand, very little notice of them have we before the time, and then, perhaps, gives us but little respite; but O when one

trial

trial is gone, God does with us as masters do with their scholars, turns over a new leaf with us; and when one trial is over, teaches us another; hence our trials are not only new, but constant; hence many a believer is apt to say, *My trials rise out of the ground*; and many believers are saying, who would have thought such a trial would have befallen me at such a time, from such a hand? this may, perhaps, open to us a gloomy scene; it would be gloomy indeed, if we were not living in a state of preparation; it would be gloomy indeed, if God was to afflict without a cause; but there is so much corruption, such remainders of indwelling sin, even in God's own children that are to stand nearest to him in glory, that are the dearest to him, and who are to be blessed with being in his bosom, that if God was not to send them afflictions, there is not a child of God but would overset even with the comforts God vouchsafes to them. We find it so with our bodies, that if we live without exercise we are liable to have a variety of diseases, we therefore submit to various ways and means that a physician can prescribe; and if the disorders to which we are exposed in our bodies, make us willing to submit to a regimen prescribed

scribed by a skilful physician, does it not follow by a parity of reasoning, that we for our souls want sometimes lenitives, and corrosives, and something like a caustic to eat off the proud flesh that cleaves to us? and it vindicates God's ways to man, that there is an hereafter appointed for us, that there is another world, to which, perhaps, we shall be called to go before the morning, *where the inhabitants shall no more say,* **I am sick.** Believers know this, and if they cannot keep a ledger book, if they cannot post a merchant's book, they may learn so much of divine arithmetic, as to know that *the light afflictions which are but for a moment, work for us a far more exceeding and eternal weight of glory.* The way to heaven, good bishop Beveridge says, is narrow, but it is not long; the gates are strait, but open to everlasting life; and therefore *God has chosen us in the furnace of affliction,* because if we were not afflicted, we should never know what we were made of. Mr. Bohem, who was chaplain to the prince of Denmark, that was married to queen Anne, in one of his excellent sermons upon affliction, has this observation, " Afflictions and temptations are like sunbeams falling upon a dunghill; they do not bring

bring vapours into the dunghill, but they exhale the vapours." So afflictions do not bring the corruptions into us; we blame such and such a one for stirring up such and such corruptions in us, but these tend to draw out the vapours, and prepare us for the more lasting sunshine of a smiling God. God does not intend to destroy thee, but to refine thee, and to humble thee by it. The devil wants to sift thee as wheat; he thinks to let the grain go through the sieve, but Christ will only let the chaff fall through, and the sooner that is gone the better: so it is no ways derogatory to the honour of Christ, but agreeable to the state in which we are, agreeable to the state and the preparations to be made for eternity, agreeable to the militant disposition that our graces must retain. Hence our Lord was content to be called God's servant, *Behold my servant whom I have chosen, mine elect in whom my soul delighteth.*—*Though he was a son, he learned obedience by the things that he suffered*; he was made perfect by his sufferings. We cannot avoid trouble as men, as Christians we should not attempt it: *man is born to trouble as the sparks fly upwards*; and Christians, especially the man new-born. *If these things were done* to the green tree, what shall be done to the dry? The cross is the high-road to heaven, and so the king's highway: you know there is always a bar upon the king's road, the king has a particular road for himself; but the King of kings will make all bars to be removed, and then his people go the same road he himself went: this was the road of all the children of God; there is not an heir of God in heaven, but is now thanking God for his sufferings here below; there is not a child of God ever received into glory, but, I believe, as soon as he comes there, is made to know why he met with such a trial, and from such a quarter; why he was under such a rod, why under it so long; why it was shifted, why it was changed, why the whip sometimes was turned to a scorpion, and the furnace heated seven times hotter; then the believer sees the need of it: in heaven, it makes him wonder he was not afflicted seven times more on earth. I remember Virgil makes his hero in the Æneid to say, *'twould all end well* [*]. He comforts himself with this consideration under his trouble, that the discharge from it would be the better;

and

---

[*] Dabit Deus his quoque finem.
 Forsan et hæc olim meminisse juvabit,
 Per varios casus, per tot discrimina rerum,
 Tendimus in Latium.

and if a child of God would think of that, hereafter he will look with pleasure on what he suffered here; much more a Christian enriched with the grace of God, will be willing to die when he considers he is hereafter to sit in Abraham's bosom, and God says to him, *Remember thou in thy life-time received thy evil things.* O my brethren, a fine school is the school of Christ! I never knew any one of my acquaintance that were believers, and I have been acquainted with some these twenty-eight years last past, but what flourished most under the afflicting hand of God. I believe if the devil had his will, he would bid too high for every believer; he does not love money; a covetous man is worse than the devil, he loves that which the devil squanders away; but say they, we think we should be very good if we had a coach and six; so when they have it, they think they are too good to go to that chapel or foundery; it was a good place when we walked a-foot, but now we have a coach we will drive by. Happy is it for us that we are chosen in the furnace of affliction; that is a glorious petition in our litany, *That in all time of our tribulation, good Lord deliver us!* You may very well excuse me for preaching from such a text as this, because I have been in the furnace, and I find it is very sweet; it is very sweet walking in a burning fiery furnace when the Son of God leads by the arm. In the account we have of the three children being in the fiery furnace, the king could say, *I see one walking with them:* what an emblem of the children of God! O, say you, does the Son of God walk with you in the furnace? I answer, yes; make the worst of it, tell them the enthusiast, the babler says, God walks with his people in the furnace; he walks with all that walk with him, and never walks closer with them than when they are in the furnace. Daniel is generally painted young, but he was four-score years old when he was thrown in among the lions, there he sits as sweet and easy, and no lion dare to touch one of his grey hairs. Nothing proves the truth of grace, and shows the love of God more, and you may be assured of it as you are of being in this place alive, that sanctified afflictions are the greatest evidence God can give you of his love; so that if we are chosen in the furnace of affliction, we are to expect it; and is it not a great shame for us, that the heathens out-do us? when one came and told one of the

heathens

heathens that his son, a darling son, was dead, he said, "I know that I begot him mortal." So Job said, *The Lord hath given, and the Lord hath taken away*. O that God may bless this poor preaching to the raising up some drooping soul. Underneath thee, O believer, O sufferer, are God's everlasting arms; therefore *the beloved of the Lord shall dwell in safety*, because they dwell near him, and *he that toucheth them, toucheth the apple of God's eye*.

This may teach us, when one trouble is over to expect another; none of your requiems here. Abraham, I believe, thought when he had got his Isaac, he was to be tried no more; but *after these things God did tempt Abraham*. We know not what trials we are to have, but remember they are marks of our adoption: not that all afflictions do prove us children of God, because there are some afflictions that are not sanctified: God give us all to have sanctified afflictions!

If this is the case, let young believers know what they are to meet with; God forgive those, and visible churches are too much pestered with them, that daub with untempered mortar: formerly, when the church was under persecution, they would forsake father, mother,

mother, and all; but *now, blessed be God, we are for becoming Christians; we live in London, we live where the church is smiled upon, we may live where we are at ease.*—My dear hearers, do you think that all the Londoners are converted? do you think they all bring forth the fruits of the Spirit; or have you heard that the devil is converted? can any body prove to me that the devil is not the same; can you prove that God is not the same; can you prove that the world is not the same, that the human heart is not the same? if you can prove that neither of these are what they were when Christ came into the world, I will give up the point; but if they are the same, we must expect the same trials our forefathers met with, if ever we hope to meet with them in glory; *God forbid I should glory, save in the cross of Jesus Christ.* Therefore, if any of us have a mind to set out for heaven, expect trouble. Indeed, if we have enlisted under the devil's banner, he shows you the kingdoms of the world, and the glory of them. When Peter said to our Lord, concerning his sufferings, *far be that from thee;* after having shown his displeasure at it, as a suggestion of satan's, he says to all his disciples, *If any man will come*

come after me, let him take up his cross and follow me. And I remember Mr. Law, who was a great man, notwithstanding some great blunders and mistakes, told me thirty-two years ago, all principles, all doctrines, are comprehended in these few words, *If any man will come after me, let him deny himself and take up his cross and follow me.* And if you do not chuse the furnace of affliction, if you are too nice to enter in, you forsake the Lord, and are only preparing to be company for the damned in hell. This was the case with Dives; *Son, thou in thy life-time received thy good things:* and for a man that fares sumptuous every day; for a man that is cloathed in fine linen, to be tormented by the devil; to see God, Christ, heaven, with all he had, lost; and the torments must never cease. One moments thought of this is very awful! God grant this may not be the lot of any of us! Come, my dear hearers, may God of his infinite mercy grant this night, that some poor soul may be rescued from the devil, and enlist under Christ's banner! I have bore the cross thirty-four years; I never wore it long, but I found to my great comfort it was lined with the love of God. *My yoke is easy, my burden*

burden is light, faith our blessed Lord. Suffering grace is given for suffering times; the reason we have not more comfort is, because we have not more crosses: happy they that say in this visitation, my Jesus, my Lord, I give up all for thee; my life, and all things, I cast behind.

> *A heart that no desire will move,*
> *But still to adore, obey, and love,*
> *Give me, my Lord, my life, my all.*

I wish you joy that run this course; don't be weary of it, don't think hard of God, don't say, never was any body tried as I am, never was any body tempted as I am, for if you was to go and tell your cross, there are a thousand in the congregation would, perhaps, say, dear I have had that and ten times worse. One Mr. Buchanan, a Scotchman, who died the other day, having lost his last child, said, " I am now childless, but, blessed be God, I am not Christless." A noble lady told me herself, that when she was crying on account of one of her children's death, her little daughter came innocently to her one day and said, " Mamma, is God Almighty dead, you cry so? the lady blushing, said, no; she replied, Madam, will you lend me your glove? she let her take it,

and

and after that asked for it again; upon which the child said, Now you have taken the glove from me, shall I cry because you have taken away your own glove? and shall you cry because God has taken away my sister." *Out of the mouths of babes has God perfected praise*, and will for ever. O glorify God in the furnace!

If any of you are saying, don't tell me of your afflictions, I will live, I will drink, *tomorrow shall be as to-day, and so much the more*. If there be any of you that say so, take care, take care, God himself can't issue out a worse sentence against you than this, *Let him alone, let him alone*; whom the Lord loves he chastens. What a pretty creature would you make in heaven, if you was to go there, without one of Christ's crosses on your back, you would be turned out; no, there are none such there.

Christians endure the cross; happy ye that are tried, and happy they that are gone to glory. Where is Mr. Middleton now? where is my dear fellow-labourer, that honest, that steady man of God? Oh! he was thanking God for the gout in his head, in his feet, in his stomach, all decays; thanking God for

that

that last trouble that cut the thread of life, and gave the soul a passage for heaven; if, in the midst of that torture, he could answer his daughter and say, *heaven upon earth, heaven upon earth*, and went to heaven but a little after; now surely he must say, *heaven in heaven*; must he not now he sees God, and sees Christ? and by his comfort, though in such great pain, it shows that God was kissing away his soul, he died at the very mouth of God. O may the blessed God bless his parents and children that are here to-night; I believe you may be glad that God has chosen him in the furnace of affliction. I am glad to hear that so many are desirous that something may be done for his family, and Mr. ——, and Mr. ——, and Mr. ——, are willing to take in the subscriptions that any may be inclined to send them. May God bless the family, and grant that his children may not disgrace the memory of their father; that they may live as followers of his faith, who is now gone to inherit the promises of God. You know not how your children may be left by you, though there is not one of you here but may be called that have children, to say, by and by my children must be left to the goodness of God; and it is

a great

a great happiness to see so many fatherless children provided for of late: there was never a time when persons were more beneficent to the distressed; let it not be said that believers in London live on bread alone, but may they be continuing to lay up treasure in heaven! when we plead, not by way of merit, remember me, O Lord, I did so and so when others were in trouble. Lord Jesus, I plead thy promises, if thou hast chosen me in the furnace of affliction; O Lord, help me to lay hold on thee: O that this may be your and my lot. I am hastning to the grave; I am astonished that I have again an opportunity to preach the word of God. May God prepare us to follow those that have gone before us, *where the wicked cease from troubling*, and the weary soul enjoys everlasting rest with thee, O Father, with thee, O Son, and with the Holy Ghost; to whom, three persons but one God, be all honour and glory, now and for evermore. Amen.

SERMON IX.

The Lord our Light.

ISAIAH lx. ver. 19, 20.

The sun shall be no more thy light by day, neither for brightness shall the moon give light unto thee, but the Lord shall be unto thee an everlasting light, and thy God thy glory. Thy sun shall no more go down, neither shall thy moon withdraw itself, for the Lord shall be thine everlasting light, and the days of thy mourning shall be ended.

UPON reading these words, I cannot help thinking of what the royal Psalmist said, *Glorious things are spoken of thee, O city of God. Selah.* I am afraid, my dear hearers, that even believers themselves, who have tasted of the grace of God, reflect not and meditate as they ought, on the glorious and amazing felicity they are called

called by the Spirit of God to experience in this life. We content ourselves too much with our hopes, and if we attain to *a good hope through grace,* we are ready to think we have got up to the last step of the gospel ladder, and have nothing more to do but to rest in that hope, without ever attaining to an abiding, full assurance of faith. If we would examine the scriptures, and not chuse to bring them down to us, but beg of God to raise our hearts up to them, we shall find the believer is made partaker of the grace of life, as well as an heir of it; the one is on earth, the other in heaven, and one is only a prelibation of the other. This blessed prophet Isaiah, speaking of the privileges of the children of God, saith, *Eye hath not seen, nor ear heard, neither hath it entered into the heart of man to conceive the things that God hath prepared* (and that even here below) *for those that love him:* God grant that we may be of that happy number! Hence, like an evangelist, the prophet draws aside the veil, and as one inspired by the Spirit of God, and filled with the rays of divine light, gives us a transporting view of the gospel state, and the glory which the church militant enjoys below, before its triumphant state above.

The text, probably, refers to the great change that should be made in the affairs of the Jews after their captivity, how wonderfully God would appear for them, after their harps had been long hanging on the willows, and they could make no other answer to their insulting foes than this mournful one, *How can we sing the Lord's song in a strange land?* The gospel is, doubtless, glad tidings of great joy; and however the people of God might be encouraged to hope that the time would come, when they should tread on the necks of their enemies, the prophet teaches them to look further, and lets them know that their happiness was not to consist in any external created good, but in a larger possession of the graces and comforts of the Holy Ghost. So that this chapter speaks not only of a temporal deliverance and rest, which they should enjoy after their trouble, but a spiritual rest, which, by faith, they should enter into here, as the earnest and pledge of the rest and enjoyment of the better world hereafter. As we know no more of heaven than is discovered by the eye of faith, for even St. Paul acknowledges, that the things he saw were unutterable, 'tis observable that heaven in scripture is described to us more by what it is not, than by what it is. So in the words of the text, *Thy sun shall no more go down, neither shall thy moon withdraw itself, for the Lord shall be thine everlasting light, and the days of thy mourning shall be ended.* Here are three negatives, and but one positive, namely, *the Lord shall be thy everlasting light*, which is a beautiful allusion to the sun, that should teach us to spiritualize natural things; and if we feared God, and lived near to him as we ought, there is no object of our bodily eyes but might improve our spiritual sight. You cannot suppose the prophet meant a time should come, when the sun should not literally go down, that there should not be night and day as now; God indeed permitted a man once to say, *sun, stand thou still*, and it was done; but, perhaps, there never will be any such thing again till the sun is removed from its station, and the moon forsake her orbit, and be turned into blood. The word must therefore be understood in a figurative sense; and then comparing spiritual things with spiritual, it must certainly import, that Jesus Christ, the Sun of Righteousness, shall be what the sun is to the visible world, that is, the light and life of all his people;

people; I say, all the people of God. You see now, the sun shines on us all: I never heard that the sun said, Lord, I will not shine on the Presbyterians, I will not shine on the Independants, I will not shine on the people called Methodists, those great enthusiasts; the sun never said yet, I will not shine on the Papists; the sun shines on all, which shows that Jesus Christ's love is open to all that are made willing by the Holy Ghost to accept of him; and therefore it is said, *the sun of righteousness shall arise with healing under his wings.* If you were all up this morning before the sun arose at five o'clock, how beautiful was his first appearance! how pleasant to behold the flowers opening to the rising sun! I appeal to you yourselves, when you were looking out at window, or walking about, or opening your shop, if in a spiritual frame, whether you did not say, Arise thou sun of righteousness with healing under thy wings, on me. All that the natural sun is to the world, Jesus Christ is, and more, to his people; without the sun we should have no corn, or fruit of any kind: what a dark place would the world be without the sun, and how dark would the world be without Jesus Christ; and as the sun does

really

really communicate its rays to the earth, the plants, and to all this lower creation, so the Son of God does really communicate his life and power to every new created soul, otherwise Christ is but a painted sun; and is Christ nothing but a painted Christ to us, while we receive heat and benefit by the Holy Ghost, on account of the virtue of his blood? Sometimes the sun shines brighter than at other times, and does not always appear alike; clouds intervene and interrupt its rays; so it is between a renewed soul and the Lord Jesus, the sun of righteousness; O my brethren, I believe you know it by fatal experience: hold but your hand now, when the sun shines in its meridian, between it and you, and if by the breadth of that you can keep the sun from you, ah! how very little earth will keep off thy heart from Jesus Christ! It was a very excellent saying of one of the antients, that God never leaves a person till he first leaves him. Some people think God does so of his sovereignty, but I am apt to think when the sun shines, we shall find some people have taken up with something short of the sun of righteousness; and I believe there are times, when the poor believer thinks his sun will quite go down, and rise no more:

he

he loses his relish, his taste and evidence of divine things; not only are the rays intercepted for a while, but doubts and fears, a dreadful cloud of them, come on. Though I hold with a full assurance of faith, yet I am of opinion that 'tis not always in a like exercise; and therefore pray that doubting people will not take hold of that, and say, Blessed be God, I am in a doubting state, and I am content. The Lord deliver you from a mind to stay in prison, and prevent the devil from locking the door upon you, and keeping you there as long as he can. The Lord help you to come; come, come, and break out of prison, that you may know how pleasant it is to behold the Sun, and praise his name.

Sometimes, instead of the sun there is only moon-light, which shews the difference a believer feels in his soul, both in relation to grace and comfort. Both sun and moon give light, but O how far superior is the one to the other: the moon gives a very faint, uncertain light, waxes and wanes, and at best is almost nothing when compared with the light, and the blessed reviving heat of the sun. Hence, my brethren, this world sometimes is a world of mourners: it is said, *that the days of our mourning shall be ended*; for if the text refers to the future state, as no doubt it does, it means that the days of believers here below are very often mournful, trying, and afflicting, though they end in joy, as our Lord intimates in his opening his gospel-sermon almost with these very words, *Blessed are they that mourn, for they shall be comforted.* Some, perhaps, may think it is an odd kind of blessing; and though worldly people are fond of the fifth of Matthew, and wonder that Methodists and gospel-ministers do not preach oftner on that chapter, I am apt to believe, when you come to preach and open that word, they will not like that chapter any more than any other, because they are for a joyful Christ, and not for any mourning at all. Do you know God in Christ? let me tell you, the more you are acquainted with him, the more your souls will be kept in a mourning state. A mournful state!—O, say you, people will mourn before they are converted.—Ah, that they will.—I don't love to hear of conversions without any secret mourning; I seldom see such souls established. I have heard of a person who was in company once with fourteen ministers of the gospel, some of whom were eminent servants of Christ, and yet not one of them could tell the time God first manifested himself to their soul. Zaccheus's was a very quick conversion, perhaps not a quarter of an hour's conviction: this I mention, that we may not condemn one another. We do not love the pope, because we love to be popes ourselves, and set up our own experience as a standard to others. Those that had such a conversion as the jaylor, or the Jews: O, say you, we do not like to hear you talk of shaking over hell, we love to hear of conversion by the love of God; while others that were so shaken, as Mr. Bolton and other eminent men were, may say, you are not Christians because you had not the like terrible experience. You may as well say to your neighbour, you have not had a child, for you were not in labour all night. The question is, whether a real child is born, not how long was the preceding pain, but whether it was productive of a new birth, and whether Christ has been formed in your hearts; it is the birth proves the reality of the thing.

Some allow that there is mourning before, but no mourning after conversion; pray who says so? none but an Antinomian, a rank Antinomian; and when you hear a person say,

that

that after conversion you will have no mourning, you may be assured that person is at best walking by moon-light; he does not walk by the sun, he has got some doctrine in his head, but very little grace, I am afraid, in his heart. How! how! my brethren, not mourn after we are converted; why, till then there is no true mourning at all. The damned in hell are mourning now, they put on their mourning as soon as they get there. How am I tormented in this flame, says Dives; and Cain, my punishment is greater than I can bear. How many worldly people break their hearts for the loss of the world: they cannot keep their usual equipage, nor do as they would; and come not to worship on Sunday, because they cannot appear so fine as formerly they did: this is a sorrow of the world that worketh death; but there is a blessed, a more evangelical mourning, which is the habitual, blessed state and frame of a converted soul. How strong the expression, *They shall look on him whom they have pierced, and shall mourn:* how shall they mourn? *as one mourneth for a first-born, an only child.* Have you ever been called to bury a child? is there any tender mother here? were you merry directly after the child was dead? no, perhaps till this very day, you continually call to remembrance your little one and shed a tear; every thing relating to it, causes the repetition of your sorrow. When a poor believer is acquainted with Jesus Christ, he mourns for having crucified the Son of God, and you will mourn for the same sin after conversion as before. Surely, says some, I mourn for my sins I committed before my conversion. I do not know whether you do or no, but I know you should. O, says David, *Remember not against me the sins of my youth*, in a Psalm which was wrote when he was an old man; and Paul says, *I was a blasphemer and injurious, and therefore not worthy to be called an apostle, because I persecuted the church of God*; and this after he had been wrapped up to the third heaven. See Mary rushing into the house, washing her Lord's feet with her tears, and wiping them with her hair: I don't suppose she was dressed as our ladies are now; they did not make such apes of themselves; but her hair was very fine in an honest way: though she breaks the allibaster box of ointment given her, perhaps by some poor silly creature that would die by her frowns, and live upon her smiles, see her at the feet of her

her Saviour; and Jesus Christ answers for her, some having thought she was profuse, that having had much forgiven, she loved much. The more the love of God is manifested, the more it will melt the soul down: I appeal to you Christians, whether the sweetest times you ever enjoyed, were not those when you were much melted at the sight of a crucified Saviour; when you could say, Lord, thou forgavest me, I feel it, I know it, but I cannot forgive myself; this will always be the effect of an ingenuous mind; and a person that is really converted will thus mourn, and if you do not know this, you may be assured you know nothing savingly of Jesus Christ. You may go and hear this and that warning, and you are right to gather honey from every flower, but you have not got within the inner court, but are yet without. God give you to see your folly herein.

A true believer will mourn over his corruptions: I wonder what they can think, who suppose they have no corruptions. I remember a poor creature of Rhode-Island, who looked the most like the old Puritans I ever saw, when I was talking with him, and said, some people say there are some men that have no sin; he said, if you send such a man to me, I will pay his charges even from England and back again. I have often learned something from the difference of glasses: you look into the common glasses, and see yourselves there so fine, and admire your person, dress, &c. but when you view yourselves through a microscope, how many worms are discovered in that fine skin of yours, enough to make you ashamed of the vermin and filth that is seated there: so it is in faith, that glass would show you so much corruption cleaving to every action of your lives, that would make you sin-sick, and mourn that you have known God so long, and are like him so little. What says Paul? *Who shall deliver me from the body of this death?* Notwithstanding he knew that *there is no condemnation to them that are in Christ Jesus*, yet cries out, *O wretched man that I am!* I should have thought, O happy man that thou art! formerly a persecutor, and now a preacher; a man that has been honoured so much above every man in planting churches, which is the highest honour a man can have under heaven; here is a man that hath been wrapt up to the third heaven,—what of him? *O wretched man that I am, who shall deliver me me from this body of sin and death?* Do you think that it was only a little qualm of conscience? no, it was the habitual temper of his heart. Some people are much humbled by fits and starts, but Paul felt this daily: many things that we are not concerned about, Paul looked upon them as such that made his heart ach, because he thought he could not live near enough to God. He not only watched to do good, but he watched how he did that good; and nature was so mixed with it, that he said, I cannot do as I would do, I would have served God like an angel, but I find myself to be a poor sinner after all; and if we are like-minded with Paul, we shall mourn over our corruptions, we shall mourn over our hidden sins that none know but God and ourselves. It is a very dangerous thing to trust gospel-gossips, who being strangers to themselves, hear with wonder and contempt, and often betray; however, a judicious friend, into whose bosom we can pour out our souls, and tell our corruptions as well as our comforts, is a very great privilege. When our corruptions do not drive us from Christ, but drive us to him, it is the greatest blessing to commune with Christ on this side heaven: and, my

brethren,

brethren, if your hearts are right with God, you will see such things as nobody else could think of. A good woman, who was charmed with Dr. Manton, said, O, sir, you have made an excellent sermon to-day, I wish I had your heart; do you so, said he, good woman, you had better not wish for it, for if you had it, you would wish for your own again. The best of men see themselves in the worst light.

How many thousand things are there that make you mourn here below! who can tell the tears that godly parents shed for ungodly children! O you young folks, you don't know what plague your children may be to you! O they are pretty things while young, like rattle-snakes and alligators, which I have seen when little, but put them in your bosom and you will find they are dangerous. How many are there in the world that would wish, if it were lawful, that God had written them childless: there is many a poor creature that makes his father's heart ach. I once asked a godly widow, madam, how is your son; she turned aside with tears, and said, sir, he is no son to me now. What in the world can come up to that! here, says one, I have bred up my children, I cannot charge myself with educating

them

them wrong, though few parents can say that, for many parents lead them into the paths of death, and so are murderers of their own children, and by their manner of education help to damn them for ever; but if you can say, I have done all I could, and yet, O my God, my children are worse than any other peoples; this is a dreadful state indeed; and the more you mourn, the more they laugh at you; O these are my godly parents. They increase their trouble, like Dr. Horneck's son, who said, *There is not a post in my father's house but stinks of piety.* I once saw a man that was awakened at the Orphan-house, fall down and throw himself on one of their beds, crying out, O, sir, what will become of my poor grey-headed father, who knows nothing of this birth! It is a difficulty with some to know how to behave towards unconverted relations; if you don't go to them, they will say you are precise; if you do, and are faithful, they will soon show you they have enough of your company: this sends a godly person home mourning; and then there comes a thought, shall I speak to them any more, or let them go to the devil. This is not like parting from your friends by death, but burying them alive:

when dead, we know we must submit, but to part from friends, those we loved, and thought to have lived with till we came to heaven, is mournful indeed.

Moreover, the poor state of the church makes many a minister and close-walker with God to weep over the desolations of the sanctuary, and to mourn for those that will not mourn for themselves: thus our Lord wept over Jerusalem, *O Jerusalem, Jerusalem, how often would I have gathered thy children, as a hen gathereth her chickens*, but it is over with thee now; the decree is gone forth, and Jerusalem shall suffer.

Brethren, the time will fail, and therefore I leave it to you to supply more cases; for if I was to preach till to-morrow morning, I doubt not but a thousand here would say, there are many things you have not mentioned yet. You know the state of your own hearts, and the many particular trials in your own case; and you may also know, though your trial seems over, it is only changed: but let it be observed, the day of your mourning shall be ended; mind, it is but days, though sometimes made very sad ones indeed, by the neglect and ingratitude of those who have made the people of God ferve them with rigour, as though all the world was made for them, as well as their incapacity to help themfelves, by poverty, pain, fore ficknefses, and of long continuance. This has been, and is the lot of many a child of God; blefsed be fovereign mercy, 'tis but a few days. An end fhall arrive, and that end fhall be happy, when death, the believer's friend, fhall come with an angel's face, to difmifs them from all their fin and forrow. When I was laft at Briftol, I could not help remembring good Mr. Middleton, who ufed you know to have the gout very much, and in that clofet were kept his crutches: now, thought I, he needs them no more, the days of his mourning are ended, and fo fhall ours by and by too, when we fhall no longer want our fpiritual crutches or armour, but fhall fay to the helmet of hope, the fhield of faith, I have no more need of thee; and the all-prevailing weapon of prayer be changed into fongs of endlefs praife; when God himfelf fhall be our everlafting light, a fun that fhall never go down more, but fhall beam forth his infinite and eternal love in a beatific ftate for ever. The profpect of this made one of the fathers cry out, O glory! how great! how great!

great! what art thou? a friend asking him what he saw? he answered, I see the glory of the only begotten Son of God. And if a sight of Christ on earth is so great, as could make good Mr. Wardrobe, an excellent Scotch minister say, after he was given over, starting up in the arms of an excellent friend who told it me, in a rapture of joy, crowns! crowns! crowns of glory shall adorn this head of mine e're long! and stretching up, added, stars! stars! stars shall e're long fill these hands of mine! and so sweetly fell asleep in Jesus: what a pleasing, awful trial is that for an affectionate friend! So our dear sister, who is to be buried to-morrow night at Tottenham-court, talked with her friends for an hour or two, and took leave of her husband and children, and said, Now come, ye heavenly chariots! We shall thank God then for all our losses, crosses, and disappointments; and I believe those things which we mourn for most, and puts us most to the trial, will give us most comfort when we come to die: God shall be our everlasting light, as well as the days of our mourning shall be ended.

Take care, don't be secure, pray don't think the day of your mourning to be ended yet:

yet: you may put off mourning for your friends, but may have fresh cause of mourning for your souls; whilst you remember that holy mourning is consistent with holy walking, following the Lord in all his ways. You have often heard me speak of one of our ministers, who was not one of your fine velvet mouths, that said once in the pulpit, As sure as you see the sun shine on my breast, which at that time it did, so sure does the Spirit of God dwell in the souls of true believers. How often has he told you, *I am for having you have godly sorrow, I wish your hearts were full of it, because it will end in everlasting joy.* Comfort, my brethren, one another with these things, the day of your mourning shall soon be ended for ever.

But what am I to say? I apprehend I shall grow forgetful to-night;—I have spoken so much to saints, I am afraid I shall have but little time to speak to sinners: I mean, I have taken so much time up in speaking to you that know God, that I have but little to speak to you that know him not. How different your state, poor hearts! poor hearts! my soul mourns for you; my blood, whilst I am speaking, is ready to curdle in my veins. The seraphic

raphic Mr. Hervey, when he did me that honour to sojourn under my roof, said, My dear friend, it is an awful thing when we see an unconverted man die, and his eyes closed, to think that that poor soul will never see one gleam of comfort or life more; to have a sight of God, of Christ, and the heavenly angels and saints; but to see what the rich man saw, a God they want; to see Lazarus, whom he would not permit to be seen at his door, now taken particular notice of in heaven; and to see himself now a beggar in hell. The Lord help you to think! O think how soon your sun will go down, and even your bodies will feel damnation, not only in respect to pain, but loss.

Bishop Usher's opinion was, and I heartily concur in it, that those who value themselves most on their beauty and dress, and do not love God on earth, will be most deformed in hell, and their bodies suffer proportionally there. There is no dressing in hell, nothing but fire and brimstone there, and the wrath of God always awaiting on thee, O sinner, whoever thou art, man or woman. It was a fine saying of Maclane, who was executed some years ago, when the cap was pulling over his eyes,

eyes, Muſt I never ſee the light of yon ſun any more; Lord Jeſus Chriſt, thou ſun of righteouſneſs, ariſe with healing under thy wings on my departing ſoul! May the Lord Jeſus Chriſt do that for us all! When you are damned, the days of your mourning will be but at their beginning; there is no end of your mourning in hell. There is but one ſong, if it may be called ſo, in hell, to wit, that of Dives, which will be always repeating, *How am I tormented in this flame!* Conſider this, ye that forget God; and O that God may bleſs you to-night with godly ſorrow. Believers, pray for them: Lord help you, ſinners, to pray for your vile ſelves. Some may think, what do you cry for? why, I cry for you. Perhaps you will ſay as a wicked one did to a poor woman in Scotland, when thouſands were awakened there; ſeeing her weep, he ſaid, what do you weep for? for this people, ſays ſhe; weep for yourſelf, ſays he; ſhe replied, I do; but what is my ſoul, to all theſe poor ſouls! O that miniſters may never riſe up in judgment againſt you: O may Moſes, in the hand of the Spirit, make you mourn! may the love of God make you cry! may you not go home to-night without

an

an arrow steeped in the blood of Christ. It was wonderful what a good woman awaking thought she saw written over her head, *O earth, earth, earth, hear the word of the Lord!* May every earthly soul be made to hear it; to awake, arise from their sleep in sin. The sun is going down, and death may put an end to all to-night: the Lord help you to come, though it is the eleventh hour: O that you would fly, fly this night to Christ, lest God destroy you for ever. Jesus stands ready with open arms to receive you whom he has first pricked to the heart, and made you cry out, *What shall I do to be saved!* he will then make you believe in his name, that you may be saved: God grant this may be the case of all here to-night. Amen.

SERMON X.

Self-Enquiry concerning the Work of God.

NUMBERS xxiii. ver. 23.

According to this time it shall be said of Jacob and of Israel, what hath God wrought?

WHEN I read you, my dear hearers, these words; when I consider what occasion, and by whom they were originally spoke, I can't help thinking of that triumphant expression of the royal Psalmist, *Why do the Heathen rage?* When Pontius Pilate and the Jews conspire to destroy the cause of God, *he that sitteth in heaven laughs them to scorn; the Lord not only has them in derision*, but over-rules even their malice and violence (no thanks to them) to promote that very cause they attempted to destroy; so that 'tis a very wrong maxim, and argues great ignorance in us, to imagine that God never brings about his designs by the means and instrumentality of wicked men. This is the Papists objection against the reformation: great pains have been taken to blacken the reformers, and to make it believed that a reformation could not be good that was begun by people of bad character, and a king of an immoral life. But so far is this from eclipsing, that it illustrates the wisdom and goodness of divine Providence, in obliging the wicked to do what they never designed, and over-ruling their counsels for the fulfilling God's holy, wise, and sovereign decree. This observation naturally arises from the words of our text, which were spoken by, as far as I can judge, one of the vilest men upon the earth, you doubtless know his name, Balaam, who, though florid in his expressions, and high in profession of intercourse with God, and puts on a fine face of religion, was but a rotten-hearted hypocrite, for he divined for money, made a trade of religion; and so loved the wages of unrighteousness, as to have wished to curse even those whom God had blessed. I need not inform you, that this was the end for which Balak sent for him; and no wonder he was so willing to go, when he knew he was to be well paid

paid for his journey. Achilles, the Græcian hero, is said to be capable of being wounded only in the heel, but bad priests, ministers, and people, have a great deal more dangerous part to be wounded in, that is, the palm of the hand; if you can keep that secure from being wounded with gold, never fear; the devil can't have his end. Balak promised him great preferment, if he would but come and curse the people of God. A prophet, or soothsayer, is one that pretends to have intercourse with God or the devil, and Balak did not care by which of them it was, so that he could but get the Israelites cursed; Balaam catches at the golden bait, pretends to ask counsel of God; and what seems strange, God bids him go, and yet sends an angel to meet him in the way, who stands ready to slay him for going. Does it not seem very strange, that God should bid a man go, and then offer to slay him for going; but people that read this passage, should carefully mind the particulars of it. God said, if the men come and call thee, go; but he did not wait for that, but saddles his ass and goes: this is called by St. Peter, the madness of the prophet: witness his rising early in the morning, not waiting for the call of the princes, which shewed how eager he was to be gone; and though this solution should not be allowed, God was justly angry for his going with an ill design, that is, maliciously to curse a people whom he knew God resolved should be blessed, and that for the sake of the wages of unrighteousness *. The king and his nobles wait upon him, in hopes this soothsayer will answer their purpose; but after all he can do nothing without God's leave: however, no cost is spared to obtain the end; so true is it, that the devil's children are ten thousand times more expensive in persecuting the people of God, than God's people are in promoting his glory. This soothsaying priest pretends to go to God, which is permitted, but forced to speak what God would have him; once and again his mouth is stopped, or rather his curses are stopped, and turned into a blessing. Balak, enraged at his repeated disappointment, bids him neither to curse or bless them at all; and thinking, perhaps, that the sight of the people affected him,

---

* It is no unusual thing in holy writ, for heaven to resent and punish even those actions that it has permitted. Witness Deut. i. 20—35. comp. with Numb. xiii. 2.—Hof. xiii. 11. comp. with 1 Sam: viii. 7. cap. xv. 23. cap. xvi. 1. Psal. 81, 11, 12. &c. &c.

him, carries him to a place where he would see but a small part of them; he goes, and there God made him confirm the blessing instead of the curse, more abundantly than before. Oratory is beautiful, though out of the mouth of the worst of men, *Surely*, said he, *there is no enchantment against Jacob, neither is there any divination against Israel. Behold, the people shall rise up as a great lion, and lift up himself as a young lion; he shall not lie down until he eat of the prey, and drink the blood of the slain*; having said just before, *According to this time it shall be said of Jacob and Israel, what hath God wrought!*

What words are here out of the mouth of a wicked man! and yet I hope it will do no hurt to chuse them as a proper subject for an evening meditation. Let us leave this prophane diviner, and the king his employer, vexed that they could not get their end of the people of God: let us snatch the words out of the vile prophet's mouth, and see if we can serve him as David did Goliah, take his sword and cut off his head. Some people run to extreams, and because some have abused religion, therefore they think there is no religion at all. Perhaps it is for this reason, that so many

offences

offences are permitted to happen in the churches, that one of the twelve should be a traitor, and that the devil should come with his bible under his arm to tempt us to disbelieve or abuse it, by which God stirs up the people of God to watch, fight, and pray.

How should we take the words of our text? by way of interrogation? or admiration? as speaking in a prophetic strain how God had wrought, and did then work, and would afterwards work for the prosperity of his faithful Jacob and his posterity, the Israel of God.

Suppose we take them in the way of question, which, perhaps, is most agreeable to the context, and it may be most serviceable to you and to me; and in order that I may not run into too great a field to-night, I will confine myself to what Balaam confines himself, *from this time it shall be said of Jacob and Israel*, in a way of enquiry, *what hath God wrought?*

If we look round the world and survey the works of creation, *the heavens declare God's glory: and the firmament sheweth his handy work*. If we look further, my brethren, down upon these bodies of ours, if we consider the curious form of them, we may cry, *what hath*

hath God wrought! surely I am fearfully and wonderfully made; and when we consider that we are made up of the four elements; when we consider to what casualties we are exposed, how wonderfully these bodies have been kept up, when thousands have dropped into the grave before us, we may well say, *what hath God wrought!* but I rather chuse to confine myself to that better part; and I am persuaded of it, we shall never go to heaven unless God works powerfully on our souls: supposing you and I now were to forget all created beings, supposing we were to forget our neighbours to-night, and to hear only for ourselves, as the shades of the evening are coming on, and as we are going shortly to rest, may be to rise no more in this lower world, what if we should steal a little time from our shop, a little time from our worldly business, as we know not but we may be called to judgment to-morrow, and ask and say, O my soul, what hath God wrought in thy heart? I am glad to hear you are so inquisitive. Observe, what hath God wrought; now whatever is done in us, is all done by God; it is all done by an Almighty power, and it is all the effect of infinite wisdom; supposing then you and I are new creatures,

tures, hath God, O my soul, wrought in thee a deep, a penitent, a humbling sense of thy transgressions against his holy law; this is a most important question, this is the very beginning of religion, this is the very first letter of the Christian's alphabet, the first line in his book; with this Christ himself began to teach fallen man. *Adam, where art thou*, was the first question that the Son of God put to his fallen creatures; what condition art thou in? how art thou fallen, thou son of the morning! and when he came to the woman, he took the same way, he preached, and ministers should preach conviction first; *what is this*, saith God, *that thou hast done?* to break thy husband, and bring all thy posterity unto ruin; and it seems to me that there was a consciousness in this; and I wonder sometimes, the Deists have not run so far as to do it in jest. I don't know that I ever heard of a female child's name called **Eve**; probably, we are ashamed to call a child by that name, because of the guilt of our mother Eve, that brought us all into sin. Now hath God wrought in you? hath he even given this conviction to you; not a little flight now and then, or a qualm of thy conscience; the devil and natural conscience may do this; but when it is wrought in thy heart by the Spirit of God, it goes to the bottom, the arrow sticks fast, and a poor soul sometimes endeavours to pray, endeavours to pull it out, but in vain. Hath God wrought this in thy soul? now when God works this change in the soul, the devil is always busy in tempting the poor convicted sinner to despond, if not despair. Ignorant formalists, who are some of the worst people under heaven, when a person is under conviction, think the devil is got into them, whereas the devil is in themselves; for the devil hoodwinks people, and he endeavours to persuade them, that there is no harm done to God by sinning against him. It is God wounds the soul, and it is he that heals it; has he wrought in thee not only a deep and humbling sense of the outward acts of sin, but a humbling sense of the inward corruptions of thy heart? has he led thee beyond the streams, through the powerful operations of his Spirit, to the fountain-head? when he has done so, then are we Christians indeed; and this cannot be the work of the devil, who never did, nor do I know whether he can, show a person the inward corruptions of his heart; it must be the Spirit of God: the devil may frighten a person, as to outward things, but I very much question whether it is in the power or will of the devil to show a person that he is totally depraved, that the whole fountain is corrupt; this cannot be, because this would make the devil omnipotent, of equal power with the Holy Ghost, who alone shows thee the guilt and corruption of thy heart. This I have found to be the fact, from thirty years observation and experience of thousands, thousands, thousands, with whom I have spoken about their hearts. So it was, I remember, when I went first to Georgia, when I was about twenty-five years old, I had them day after day, week after week, and night after night, saying, *What shall I do to be saved?* O my wicked heart, my deceitful heart, from morning to night. Hath God wrought this in any of you? are you complaining of your wicked heart and corrupt nature? have you found out that your hearts are cages of unclean birds, only a lodging for vain thoughts to dwell in? O my friends, my dear hearers, O may you turn the question into a note of admiration, and say, *what hath God wrought!* he has not only convinced me of my outward sins, but powerfully convinced

me

me of the corruptions of my heart. Do aſk yourſelves this queſtion, has God wrought in me a view of the ſpirituality of his holy law? till this is done, you are as faſt in the devil's arms as he can claſp you. Of all the children the devil has in the world, I believe he moſtly loves his Phariſaical children: I was talking with one of them ſome time ago, and ſomebody very innocently aſked me where the Phariſees lived, O, ſaid I, they live every where. Some people think that they only lived in the times of the apoſtles. Do you know, vipers and toads have the moſt eggs and moſt numerous progeny? if you was to ſee the eggs of a toad through a microſcope, you would wonder at the innumerable multitude; and the Phariſees are an increaſing generation of vipers, which hatch and ſpread all over the world: if you want to know what a Phariſee is, he is one who pretends to endeavour, and talks about keeping the law of God, and does not know its ſpirituality; they are ſome of them very great men in their own opinion, and always made the greateſt figure in the church: one of them, a gentleman's ſon, becauſe he had not broke the letter of the law, thought he was right and without sin; O, says he, if I have nothing else to do but to keep the commandments, I am safe; I have honoured my father and mother; I never stole; what need he steal that had so good an estate? I never committed adultery; no, no, he loved his character too well: but our Lord opens to him the law, *this one thing thou lackest, go sell all thou hast*; he loved his money more than his God: Christ brought him back to the first commandment, though he catechized him first in the fifth. So Paul was a Pharisee; he says, *I was alive without the law once; I was, touching the law, blameless*; how can that be, can a man be without the law, and yet, touching the law, blameless; says he, *I was without the law*; that is, I was not brought to see the spirituality of it; I thought myself a very good man, no man could say of Paul, black is his eye; but, saith he, when God brought the commandment with power upon my soul, then I saw my specks, and do now. Pray mind and say the commandments, if you go to church you see them, and if you go to meeting I hope you have not forgot them; *thou shalt not bear false witness against thy neighbour, thou shalt not covet*; from repeating the last commandment,

we

we are taught that God's law is spiritual, *I should not have known sin*, as the apostle said, *if the law had not said, thou shalt not covet*; now has God wrought in you these things? hast thou really seen his law that it is spiritual? have you been made to see that the law of God requires perfect, sinless obedience? have you been made to see that you are under the curse, because you have sinned, by the inward teaching of the blessed Spirit of God? for then be assured, as sure as thou art in this place, God has wrought this in thy soul, and thou mayst turn the question to admiration, and say, *what has God wrought!* has he wrought in thee a sense of unbelief, that thou canst no more believe than thou canst create a world? I mention this, because I have told you often, and I am in the same mind; yet there are very few books that talk about unbelief, there is a long catalogue of sins, but not one word about unbelief; why? O because these good folks, that have wrote communion books, take it for granted, all folks that go to church are believers; I take it there are more unbelievers in the church than out of it; why, say you, do not they assent to the gospel? so does the devil; do not they assent to all the articles of the
Christian

Christian faith? so does the devil; the devil is a stronger believer than an Arian; the devil is a stronger believer than a Socinian, he believes Christ is God, for he has felt his power by his damning him to hell; *we know thee who thou art, the holy one of God.* But remember Christ says, when he is gone the Spirit of God shall come to reprove the world, in the margin it is, convince, and not a transient conviction, but a conviction that fastens, that brings salvation with it; if conviction brings its own evidence, surely faith must bring its own evidence along with it too; *now he shall convince the world,* saith our Lord, *of sin;* what sin? the sin of unbelief, *because they believe not in me.* It is mentioned by the dear Mr. Hervey, by the dear Mr. Marshall himself, and also by somebody else, that when complaining to a minister that he could get no ease to his soul, and told the minister he confessed his sins every day, he put them all down, (a man must have a good memory that can do that) the minister said to him, I think your catalogue is worth nothing at all, the grand sin is not mentioned; what is that? sir, said he, the sin of unbelief, a sin the poor creature thought he had never been guilty of. Has God wrought

wrought in thee a sense of thy unbelief? what blessed times have I seen in New, as well as Old England and Scotland, when thousands were awakened at Edinburgh, at Glasgow, and many other places, when I have seen them taken out of the congregation by scores, and asked what is the matter? what do you want? I can't believe! I can't believe! I can't believe! We think we can believe when we will, but the Spirit alone can convince us we have no faith, the Spirit alone can convince us of our want of faith, and can alone impart it to the poor awakened sinner; consequently, you may ask yourselves whether God has wrought in you, not only a sense of your own misery, but also a sense of your remedy; set you upon hungering and thirsting, such a hungering and thirsting as has never been satisfied but by an application of the blood of Christ imputed to you. I do not want to dispute upon the scriptures with any body: there are a great many good men have been prejudiced by Antinomian principles and practices, and because some people have run to a dangerous extream, and have not thought proper to make use of the word *imputed* at all. The best truth may be spoiled by bad books; but, for my part, I

am

am more than ever convinced, that the doctrine of imputed righteousness is a doctrine of the gospel; and that as Adam's sin is imputed to me, so the righteousness of Christ must be imputed also: I stand not only as a pardoned sinner, but as a justified sinner; I stand before God justified, and so do all whom Jesus Christ has purchased. Now has God wrought this in thee, O man; in thee, O woman? I am not going to ask, whether it was wrought in thee by hearing a sermon or reading a book, God may make use of a minister, or of a book; and I don't like people to get above ministers and books, saying, we do not want these. God draws with the cords of a man, and generally draws us with cords by men such as ourselves. Canst thou say, there is a book, there is the minister, in reading or hearing which, Christ's blood was applied, and the Spirit of God witnessed with my spirit that I was one of his children? now this is all God's working, indeed it is, the devil can't do this, it is out of his power; he may attempt to persuade them that he has done it, when he has not, and cannot. The magicians turned their rods into serpents, but the rod of Jehovah swallowed them all up. Has the Lord God wrought

a change

a change of heart in thee, and a change of life as a consequence of that; I mention this, but I would have every body that stands up for Christ's imputed righteousness, especially as some good people are apt to speak of it and carry it very high, to be careful in the same discourse to speak as highly of obedience too, to Christ's commandments. I don't like only to mention the word promises; when people tell me they hang upon the promises, I always ask them how do you hang upon them? have you got the thing promised? the promise is, that the Promiser should come to my soul; the promise is, what, my brethren? the promise is, for this and that good thing; have I got it? How would you do if you was to take false bank notes, if you was to take false bills? the people generally ask, is the man that has given me this note worth any thing? if you have a bad note you go to the notary and note it, you say, I was to have had this note paid ten, twenty, thirty days after sight, or upon sight; where is the notary? they note it and protest it: let us be careful then to see that God pays his notes, as we are that man does. Hast thou got the thing promised? the thing promised is, all peace and all joy; the thing

promised

promised is, a new heart; the thing promised is, a new nature; and therefore David goes to God for the thing promised, and says, *Create in me a clean heart, O God, and renew a right spirit within me.* Now is this the case of thy heart? the devil never can make a new creature; I am sure nothing but an Almighty power can take away the heart of stone, and give a heart of flesh: has God wrought this in thee? if he has, though it is not come to such a heighth as thou would wish, yet be thankful for what he has done, and say, what has God wrought in me! Attend to the word, I do not mean lazily, there is not a thing upon the face of the earth that I abhor so much as idleness or idle people; I am so far from having a love to people that are lazy, that if I had the dealing with a number that are called Christians, they should go to bed sooner, and get up sooner; there is one thing that will make people rise sooner in the morning in London, and that is, for merchants to agree to have the 'Change opened at six, and that will make people as much alive in the morning, as the markets are after people have been travelling all night to prepare for them.

Has God wrought in you a spirit of zeal and love? has he wrought in you a love to his name, a zeal for his cause? has he wrought in thy heart a deadness to the world, that you can live above it from morning to night, having your conversation in heaven? has he wrought in thee a love to his people, not people that are Calvinists only; not people that hold universal redemption only; O be careful as to that; O what nonsense is that, for people to hold universal redemption, and yet not love all mankind; what nonsense is it to hold election, and not *as the elect of God to put on bowels of mercy, kindness, humbleness of mind, meekness and long-suffering*; as the woman said, I have a house will hold a hundred, a heart ten thousand. Has he wrought in thee a love to thy enemies, so that thou dost not only love them that love thee, but them that hate thee? what say you? must I put a snake in my bosom, no, no; I may hate the conduct, and at the same time pray to God for them. Enmity is, *an eye for an eye, a tooth for a tooth.* Love as archbishop Cranmer did, that it became a proverb concerning him, that if any man would make him his friend, he must do him an injury. Has he wrought in thee a desire to go to heaven? has he wrought in thee such a love to Jesus, that you prefer him to the heaven he dwells in? We count heaven a fine place, and we may say, I am glad to see the departed saints and the angels, but all that will be nothing unless I see the Lamb in the midst of the throne. Has God wrought in thee a desire to promote his glory, to be upon the stretch for God, to deny thyself, to take up the cross daily and follow him? if God has wrought this in thee, and I verily believe from my soul he has wrought it in some degree in many of you, O you may well say, *what has God wrought!* especially if you consider the manner, and the time in which he wrought it; if you consider the instruments he made use of, when, and by which he wrought it; and if you consider the inestimable price that was paid for it, and the Spirit taking possession of your hearts. One part of our entertainment in heaven will be, to count the steps of the ladder by which God brought us there; one will say, God wrought in me when I was young; another, when I had grey hairs. Mary Magdalen will say, God wrought in me when I was a sinner; the expiring criminal will say, God wrought it in me just as I was turned off,

I was

I was a brand plucked out of the burning. The anthem, as good Mr. Erskine observes, will be in heaven, *what has God wrought!* Curiosity led me to hear the preacher, and God touched my heart; there was a young fellow, called emphatically *wicked Will of Plymouth*, who came, as he said, to pick a hole in the preacher's coat, and the Holy Ghost picked a hole in his heart. What has God wrought, to work it in you, and not in your father; you, and not your children; work it in you, and not a fellow-servant; work it in one brother and not in another; all these things will make us cry, *what has God wrought!* Well, I do not want you to rest in this by no means; I do not like to hear people talk, and speak against inward frames and inward works, nor do I like to hear people legal, let every thing have its proper place. It is about thirty-three years ago, or very near, when a man came to me, after I had preached upon marks and evidences, at Whitechapel I think it was, and said, I am come to tell you, that I don't chuse any marks at all; then, said I, you must be content with the marks of the devil, for you must have the one or the other.

Now,

Now, my brethren, if God has wrought this in us, what shall I say? why, I pray the Lord Jesus Christ that your life and mine may be a life of praise. I would have you not only dwell upon particular words of God set home upon your hearts, but his various providences, the numerous trials he has brought you through: O think how often you have been kept, think how often you would have run away from God if he had not stopped you; what has God wrought, by preventing me from sin; what has God wrought, by delivering me from blasphemous thoughts; what has God wrought, in snatching me out of the jaws of ruin; even after conversion, when I was damning my own soul, his grace arrested me. Have we brought ourselves into trials, how has he made these very trials work for good; made our scolding husbands and wives, persecuting fathers, friends and relations, that you have thought would devour you, made the bulls of Bashan instruments of bringing you nearer to God; and eternity will be too short to cry perpetually, *what hath God wrought!*

And if God has not wrought this in any of you that are here, which, perhaps, may be the case, though I cannot think what should

bring

bring any body here if they had not a desire of the salvation of their souls; if God hath not wrought it in you yet, O that this may be the time; O that God may give us some parting blessing; that some poor creatures that have nothing but the devil's work in them yet, may now seek after the blessed work of the Holy Ghost. If we may ask what God has wrought, let me ask you what the devil hath wrought in you; O thou unconverted soul, sin has made thee a beast, made thy body, which ought to be the temple of the living God, a cage of every unclean bird; what hath satan wrought in thee? but made thee a nest of vile stinking swine; and what will he give thee? hell, hell, hell. The wages the devil gives no man can live by; *the wages of sin is death:* and here I come to bring you good news, glad tidings of great joy; O that God may now counter-work the devil, and take thee into his own workmanship, create thee anew in Christ Jesus, give thee to feel a little of his Spirit's work on thy heart, and make thee, of a child of the devil, a child of God! Say not, it cannot be; say not, it shall not be; say not, it is too late; say not, it is for others but not for me; my brethren, God help you to cry, and to try
to-night,

to-night, if thou canst turn the text into a prayer, Lord God, I have felt the devil work in me, now, good God, let me know what it is for thee to work in me; make me a new creature, create a new spirit within me, that I may join with thy dear people in singing, *what hath God wrought!* O remember, if this is not the case with you, you must have a dreadful different ditty in hell; the note there will be, what hath the devil wrought! what hath sin wrought! how am I come to this place of torment! I sold my birthright for a mess of pottage! Heaven or hell is set before you to-night; Jesus grant, that the terrors of the Lord may awaken you to-night, and that you may not rest till you have comfort and support from God.

You that have this work begun in you, look still for better things to come, even after death, when our bodies are made like Christ's glorious body, and our souls filled with the fulness of God, we shall then cry, Churchmen and Dissenters, Methodists and Foundery-men, and the Lock too, we shall all then join without any bickerings, saying, *what has God wrought!*

I could enlarge, but I am afraid I have been too long already; yet as I think the providence

Ser. X. *the Work of God.* 249

vidence of God calls me, and I shall give a particular account of my call to-morrow evening, at the other end of the town, I think if I should keep you a few minutes longer, it might be excused. I begin to feel already it must be executed in a few days; I feel already that I shall soon part from you, and O that God may awaken many of you poor unawakned souls; my heart bleeds for you; O may the oil of the blessed Spirit soften every hard, unconverted heart, that we may go away praising and blessing God that we shall at last meet, whether we go by land or by water, before the throne, where we shall ascribe glory, and honour, and power, to him for evermore. Amen.

K k SERMON

SERMON XI.

The Burning Bush.

EXODUS iii. ver. 2, 3.

And he looked, and behold the bush burned with fire, and the bush was not consumed; and Moses said, I will now turn aside, and see this great sight, why the bush is not burnt.

IT is a common saying, and common sayings are generally founded on matter of fact, that it is always darkest before break of day; and I am persuaded, that if we do justice to our own experience, as well as consider God's dealings with his people in preceding ages, we shall find that man's extremity has been usually made God's opportunity, and that *when the enemy has broke in like a flood, the Spirit and providence of God has lifted up a standard against him:* and I believe at the same time, that however we may dream of a con-

continued scene of prosperity in church or state, either in respect to our bodies, souls, or temporal affairs; we shall find this life to be chequered; that the clouds return after the rain, and the most prosperous state attended with such cloudy days, as may make even the people of God sometimes cry, *all men are liars, and God has forgotten to be gracious.*

The chapter in which is our text, is an instance of this. What a glorious day of the son of man was that when Joseph sent for his father to Egypt; and the good old patriarch, after he had thought his son had been dead many years, agreeably surprized by a message from him to come to him, with all his family, and are by him comfortably settled in Goshen; where the good old patriarch, after many a stormy day, died in peace, and was highly honoured at his funeral by Pharaoh and his servants, and attended to the sepulchre of his fathers in Canaan by all his sons. After which, Joseph continued to live in splendor, lord of all the land of Egypt; and his brethren, doubtless, in the height of prosperity: but how sadly did the scene change at Pharaoh's death, soon after which, *another king arose that knew not Joseph,* verifying the observation, New lords,

lords, new laws, by whom the descendants of Jacob, instead of reigning in Goshen, were made bond-slaves; many, many long years, employed in making bricks, and, in all probability, had what we call their bibles taken from them, by being forced to conform to the idolatry of Egypt, and so were in a worse state than the unhappy Negroes in America are at this day. No doubt, numbers of them either wondered that ever they had been prospered at all, or that God had forgot them now; but what a mercy it is that *a thousand years in God's sight are but as one day*, and therefore when God's time is come, the set time that he has appointed, he will, maugre all the opposition of men and devils, he will come down and deliver his people, and in such a manner, that the enemy shall know, as well as friends, it is the Lord's doing. A deliverer is born and bred in Pharaoh's court, a Moses is brought up in all the learning of the Egyptians, for Pharaoh intended him for a high and exalted post: but when offers of the highest preferment are made to him, he did not catch at them as some folks now do, who are very good and humble till something occurs to take them from God. Young as he was, he refused

fused the highest dignity, and spurned at it with an holy contempt; and chuses rather to suffer affliction with the people of God, than enjoy all the grandeur and pleasures of, perhaps, one of the greatest courts on earth. Forty years continued he in this state of obscurity, in which time he acquired such a competent degree, and variety of knowledge, as qualified him for every thing God intended him for: the occasion of this, was his kind attempt to compose a difference between two of his brethren, one of whom accused him of murder, on which he that was to be king in Jeshurun, is forced to fly into a strange land; there he submits to the humble office of a servant, marries, and lives in a state of subjection for forty years, as was said before. At length, when he was eighty years old, dreaming of no such thing, behold God calls, and commands him to go and deliver his people; as he himself informs us, who is the author of this book, ver. 1. *Now Moses kept the flock of Jethro his father-in-law, priest of Midian:* he might have said, what such a scholar as I keep a parcel of sheep! such a learned man as I am employed in such a menial service! some proud hearts would break first, but you never knew a truly great man

man but would stoop; some that are called great men, swell till they burst; like sturdy oaks, they think they can stand every wind, till some dreadful storm comes and blows them up by the roots, while the humble reed bends and rises again. Moses was one of the latter; he keeps the flock of Jethro his father-in-law, and leads them to the mountain of God, even to Horeb. This shows how persons ought to methodize their time; but however the name of a Methodist is despised, they will never be bad servants and masters; you would be only weathercocks, unless you took care to order things in proper seasons: the devotion and business of a Methodist go hand in hand; I will assure you, Moses was a Methodist, a very fine one, a very strong one too; he kept his flock, but that did not hinder his going to Horeb, he took them to the desert, and being thus employed in his lawful business, God met him. Some say, we encourage people in idleness; I deny it; we say, people ought to be industrious; and I defy any one to say, a person is called by God that is negligent in his calling. *The angel of the Lord appeared to him in a flame of fire out of the bush:* some think this angel was Gabriel, but most agree, and

and I believe with the greatest probability, that it was Jesus Christ, *the angel of the everlasting covenant*; and an expositor tells you, that the eternal *Logos*, longing to become man, often visited this earth in that form, as an evidence of his coming by and by, and dying a cursed death for man. The manner of this angel's appearing is taken particular notice of, it was to Moses when nobody was with him; I do not hear he had so much as a boy, or one companion; and I mention this, because I believe we have often found that we are never less alone than when with God; we often want this and that companion, but happy they that can say, Lord, thy company is enough. Moses was startled at the sight, and I don't know that he is to be discommended for it, it was not to gratify a bare curiosity, but seeing a bush burning it engaged his attention, and made him think that something was uncommon; *the bush burned with fire and yet was not consumed*; this startled him, as it was intended to do; for where God designs to speak, he will first gain attention from the person spoken to; Moses therefore says, *I will now turn aside and see this great sight, why the bush is not burned*; he did not know but the

bush

bush might take fire by some accident; he saw no fire come from above, he saw no fire round the bush, yet that did not so much startle him, as to see, though it did burn, it was not consumed, or in the least diminished; it was a strange sight, but it was, my brethren, a glorious one; a sight which, I pray God, you and I may behold with faith and comfort this evening; for, my dear hearers, this bush, and the account of it, was given for our learning; and I will venture to say, could Moses arise from the dead, he would not be angry with me for telling you, this is of no private interpretation, but is intended as a standing lesson, as a significant emblem of the church, and every individual child of God, till time it self shall be no more. I would therefore observe to you, that this bush,

In the first place, is typical of the church of God in all ages; the bush was burning, why might it not be a tall cedar, why might it not be some large or some glorious tree, why should the great God chuse a bush, a little bush of briars and thorns, above any other thing? but because the church of Christ generally consists of poor, mean, despicable creatures: tho' it is all glorious within, yet it is all despicable
without.

without. It is observable, that when the church came to prosper, when Constantine smiled on it, it was soon hugged to death; and that great poet, Milton, observes, that when that emperor gave ministers rich vestments, high honours, great livings, and golden pulpits, there was a voice heard from heaven, saying, this day there is poison come into the church; and I have sometimes said in discourse, I don't doubt but if any one made an experiment, and left 100,000*l.* or 200,000*l.* only among the Methodists, there would be hundreds and thousands that would not be reckoned Methodists now, that would turn Methodists presently, that would buy an hymn-book, because a part of the legacy would pay for the hymn-book, and would wish to have a living into the bargain: but though *not many mighty men, not many noble are called*, yet some are; if any of you are rich here, and are Christians, thank God for it, you ought to be doubly thankful for it; God's people are but like a little bramble bush. I remember an eminent minister said once, when I heard him preach upon Christmas-day, *Christ personal is very rich, but Christ mystical is very poor;* and Jesus Christ does this on purpose to confound the world. When he comes to judgment, millions that have their thousands now, will be damned and burn to all eternity, and Chrift's church will be rich to all eternity, that is now like a bramble all on fire.

The bush burned, what is that for? it shewed that Chrift's church while in this world, will be a bush burning with fiery trials and afflictions of various kinds; this was a lively emblem of the state of religion, and liberty of Ifrael at that time: they were busy making of brick, and there consequently were burning continually; as though the Lord had said, this bush is burning with fire, so my people are burning with flavery. Ah but, say you, that was only the case of the Ifraelites when they were under Pharaoh; pray is not that the case of the church in all ages? yes, it has been; read your bibles, and you may inftantly see that it is little elfe than an hiftorical account of a burning bush; and though there might be some periods wherein the church had reft, yet these periods have been of a short date; and if God's people have *walked in the comforts of the Holy Ghoft,* it is only like a calm that preceeds an earthquake. If you remember, before the laft earthquake it was a fine morning,

and

and who, when they arose in the morning, would have thought the earth should shake under them before night; and so with the church when they are in a calm, and all seems safe there, then comes a storm: God prepare us for it.

But this is not only the case with the church of Christ collected, but also it is so with individual believers, especially those that God intends to make great use of as prophets in his church. I know very well that 'tis said, that now the case is altered: modern commentators therefore, and our great Dr. Young, calls them downy Doctors; they tell us, now we have got a Christian king and governor, and are under the toleration act, we shall have no persecution; and, blessed be God, we have had none since this family has been on the throne: may God continue it till time shall be no more. Yet, my dear hearers, we shall find, if God's word is true, whether we are born under a despotic power, or a free government, that they that will live godly in Christ Jesus must suffer persecution. You have heard of that saying, *Wonder not at the fiery trial wherewith you are to be tried*; and God saith, *I have chosen thee*, which is applicable to every believer, *in the furnace of affliction*. Now the furnace is a hot place, and they that are tried in the furnace must be burnt surely. Now what must the Christian burn with? with tribulation and persecution. I heard a person not long ago say, I have no enemies. Bishop Latimer came to a house one day, and the man of the house said, he had not met with a cross in all his life; give me my horse, says the good bishop, I am sure God is not here where no cross is. But suppose we are not persecuted by the world, is there one Christian but is persecuted by his friends; if there is an Isaac in the family, I warrant there is an Ishmael to mock at him, *Woe is me*, says David, *that I must dwell with Meskeck, and in Kedar:* and in one's own family, one's own brothers and sisters, one's own dependants, though they wait for our death, and, perhaps, long to have us gone, that they may run away with our substance, to have these persons mock at us, and if they dare not speak out, yet let us see they hate the God we worship; if this is thy case, why, God knows, poor soul, thou art a burning bush: but if we have no such thing as mocking, yet if we are surrounded with afflictions,

domestic

domestic trials, the loss of dear and near friends, the bad conduct of our children, the dreadful misconduct of those that are dependant upon us; O there is many a parent here that is a burning bush; burning with what? with family afflictions; some don't care what becomes of their children; O, I thank God, I have left my boy so much, and my daughter a coach, perhaps; ah! well your son and daughter may ride in that coach post to the devil: but the godly man says, I want an eternal inheritance for my son; I want God's blessing for him; this is the poor man's prayer, while the poor deluded youth mocks him: or, supposing this is not the case, a person may burn with inward temptation; you have heard of the fiery darts of the devil, and was you to feel them, I believe you would find them fiery darts indeed! and you have great reason to suspect your experience, your having any interest in the love of the Son of God at all, if you never found the fiery darts of the devil. O, says one, I never felt the devil; I am sure thou mayst feel him now; thou art dadda's own child; thou art speaking the very language of the devil, and he is teaching thee to deny thy own father; therefore, graceless child of the devil,

devil, you never felt the devil's fiery darts, it is becaufe the devil is fure of thee; he has got thee into a damnable flumber; may the God of love wake thee before real damnation comes! The fiery darts of fatan are poifoned, and wherever they ftick they fill the perfon with tormenting pain like fire; this I mention, becaufe there are fome poor fouls perhaps here to-night, whom the devil tells, thou haft committed the unpardonable fin; you are afraid to come to facrament, you are afraid to go to prayer, becaufe at thefe feafons the devil difturbs thee moft, and tempts you to leave thefe feafons; and there are fome go on thus burning a great while. My brethren, the time would fail, and I fhall draw this difcourfe to too great a length, and hinder you from your families, if I was to mention but a few more of thofe thoufands that the believer burns with, the trials without, and, what is ftill worfe, their trials within. Why, fays one, it is very ftrange you talk thus to-night; I am forry it is ftrange to any of you; fure you are not much acquainted with your bibles, and lefs with your hearts, if you know not this. Why fure, fay fome, you make God a tyrant; no, but having made ourfelves devil's incarnate,

we

we are now in a state of preparation, and these various trials are intended by the great God to train us up for heaven; and therefore, that you may not think I am drawing a picture without any life, give me leave to observe, that it is particularly remarkable, that though *the bush burned, it was not consumed:* it was this struck Moses, he looked to see why the bush was not consumed. But the burning I have been here painting forth to you, is not a consuming, but a purifying fire; is not that enough to answer the shade that has been already drawn; it is true the bush burns, the Christian is persecuted, the Christian is oppressed, the Christian is burned with inward trials, he is perplexed at times, he is *cast down, but,* blessed be God, *he is not destroyed,* he is not in despair. Who is that, that says he has got into such an estate that nothing disturbs him? vain man! he discovers an ignorance of Christ; are you greater then than the apostle Paul? some people think that the apostles had no trials; so they think, perhaps, of some ministers, that they are always on the mount, while, perhaps, they have been in the burning to get that sermon for them. We that are to speak for others, must expect to be be tempted in all things like to our brethren, or we should be only poor whip-syllabub preachers, and not reach mens hearts. But whether ministers or people burn, the great God, the angel of the everlasting covenant, spoke to Moses out of the bush; he did not stand at a distance from the bush, he did not speak to him so much as one yard or foot from the bush, but he spoke to him out of the bush; he said, Moses, Moses, my people shall burn in this bush to the end of time, but be not afraid, I will succour them; when they burn, I will burn too. There is a scripture vastly strong to this purpose, in which it is not said, *the good will of him that* was *in the bush*, but *the good will of him that* dwelt *in the bush*. Amazing! I thought God dwelt in heaven; but as a poor woman who was once in darkness fourteen years, before she was brought out of it, said, God has two homes, one in heaven, the other in the lowest heart. He dwells in the bush, and I am sure if he did not, the devil and their own cursed hearts would burn the bush to ashes. How is it that it is not consumed? why, it is because God has declared it shall not be consumed; he has made an everlasting covenant, and I pity those

that

that are not acquainted with an interest in God's covenant; and it would be better that people would pity them, than dispute with them: I really believe a disputing devil is one of the worst devils that can be brought into God's church, for he comes with his gown and book in his hand, and I should always suspect the devil when he comes in his gown and band, and this is the cause they agree and disagree. Some, who it's to be hoped are God's children, if you tell them that God has loved them with an everlasting love, they are afraid to suck it in, and especially if you pop out the word election, or that hard word predestination, they will be quite frightned; but talk to them in another way, their dear hearts will rejoice. God has said, *As the waters of Noah shall cease for ever, so he will not forget the covenant of his peace; nothing shall pluck them out of his hand.* Ah! say some, the apostle has said, *that neither things present, nor things to come, shall separate us from the love of Christ;* but he has not said an evil heart shall not; I fancy that is one of the *present things*. The bush is not consumed, because if the devil is in the bush, God is in the bush too; if the devil acts one way, the Lord, the Spirit, acts another to balance it, and the Spirit of God is engaged to train up the souls of his people; and God has determined the bush shall not be consumed; his Spirit stands near believers to support and guide, and make them more than conquerors: all that are given to Jesus Christ shall come, he will not lose one of them; this is food for the children of God; a bad mind will turn every thing to poison; and if it was not for this, that God had promised to keep them, my soul within these thirty years would have sunk a thousand times over. Come then, O suffering saints, to you the word of this salvation is sent. I don't know who of you are the followers of the Lamb; may the Spirit of the living God point them out, may every one be enabled to say, I am the man. O, says one, I have been watching and very attentive to-night, but you have not mentioned my burnings; what do you think of my burning lusts? what do you think of my burning corruptions? what do you think of my burning pride? O, perhaps some of you will say, thank God, I have no pride at all; like the bishop of Cambray, as mentioned by Dr. Watts, who said, he had received many sins from his father Adam, but, thank God, he

had

had no pride. Alas! alas! we are all as proud as the devil. Pray what do you think of paffion, that burns not only themfelves but all around them? what do you think of enmity? what do you think of jealoufy, is not this fomething that burns the bufh? and there are fome people that pride themfelves, they have not got fo much of the beaft about them, they never got drunk, fcorn to commit murder, and at the fame time are as full of enmity, of envy, malice, and pride, as the devil: the Lord God help fuch to fee their condition. Happy is it Chrift can dwell in the buth when we cannot dwell ourfelves there: there are few Chriftians can live together, very few relations can live together under one roof; we can take that from other people that we can't bear from our own flefh and blood; and if God did not bear with us more than we bear with one another, we fhould all have been deftroyed every day. Does the devil make you fay, that you will give all up; I will go to the Tabernacle no more; I will lay upon my couch and take my eafe; Oh! if this is the cafe of any tonight, thus tempted by fatan, may God refcue their fouls. O poor dear foul, you never will have fuch fweet words from God as when you are in the bush; our suffering times will be our best times. I know we had more comfort in Moorfields, on Kennington-Common, and especially when the rotten eggs, the cats and dogs were thrown upon me, and my gown was filled with clods of dirt that I could scarce move it; I have had more comfort in this burning bush than when I have been in ease. I remember when I was preaching at Exeter, a stone came and made my forehead bleed, I found at that very time the word came with double power to a labourer that was gazing at me, who was wounded at the same time by another stone, I felt for the lad more than for myself, went to a friend, and the lad came to me, Sir, says he, the man gave me a wound, but Jesus healed me; I never had my bonds broke till I had my head broke. I appeal to you, whether you were not better when it was colder than now, because your nerves were braced up; you have a day like a dog-day, now you are weak, and are obliged to fan yourselves: thus it is prosperity lulls the soul, and I fear Christians are spoiled by it.

Whatever your trials are, let this be your prayer, Lord, though the bush is burning, let it not be consumed. I think that is too low,

low, let it be thus; Lord, when the bush is burning, let me not burn lower as the fire does, but let me burn higher and higher: I thank thee, my God, for trouble; I thank thee, my God, for putting me into these afflictions one after another; I thought I could sing a requiem to myself, that I should have a little rest, but trouble came from that very quarter where I might reasonably expect the greatest comfort: I thank thee for knocking my hands off from the creature; Lord, I believe, help my unbelief; and thus you will go on blessing God to all eternity: by and by the bush shall be translated to the paradise of God; no burning bush in heaven, except the fire of love, wonder, and gratitude; no trials there, troubles are limited to this earth, above our enemies can't reach us.

Perhaps there are some of you here are saying, *burning bush, a bush burnt and not consumed!* I don't know what to make of this nonsense: come, come, go on, I am used to it, and I guess what are the thoughts of your hearts: I pray God, that every one of you here may be afraid of comfort, lest they should be tossed about by the devil. What is it I have said? how have I talked in such an unintelligible

gible manner? why, say you, what do you mean by a burning bush? why, thou art the very man, how so? why, you are burning with the devil in your hearts; you are burning with foppery, with nonsense, with *the lust of the flesh*, with *the lust of the eye, and pride of life*; and if you do not get out of this state, as Lot said to his sons-in-law, e're long you shall be burning in hell, and not consumed: the same angel of the covenant who spake to Moses out of the bush, he shall e're long descend, surrounded with millions of the heavenly hosts, and sentence you to everlasting burnings. O you frighten me! did you think I did not intend to frighten you? would to God I might frighten you enough! I believe it will be no harm for you to be frightned out of hell, to be frightned out of an unconverted state: O go and tell your companions that the madman said, that wicked men are as firebrands of hell: God pluck you as brands out of that burning. Blessed be God, that there is yet a day of grace; Oh! that this might prove *the accepted time*; Oh! that this might prove *the day of salvation*; Oh! angel of the everlasting covenant, come down; thou blessed, dear comforter, have mercy, mercy, mercy upon the unconverted,

upon

upon our unconverted friends, upon the unconverted part of this auditory; *speak, and it shall be done; command, O Lord, and it shall come to pass;* turn the burning bushes of the devil into burning bushes of the Son of God: who knows but God may hear our prayer, who knows but God may hear this cry, *I have seen, I have seen the afflictions of my people; the cry of the children of Israel is come up to me, and I am come down to deliver them:* God grant this may be his word to you under all your trouble; God grant he may be your comforter. The Lord awaken you that are dead in sin, and though on the precipice of hell, God keep you from tumbling in: and you that are God's burning bushes, God help you to stand to keep this coat of arms, to say when you go home, blessed be God, *the bush is burning, but not consumed.* Amen! even so, Lord Jesus. Amen!

SERMON XII.

Soul Dejection.

PSALM xlii. ver. 5.

Why art thou cast down, O my soul, and why art thou disquieted within me? hope thou in God, for I shall yet praise him, for the help of his countenance.

I HAVE often told you, in my plain way of speaking, that grace is very frequently grafted on a crab-stock; that the Lord Jesus picks out persons of the most peevish, churlish disposition, and imparts to them the largest measure of grace, but for want of a better natural temper, a great deal of grace does not shine so bright in them, as a small degree in those that are constitutionally good-natured: persons of this disposition are generally complaining, and are not only tormentors of themselves, but are great plagues to those that are about them; you will hear them always

always complaining something or other is the matter. What a pity it is we cannot all agree in one thing, to leave off chiding others to chide our own selves, till we can find nothing in ourselves to chide for; this we shall find will be a good way to grow in the divine life, when, by constant application to the Lamb of God, we get a mastery over those things which hitherto have had the mastery over us; but are these the only people that complain? are people of a melancholy disposition only subject to a disquietude of heart? I will venture to affirm, that the greatest, the dearest children of God, have got their complaining, and their dreary hours. Those who have been favoured with large measures of grace, even those that have been wrapped up as it were to the third heavens, basking on the mount in the sunshine of redeeming grace, and in raptures of love crying out, *It is good for us to be here,* even these must go down to Gethsemane; and if they would not be scorched with a strong burning fever from the sun of prosperity, shall find clouds from time to time overshadowing them, not to burn, but to keep them low. It is on this account, that you see good men in different frames at different times: our Lord himself

himself was so, he rejoiced sometimes in spirit, but at other times you find him, especially near the last, crying out, *My soul is exceeding sorrowful even unto death, tarry you here and watch.* And I am going to tell you of one to-night, who had the honour of being called, *the man after God's own heart*; and who, though an Old Testament saint, was greatly blessed with a New Testament spirit, and had the honour of composing Psalms, which in all past ages of the church have been, and in future ones will be a rich magazine, and store-house of spiritual experience, from which the children of God may draw spiritual armour for fighting the good fight of faith, until God shall call them to life eternal: may this be your happy lot. What frame was this good man in when he composed this forty-second Psalm? the Psalm itself can best tell. It seems composed when he was either persecuted by Saul, or driven from his own court by his fondling, beloved son, Absalom; then David appeared truly great; I honour him when I see him yonder, attending a few sheep; but I admire the young stripling, when I see him come out with his sling and stone, and aiming it at the head of Goliah, the enemy my of God; or, when exalted and filling the feat of juſtice; but to me he never appears greater, than when he is bowed down in low circumſtances, beſet on every ſide, ſtruggling between ſenſe and faith; and, as the ſun after an eclipſe, breaking forth with greater luſtre to all the ſpectators. In this view we muſt conſider this great, this good man, David, when he cries out, *Why art thou caſt down, O my ſoul, why art thou diſquieted within me? hope thou in God.*

Suppoſing you underſtand the words as a queſtion, *Why art thou caſt down, O my ſoul, though thou art in ſuch circumſtances?* pray now what is the cauſe of thy being ſo dejected? The word implies, that he was ſinking under the weight of his preſent burden, like a perſon ſtooping under a load that lies upon his ſhoulders; and the conſequence of this preſſure without was diſquietude, uneaſineſs and anxiety within; for, ſay what you will to the contrary, there is ſuch a connection between ſoul and body, that when one is diſordered, the other muſt ſympathize with its ever-loving friend.

Or, you may underſtand it as chiding himſelf, *Why art thou caſt down, O my ſoul, why art thou disquieted within me*, how foolish is it to be thus drooping and dejected; how improper for one favoured of God with so many providences, and special particular privileges, for such a one as thou art thus to stoop, and be made subject to every temptation; why dost thou give thy enemies such room to find fault with thy religion on account of thy gloomy looks, and the disquietude of thy heart? a yoke which thou wilt find to be lined with love, and God will keep it from galling thy shoulders. You see, he speaks not to others but to himself; would to God we did thus learn that charity begins at home. Then he goes to God with his case, O my God, says he, *my soul is cast down within me.* O that we could learn, when in these moods to go more to God, and less to man, we should find more relief, and religion would be less dishonoured. But see how faith triumphs in the midst of all, no sooner does unbelief pop up its head, but faith immediately knocks it down. A never-failing maxim is here proposed, *hope thou in God,* trust in God, believe in God; for I am sure, and all of you that know Jesus Christ are persuaded of it too, that all our troubles arise from our unbelief:

belief: O unbelief, injurious bar to comfort, source of tormenting fear! on the contrary, faith bears every thing. *Put thy trust in God*, as in the old translation; *hope in God*, as in the new, *I shall yet praise him.* The devil tells me my trouble is so great, I shall never lift up my head again; but unbelief and the devil are liars; *I shall yet praise him*; my God will carry me through all; I shall yet praise him, even for casting me down; I shall praise him even for that which is the cause of all my disquietude; he will be *the health of my countenance*; though my afflictions have now made my body low, suck up my spirits, and hurt my animal frame, *he will be the help of my countenance*; I shall by and by see him again, and be favoured with those transforming views, which my God has favoured me with in times past; *he is the health of my countenance, and my God:* though the devil tempts me, and my evil neighbours say, *where is now thy God?* Dost thou think thou art a child of God, and thy Father suffers thee to be cast down? I tell thee, I tell thee, O satan, that God who I have been so vilely tempted as to believe has forsaken me, will come over the mountains of my guilt, will forgive my backslidings against himself,

himself, my unbelief shall not make his promises of none effect; I shall praise him even while I live, I shall praise him before I die, I shall praise him for ever in heaven, where he will be, after death, *the health of my countenance, and my God*; thus faith will get the better in a saint. David was sometimes left to say, in effect, all things are against me; yet still in most of the Psalms, in this, the next, the cxiiith, and many of the rest, he triumphs in God; and he composed but very few without praising at the end, though he complains at the beginning: God help us thus to do!

But it is time to leave off speaking particularly of David, and to turn to you to whom these words, I pray God, may prove salutary and useful. I have had a great struggle in my mind this afternoon what I should preach from; I have been praying and looking up to God, and could not preach for my life on any other text, which has often been the case before, and whenever it was, some poor soul has been comforted and raised up; and among such a mixed multitude, there are some, no doubt, come to this poor despised place cast down and disquieted within; I shall endeavour to enquire what you are cast down for, and then I shall

propose

propose a great cure for you, namely, trust in God; and I pray, that what was David's comfort may be yours. Why should not we expect an answer when we pray, that God before you go home may make you whether you will or no, leave your burdens behind you? and God keep you from taking them up as you go home.

Probably, there may be some of you that are real believers; perhaps, I ought to ask your pardon: where am I preaching, in the Tabernacle! the most despised place in London! so scandalous a place, that many of the children of God would rather go elsewhere! God help us to keep up our scandal! But yet I believe there are many King's daughters here, many of you whom God enabled in this place first to say, *My Lord, and my God.* When you put your fingers, as it were, on the print of Christ's nails, and put your hands into his side, and were no longer faithless, but believing, you thought you should never be cast down any more, but now you have found yourselves mistaken; and I shall endeavour, in the prosecution of this text, to speak to all that are cast down, whether before or after conversion, and then to such that were never cast

down

down at all; and if you was never cast down before, God cast you down now.

What are persons cast down for? what are some of you disquieted within for? I have reason to believe, from the notes put up at both ends of the town, that there are many of you that have arrows of conviction stuck fast in your souls; I have taken in near two hundred at the other end of the town, within a fortnight; if this be the case, that God is thus at work, let the devil roar, and we will go on in the name of the Lord. And what are you cast down for? some poor soul will say, with a sense of sin, the guilt of it, the enmity of it, the very aggravated circumstances that attend it, appear and set themselves as in battle-array before me: once I thought I had no sin, at least, I thought that sin was not so exceeding sinful; but I now find it such a burden, I could almost say with Cain, *it is greater than I can bear.* And, perhaps, some of you are so cast down, as in your haste to say as colonel Gardiner, that great man of God, told me himself had said when under conviction, " I " believe God cannot be just, unless he damns " my wicked soul." Is this thy case? art thou wicked, art thou so cast down, so disquieted,

quieted, that thou canst not rest night nor day, shall I send thee away without any comfort? shall I send thee away as the legal preachers do? as a minister some time ago did, when a man told him how wicked he had been; O, says he, if you are so wicked you are damn'd to be sure, I shall not trouble myself with you. When a poor negro was taken up for thieving, another went to him and said, you are so bad I must turn my back to you; that is the law, but the gospel is turn thy face to God; think not that God is dealing with thee as an absolute God, a God out of Christ. I would have nothing to do, says Luther, with an absolute God; as such he is a consuming fire. Trust God in Christ, throw thyself upon him, throw thyself on the Son of God; cry with thy brother, and now thou art in that temper, thou wilt not be ashamed to call the thief thy brother; say with him, *Lord, remember me when thou art in thy kingdom:* thou shalt yet praise him, thou shalt yet have the forgiveness of thy sins; thy pardon shall not only be sealed in heaven, but thou shalt have it in thy heart: these are only the pangs of the new birth, the first strugglings of the soul immersing into the divine life; he shall yet be the health of thy countenance: these poor cheeks, though bedewed with tears, shall by and by have a fine blush, when a pardoning God comes with his love; it shall even make a change in thy countenance, for as a heavy heart makes a man's countenance sad, so a chearful heart makes the countenance pleasant: thou shalt know him to be thy God, thou shalt say, *my Lord, and my God:* Lord Jesus grant this may be the happy moment. Was Jesus here, was the Redeemer now in this metropolis, I am sure he would go about the streets, he would be a field-preacher, he would go out into the highways and hedges, he would invite, he would run after them; Lord Jesus, take the veil from our hearts, and let us see to-night thy loving heart as the Son of God! Trust in God, you will say, it is very easy for you to say so, but I cannot trust in God; can't you, who told you that? that is the work of God, you are not far from the kingdom of God. Who convinced thee of thy inability to believe, do you think the devil did? no, it was the Spirit of God procured by the blood of the Lamb, that was to come to convince the world of sin. If thou canst not trust as thou wouldst, say, *Lord, I believe, help my unbelief;* stretch out thy

thy poor hand. I am thinking of Sunday laſt, when I was giving the ſacrament, I obſerved there was one blind communicant that could not ſee, but he thruſt out his hand; I obſerved ſeveral lame perſons, but there were enough to give it to them; I ſaw alſo a poor barrow-woman, and I took particular care to give the cup to her; ſo I put it up to the mouth of the poor blind man: if that is the caſe, what love muſt there be in God to the poor ſoul!

But, methinks, I hear ſome poor ſoul ſay, that is not my caſe, I am not caſt down for that, but I am caſt down becauſe after that I knew God to be my God, after I knew Jeſus to be my King, and after I had mounted upon my high places, the devil and my unbelieving heart threw me down again; would you not have me caſt down? would you not have me diſquieted? a perſon of an Antinomian ſpirit would ſay, don't tell me of your frames, I have learned to live by faith, I don't care whether Chriſt manifeſts himſelf to me or no, I have got the word and the promiſe, I am content with a promiſe now; ſo theſe poor creatures go on without any frame, becauſe they will not live in it: from ſuch Antinomianiſm, good God, deliver me. How! how!

how! how! not cast down at an absent God, not disquieted when God withdraws? where are you gone? you are gone far from your father's house; if nothing else will do, may your father whip you home again. But tender hearts when they reflect how it was once, are cast down; David says, *My tears have been my meat day and night, for I had gone with a multitude to the house of God.* Here he looks back upon his former enjoyments, his spiritual prosperity, (as Job looks back upon his temporal) and says, *Why art thou cast down, O my soul*; it is because I don't meet God in his ordinances as I used to do; poor deserted, panting soul! poor disquieted soul! he must be the help of thy countenance, he will yet be thy God. Who was it sought Jesus sorrowing? what would you have thought of the Virgin Mary if she had said, I don't care whether I see my son or not; she sought him, and found him in the temple: God grant every poor deserted soul may find him to-night; I mean, in the temple of his heart. And in the case of Mary, she says, *They have taken away my Lord, and I know not where they have laid him*; if they had not taken away her Lord, Mary would have been rich: so you may say your

your corruptions, your backslidings and ingratitude, have taken away your Lord: Lord grant thou mayst find him to-night. He that said, *Mary*, can call thee to-night, and can make thee say, My dear Lord, I come to-night; he can call thee by thy name.

But, say you, I am cast down because I am wearied with temptation; not only my God is departed from me, but an evil spirit is come upon me to torment me; I am haunted with this and that evil suggestion, that I am a terror to myself. Come, come, hear what David saith in the beginning of the Psalm, *As the hart panteth after the water-brooks, so panteth my soul after thee, O God.* What say you to that? if you have a mind to see the beauty of this verse, read Mr. Hervey's Theron and Aspasio, which will live when its despisers are dead; and those that have endeavoured to disparage him will be obliged to own, that he was one of the greatest luminaries we ever had, and one that has laid down the doctrines of the gospel, in a manner to charm and allure the great and noble. Well, is it thy case that unbelief dogs thee go where thou will? well, still trust in God, *thou shalt yet praise him for the help of his countenance; he will command his loving-kindness in the day,*

and

and his song shall be with thee in the night. Though it be night, there is some moon, blessed be God, or some stars; and if there is a fog that you cannot see, God can quiet his people in the dark, he will make the enemy flee; fear him not, God will comfort thee, and punish the devil for tempting thee, if thou trust in him.

But, say you, I am cast down and disquieted within me; why? because I have one affliction after another, no sooner is one trial gone, but another succeeds; now I think I shall have a little rest, the tormentor will not come nigh me to-day, but no sooner has the Christian so said, but another storm comes, and the clouds return after the rain; then we think we must be cast down, and that we ought to be disquieted; this was David's case; what does he say? *All thy waves and thy billows are gone over me.* I believe he found after that, there were more waves to come than he had yet felt; why? says a poor distressed soul, because I have been so long in Christ, and have got these cursed corruptions yet within. I thought to have been rid of them all long ago; I thought I had no corruptions left thirty-three years ago, and that

the

the Canaanites were all rooted out of the land, that Pharaoh and his hoſt were all drowned in the red-ſea; but I find the old man is ſtrong in me, I look upon myſelf to be leſs than the leaſt of all ſaints, God knows; and you that walk near God, and have made greater advances in the divine life, if you are honeſt muſt ſay, O this body of ſin and death, if I ſhut this old man out at the fore-door, he comes in at the back-door. Come, come, come ſoul, truſt in God, he will give power to the faint, he will give ſtrength, and in due time deliver thee: go to God, tell him of them; beg thy Redeemer to take his whip into his hand, either of ſmall or large cords, and uſe it, rather than your corruptions ſhould get head again.

Time would fail to mention all that are caſt down on theſe accounts, but I muſt mention one more; perhaps, ſome of you may be caſt down with the fear not of death only, but of judgment. I believe there are thouſands of people die a thouſand times, for fear of dying once. Dr. Mather and Mr. Pemberton, of New-England, were always afraid of dying, but when they came to die; one or both of them ſaid to ſome that were intimate with them,

them, *Is this all, I can bear this very well:* and I have generally found that a poor foul, that cannot act that faith on God it once did, or in old age when the body grows infirm, as they ufed to do, yet they go off rejoicing in God, as a good foul that was buried at the Chapel the other day, faid, *I am going over Jordan.* Therefore, O poor foul, leave this to God, he will take care of thy dying hour. If any of you are poor here, and I was to promife to give you a coffin and a fhroud you would be eafy; now can you truft the word of a man, and not that of a God? Well, the Lord help you to truft in him; *having loved his own, he loves them to the end*; he is a faithful, unchangeable friend, that fticketh clofer than a brother.

Who would not be a Chriftian, who would but be a believer, my brethren; fee the precioufnefs of a believer's faith; the quacks will fay, here buy this packet, which is good for all difeafes, and is really worth nothing; but this will never fail the foul. Now I wifh I could make you all angry; I am a fad mifchief-maker; but I will affure you, I don't want to make you angry with one another: fome people that profefs to have grace in their hearts,

hearts, seem resolved to set all God's people at variance; they are like Sampson's foxes with firebrands in their tails, setting fire to all about them. Are any of you come from the Foundery, or any other place to-night? I do not care where you come from, I pray God you may all quarrel to-night; I want you to fall out with your own hearts; if we were employed as we ought to be, we should have less time to talk about the vain things that are the subjects of conversation: God grant your crosses may be left at the cross of the Lamb of God this night.

And if there be any of you here, as no doubt there are many, that are crying what nonsense he is preaching to-night, I should not wonder if they were to mimick me when they go home; if they should say, I thank God, I was never cast down; you take God's name in vain; you thank God you was never cast down, the very answer you have given makes me cast down for you; why so? why, as the Lord liveth, I speak out of compassion, there is but one step between thee and death. Don't you know the sessions began at the Old-Bailey to-day, if there were any capitally convicted, what would you think to see them playing at cards, or go on rattling and drinking, and swearing? would not you yourself cry, and if it were a child of your own, would it not break your heart? but yet thou art that wretch; I must weep for thee, my brother-sinner; we had both one father and mother, Adam and Eve; this was our sad original.

Dear Christians, pray for me to-night. I remember once I was preaching in Scotland, and saw ten thousand affected in a moment, some with joy, others crying "I cannot believe;" others, "God has given me faith," some fainting in their friends arms: seeing two stout creatures upon a tomb-stone, hardened indeed, I cried out, you rebels come down, and down they fell directly, and cried before they went away, *What shall we do to be saved?* Have any of you got apprentices, whom you have brought from time to time to the Tabernacle, but now will not let them come, because you think they grow worse and worse, and you will be tempted to leave off praying for them? don't do that; who knows but this may be the happy time. Children of godly parents, apprentices of godly people, servants of people who fear the Lord, that hear gospel-preachers, that are on the watch for every infirmity, that

go

go to their fellow-servants and say, these saints love good eating and drinking, they are only gospel-gossips; is this the case of any of you, if it is, you are in a deplorable condition, under the gospel and not convinced thereby: O may God bring down you rebels to-night; may this be the happy hour you may be cast down and disquieted within you. What can I say more? I would speak till I burst, I would speak till I could say no more. O poor soul, that hast been never yet cast down, I will tell you, if you die without being cast down, however you may die and have no pangs in your death, and your carnal relations may thank God that you died like lambs, but no sooner will your souls be out of your bodies, but God will cast you down to hell, you will be lifting up your eyes in yonder place of torment, you will be disquieted, but there will be nobody there to say, *hope thou in God, for I shall yet praise him*, &c. O my God, when I think of this, I could go to the very gates of hell to preach. I thought the other day, O if I had my health, I would stand on the top of every hackney coach, and preach Christ to those poor creatures. Unconverted old people, unconverted young people, will you have no compassion on your own souls: if you will damn yourselves, remember I am free from the blood of you all. O if it be thy blessed will, Lord most holy, O God most mighty, take the hearts of these sinners into thy hand. Methinks I see the heavens opened, the Judge sitting on his throne, the sea boiling like a pot, and the Lord Jesus coming to judge the world; well, if you are damned, it shall not be for want of calling after. O come, come, God help you to come, whilst Jesus is standing ready to receive you. O fly to the Saviour this night for refuge; remember if you die in an unconverted state you must be damned for ever.

O that I could but persuade one poor soul to fly to Jesus Christ, make him your refuge; and then, however you may be cast down, *hope in God, and you shall yet praise him.* God help those that have believed, to hope more and more in his salvation, till faith be turned into vision, and hope into fruition. Even so, Lord Jesus. Amen and Amen.

SERMON

SERMON XIII.

Spiritual Baptism.

ROMANS vi. ver. 3, 4.

Know ye not, that so many of us as were baptized into Jesus Christ, were baptized into his death? Therefore we are buried with him by baptism into death: that like as Christ was raised up from the dead by the glory of the Father, even so we also should walk in newness of life.

I BELEIVE, my dear hearers, I may venture to tell you, that the longer you live, the more you will find that the royal preacher spoke truth when he said, *There is nothing new under the sun*; for as God is always the same, so the world, the flesh, and the devil will be always the same, frail, vile, inimical and deceitful. New scenes surprize us, not because they are really new, but because

cause they are new to us: our lives are mostly taken up with viewing only the present appearance of things; we have neither time or leisure to look back as we ought, or might, upon the events of Providence, or the effects of the doctrines of grace. I will not say, my thoughts always run in a religious channel, but I will say, I wish they did. The words in our text, as connected with what preceeds and follows, contain the unchangeable truths of God: nor am I any ways staggered by opposition to the vindication of what the good old Puritans, and the Dissenters of the present age, call evangelical doctrine. I do not know a man that has wrote in a legal strain, or that reads, or talks in common conversation in a legal strain, but discovers his ignorance of, if not his enmity to the doctrine of justification by faith alone, by charging it with very bad consequences, and endeavouring to explode it as a dangerous doctrine, destructive of holiness, which they would seem to patronize; though if one were always to judge of them by their calumniating practice, one would imagine they had never read with proper attention, either the preceeding or following chapters, nor that wherein is our text, which proves it to be a doctrine

according

according to godliness, and therefore properly begins, *What shall we say then, shall we continue in sin that grace may abound?* You will say, I have been insisting upon the universal depravity of nature, I have been bringing all down upon an equal level; that I have not only mentioned the dreadful state of Heathens, but the equally dreadful state of the haughty Jews, and ignorant Gentiles, one only sinning against the light of nature, and the other sinning against the light of revelation, by which both, in one sense, stand on an equal footing, though the last, who thinks he stands upon higher ground, appears to be only superior in sin; why then, how must either or both be saved, since they have nothing to recommend them, nothing to plead as an atonement for their sins? Here comes in the blessed doctrine of justification, by the glorious imputed righteousness of Jesus Christ, to be received by faith as an instrument by the poor convicted sinner. If this be the case, *shall we sin that grace may abound?* this serves as a foil, to set off the riches of grace with a greater lustre. Is it not a very unfair deduction, to say never mind holiness, but sin that grace may abound, that God's grace may be more conspicuous?

Pray

Pray how does the apostle treat this? with the utmost abhorrence; *God forbid*, says he; how dare you charge the doctrine of grace with such a horrid consequence? God forbid that it should enter into our hearts; for *how shall we that are dead to sin live any longer therein? Know ye not*, saith he, *that as many of us as were baptized into Christ, are baptized into his death:* therefore, saith he, so far from sinning that grace may abound, we look upon ourselves as *being buried with Christ by baptism into death, that like as Christ was raised from the dead by the glory of the Father, even so we also should walk in newness of life*. This I thought a proper supplement to some discourses I have endeavoured to deliver you for some days last past, when treating on the credibility and authenticity of our blessed Lord's resurrection.

I cannot make sport for the devil by railing against infant or adult baptism; it is a strange thing how bigots can set the world on fire by throwing water at one another, and that people cannot be baptized, or sprinkled, as the others call it, without bespattering one another, and show that the chief thing they have been baptized into, are the waters of strife; this is catching at shadows, and making sport for

for the devil, while the combatants on both sides, being thus engaged in throwing the shadowy water at one another, lose the substantials of religion, while they are defending the outside of it. For my part, I do not enter into the debate about infant or adult baptism; there has been a dispute about the mode, as well as the subjects of baptism; persons equally skilled in language, pretend to bring various texts from the original, to prove that the word *baptizo*, signifies either sprinkling or plunging; and I believe you and I might as well attempt to draw two parallel lines, and bring them to meet at some certain place, as to bring these learned combatants together; for of all disputants, religious disputants are the most fiery and obstinate; therefore, I am for those that have learned to throw water upon bigotted fire, *to think, and let think,* about the mode, and consider what it imports.

It is certain, that in the words of our text, there is an allusion to the manner of baptism, which was by immersion, which our own church allows, and insists upon it, that children should be immersed in water, unless those that bring the children to be baptized assure the minister that they cannot bear the plunging.

We will allow this then, that one was plunged when he was young, another plunged when he was old; and, in fact, when adults are plunged as they ought, it is backwards at once: but whether I am plunged in a great deal, or *buried* with a little water, as a body is when it is said, *Earth to earth, ashes to ashes, dust to dust*, what signifies it, if I go in and come out, and continue just the same as before, unless you can say, *in Heathen and out Christian*; but we see very often they are not one bit the better, they have not one grain of Christianity more. Supposing a child when young grows up to a man, is sprinkled, or dipped as the children I saw at Lisbon, or in our font, as they are made large enough to dip in, though now they sprinkle; suppose one of these grows up a child of the devil, and says, I don't look upon what was done in my infancy to be baptism, I will be baptized really; and yet suppose also, that person takes up only the outward sign, and both of them die and go to the devil, would it give either of them satisfaction to say, I am in hell, but I was baptized when an infant, or adult? both of them would have to lament they were tormented in the flame. Would it not be better for us to

take

take care not to offend our brethren, not to raise one anothers spirits and corruptions, but rather, when we come together, talk of the heart, and enquire whether, when we received the outward sign by sprinkling or dipping, we really received the thing signified in our hearts, and exemplify that thing signified, in our lives.

Now pray what is the thing signified? we need not go farther for an answer than our text, *As many of them as were baptized into Jesus Christ, were baptized into his death:* and it is worthy remarking, that our Lord told his disciples, that they were *to baptize all nations in the name of the Father, and of the Son, and of the Holy Ghost.* Now I believe all persons that have but a little skill in scripture interpretation, must allow that the word name signifies Christ; my name is in him, speaking in the Old Testament of Christ's name; and when we say, *in or by the name*, it has a peculiar reference to every thing that belongs to God: and I verily believe that when the Redeemer said, *baptize them in the name of Father, Son, and Holy Ghost*, he not only intended to establish the doctrine of three persons in one God, but also to point out the nature of true baptism, namely, to be baptized into the nature of the Father, into the nature of the Son, and into the nature of the Holy Ghost, and this seems to be the meaning of our text, *Know ye not that so many as were baptized;* if we have been baptized aright, have been baptized not only in the name of Christ, but have been baptized into Christ; that is, we have not only put on Christ in an outward profession, but have been so baptized by the Holy Ghost, as to be made members of Christ's mystical body, united to him by the blessed Spirit; so that in a degree, though not in every sense, we are one with Christ, and the Father, through him. This is religion common to all, whether we are Baptist or Pœdo-baptist; for we may call one another by this and that name, it is no matter what we are called, the grand matter is, what God looks upon us to be; whether we are become by baptism, and with the powerful operations of the Spirit of God accompanying that ordinance, branches of Jesus Christ, the true vine. It has been always an argument with me, and I may plead for the same liberty that I give, that I think infant-baptism is an ordinance of Christ, because if our children are not to be baptized, they are left inferior in their privileges to the Jews,

their

their children were circumcised to God, and why should not our children be as soon initiated into Christ as they? The apostle saith, *He is not a Jew that is one outwardly, neither is that circumcision which is outwardly in the flesh,* but circumcision is *that of the heart and of the spirit, whose praise is not of men but of God;* so it may be said of outward baptism, he is not a Christian who is baptized only outwardly, but he that is baptized inwardly of the Spirit, *whose praise is not of men but of God.* When we get a proselite, we are so fond of them that we hug them to death: I have got the praise of men especially when religion walks in silver slippers; when a person says, I may get business if I get into such a church, into such a society; a man may become religious as he may go to 'Change for trade, but he is a Christian who is one inwardly, who has no worldly views, no designs but what are subordinate to the glory of God. The primitive Christians gave great proof of their sincerity, they were baptized over the dead; *what shall they do who are baptized for,* or over, *the dead?* notwithstanding they saw their fellow-creatures murdered, they dared to go openly to be baptized; though they knew very well soon after,

that

that for their baptism with water, they should be baptized with fire, and yet they dared openly to avow their profession of Christ. This is being baptized into Christ; well, what then? why, then we are baptized into his death. Can you tell me what that is? I cannot fully, I don't know that myself; and we should preach according to our experience, (a man of little true grace, he will give you a little, little, little practical application; very little, because he has but little himself; a man that has a good deal of it in his heart, he will not neglect his principles, but he will give the people a good sound meal of practical religion) though I am but a babe in Christ, though I have been in Christ four or five and thirty years, and know but little of Christ, yet I think I can tell you a little what it is to be baptized into Christ, to be baptized into his death. Am I immediately to die in the body? that does not always follow, but we are to die daily, we are to be conformed to Christ's death, which we never can till we have been baptized into Christ; we can never die till we have been enabled by his power to die. When we talk of dying the death of Christ, we mean being crucified to the world with him.

I live,

Ser. XIII.   *Spiritual Baptism.*   303

I live, says Paul, *yet not I, but Christ lives in me; and the world is crucified to me, and I unto the world.* Now we all come into the world alive to the world, the flesh, and the devil. Some people say, a child must cry in order to prove itself an heir; what do you think it cries for? I believe some people think 'tis because it is in pain, but I am afraid the child cries because he is hurt; I believe he finds the air too cool for him; and the first thing he does, is giving a proof of original sin to his parents, and all the attendants about him: this is called in scripture, the old man; and however some may find fault with the Church of England, and its forms (perhaps they may be mended, but I question whether we have men capable of mending them now-a-days, either for zeal or spiritual knowledge) yet I am sure there is something in it very good, particularly there is that prayer to be put up by a child, deserves to be written in letters of gold, *Grant, O Lord, that all things belonging to the old man may die in me;* and then follows (what I shall speak of by and by) *and all belonging to the new man may live and grow in me.* There is the whole sum and substance of religion, the Alpha and Omega, the beginning,

ginning, the middle, and the end, as Mr. Ambrose's works are intitled. We want nothing but all things belonging to the old man to die in us, and all things belonging to the new to live, to make us fit for the kingdom of Christ; and if we can find this in us, God grant we may not quarrel one with another, though I verily believe young men think the old man is very troublesome. There is one does not live very far from hence, who is a very worthy man, I remember a few years ago he came in, in his first love, saying, " he had got on the mount; the fire burnt upwards, though there was a good deal of smoak. Pray, says I, is the old man dead yet? no, said he, he is not quite dead, but spoke as if he thought he was expiring; says I, I will speak to you three or four years hence. Some time after that, meeting him, I asked him concerning the old man, he said, he thought he was alive and worse than ever, and that he was a sly creature, would lie down as if he was asleep, that he may attack you when off your guard the better." I heard of a good man in the country, who said, he found his corruptions were a monster of a thousand heads; now this is called a crucifixion, which is a painful and a

gradual

gradual death, but a certain death: God forbid any of you now should turn the food into poison, saying, this is a very good doctrine, I like it; the minister says the old man dies slow, so I will not crucify him; they tell me he will die by and by, but not yet, so I will not trouble myself much about him; why then, my dear hearer, whoever thou art, thou talkest like a stinking hypocrite, or a rank, vile Antinomian; how, how, is the old man such a pleasant companion, that you love to have him dwelling under your roof? would you chuse to have a parcel of whores and rogues to live in your houses? would you like, if you lived by letting of lodgings, two or three rooms suppose, to have a parcel of thieves and robbers, and pickpockets, come and tell you their profession, would it not be foolish for you to let such people in, would it not? and just such fools you are to let pickpockets, street-robbers, God-robbers, vile prostitutes in your wicked hearts, the lusts of the flesh, the lusts of the eye, and the pride of life, stay not only till quarter-day, but long after: before you turn them out, you may be dead; no, no, it is not an instantaneous, but a gradual, progressive work.

Then we are baptized into Christ, when we study to glorify Christ; that is the reason that God Almighty sends you so many trials, that you may be baptized into his death; and generally you will find, when you have had most communications from God, that some cross trials soon follow. Hast thou been praying for resignation? perhaps God takes away a beloved child; you have been praying for great patience, perhaps a cross wife, a Nabal of a husband, bad servants, undutiful children, or something or other, and the devil at the head of them, making you uneasy, so that you find you have not so much patience as you thought you had; you never was upon the mount in your lives, but when you came down, you were tempted to break the tables: was it not so with Moses after forty days communion with God? down he came, and seeing the people dancing round the calf, down he throws the tables, and breaks them all to pieces; and if God was not to keep us, after all our communion with him, we should break the tables to pieces and be damned. After all that person then is dying every day, who looks upon himself every morning as one that is to be crucified afresh, that looks for crosses,

crosses, and at the same time walks so inoffensively as to bring no cross upon himself. I spoke to a person yesterday about the cross; pray sir, says he, would you have me bring a cross upon myself; no, said I, only be honest, and you will find crosses enough.

Then we must be raised to newness of life, as Christ was raised from the dead by the glory of the Father; this points out to us in what sense Jesus Christ is the resurrection and the life, and shews us that every thing Jesus Christ did and suffered, must be spiritually experienced in our hearts. You have often heard me say, as he was born in the Virgin's womb, he must be born in our hearts, and as he died for sin, we must die to sin, as he rose again, we must rise to newness of heart and life. What is the new birth? says a great doctor: suppose any of these doctors were to come to any woman when her travelling pains were upon her, and she was crying out, and labour pains came on faster and faster, and they should stand preaching at the door, and say, good woman, these are only metaphorical pains, this is only a bold expression of the Easterns, it is only metaphorical, I question whether the woman would not wish the doctors some of

these

these metaphorical pains for talking so, which they would find real ones; though she could not read she might feel. But notwithstanding the reality of the new birth, and the pains that attend it, yet they say it is only a metaphorical thing. I am of an odd temper, and of such a temper, that I heartily wish they may be put under the pangs of the new birth, and know what it is by their own experience, know there is nothing in nature more real than the new birth. The apostle Paul said, *I travel in birth till Christ be formed in you:* now don't you think the apostle had this metaphorical expression of something real; the apostle's travelling in birth must be something analogous to the natural birth; must I say there is no such thing as pangs because I don't feel them: I am fearfully and wonderfully made, that my soul knows right well; and in respect to the new birth we may say, I am fearfully and wonderfully redeemed by Christ, and renewed by the Holy Ghost; the new life imparts new principles, a new understanding, a new will and new affections, a renewed conscience, a renewed memory, nay, a renewed body, by making it the temple of the living God, an habitation of God through the Spirit, and

walking

walking in newness of life; if I am not mistaken, it implies a progressive motion, going from strength to strength, from one degree of grace to another, passing from glory to glory, for grace is only glory in the bud, till grace is swallowed up in endless glory. A person that walks, though he may not walk equally fast as others, yet may get ground: hence, *not to go forward is to go backward.* Enoch walked with God; it bespoke the habitual tendency of his heart, the actual exercise of grace, that he was kept in a lively frame, walked with God among a very wicked generation, dared to be good when all were wicked around him, and he was so favoured, as to be translated to heaven; this was the case with Elijah. *Moses,* says the Lord, *go up to the mount and die:* God made him undress himself, and put on his own grave cloaths, gives him a sight of Canaan, but to let him know that he even to the very last would chastise his people, when he is even taking them to heaven; tells him, thou shalt not go into the earthly Canaan, but I will take thee to the heavenly one, which is far better. Being baptized into the death of Christ, bespeaks the habitual tendency and practice of the heart and life; the old man must die,

die, hence the new man must live; it must be emptied of self, that there may be more and more room for God: now I appeal to your hearts, how far you have experienced this. I believe the world pretty well knows the temper of my mind, both in respect to politics and church-government, and church-principles: I am a professed avower of moderation, and I heartily wish that all who are concerned in church and state, may particularly take care to let their moderation be known to all men, for if we quarrel with one another, we shall only make sport for the devil, and occasion destruction. I don't care whether you go to church or meeting; I am, I profess, a member of the church of England, and if they will not let me preach in the church, I will preach any where; all the world is my parish, and I will preach wherever God gives me an opportunity, but you will never find me disputing about the outward appendages of religion; don't tell me you are a Baptist, an Independant, a Presbyterian, a Dissenter, tell me you are a Christian, that is all I want; this is the religion of heaven, and must be ours upon earth; I say, are there any of you under the gallery, or in the green-seat, or any where,

I will

I will try to find you out before I have done my sermon, though you are come in the dark.

But I will just at present speak to you who understand the gospel, to you that are my brethren, though, in all probability, my elder brethren in the gospel. Methinks there is something solemn in meeting in the evening, something solemn in coming to worship after we have been in the labours of the day; and I verily believe, that when weekly preaching is banished from London, that all Christianity will be banished, it cannot be very long after it, there have been such instances, you may die before to-morrow. I think a good tradesman, whether he deals largely or not, will take care to keep his day-book well; if a man will not keep his day-book well, it is ten to one but he loses a good deal when he comes to count up his things at Christmas; now I take it for granted, a good spiritual tradesman will keep his spiritual day-book well: can you say, this day I hope I have died a little more to the world than yesterday, this day I hope I have been a little more alive to God than I was yesterday; and yet when I look upon my family, whether a man trades wholesale or retail, when he finds he has done but little

little business that day, great going out, and little coming in. I hope when you die but little daily, that you go to bed begging pardon, and begging grace, that you may die more to yourselves and the world, and live more to God to-morrow; for I am sure I can call you to witness, that you never lived so comfortably as when you lived near to God; you may as well pretend to say, that a person in a cold winter's day is warmest when he keeps from the fire, as to say, a soul can live near to God when he does not die daily to sin. O, says one, don't tell me of your frames, don't mind them; I will tell you of them, *don't mind your frames*, I don't in respect to justification, but I will to the well-being and comfort of my soul: a man that has got but very little spirits may be alive, but there is a wide difference between having a disorder that one can hardly speak, having no spirits at all, or but very few, and having solid health: God grant we may be healthy Christians; the more you live to God, the more you will have health; be not angry with me; assure yourselves a lukewarm Christian does more hurt to religion, than all the open infidels in the kingdom; we have God himself asserting this, *Thou art neither hot*

hot nor cold, I would thou waſt either cold or hot, but becauſe thou art neither cold nor hot, but lukewarm, I will ſpew thee out of my mouth; what an expreſſion is that! what a nauſeous thing is lukewarm water to a ſick ſtomach! *I will come and remove my candleſtick from you.* Therefore, I believe, it is the opinion of all judicious men, that if we ſhould have a ſevere rod of correction to ſtir us up, it is becauſe of the lukewarmneſs of moſt Chriſtians: my brethren, God make us all alive to Chriſt tonight; come, come, if your ſoul is for Chriſt, to arms, to arms, put on your cockades, you that have them in your pockets, for fear you ſhould be known to be Chriſt's. O you cowards; many ſoldiers put off their cockades, as if they were not ſoldiers; as many of our clergy affect to dreſs like the laity, that they may go to the plays, that the orange-women may not know them, and they don't care whether God ſees them or no. I deſire you will all appear in your proper dreſſes, let us ſee it is painted on the breaſt-plates of your hearts, by the bleſſed monitor, the eternal Spirit of God; I don't want you to wear them as the Papiſts, upon your faces, no; you that are for infant-baptiſm, were ſigned with the ſign of the croſs,

cross, for what? that you might, when you came of age, *prove Chrift's faithful foldiers to the end:* God grant, the nearer we come to the end the bolder we may be for Chrift.

If there be any of you here that are formalifts, *that have a name to live and are dead,* the Lord grant, that our Lord Jefus Chrift, who was raifed from the dead by the glory of his Father, caufe a ftirring among thefe dry bones. Think what it will be to go to hell to-night, to want a drop of water, wherewith you was fprinkled, to cool your tongues in hell; think what it will be to go to hell by the way of heaven, which is the worft way you can take; think what it will be to be juft at the threfhold, and not have religion enough to take you over; my heart bleeds for you. Had you a fon, a father, a mother, a relation, to be tried at the Old-Bailey this feffions, how would you be concerned, how carefully would you enquire when your relation would be tried, how anxious would you be to hear whether he is condemned or no; and if fomebody was to come to tell you, now he is about to be tried and caft, and now the judge is going to put his cap on, to pafs fentence on him; how would you bear it? I believe fome of you would drop a tear, and

fay,

say, O that this poor creature should be born for this; and can you blame a poor minister of Christ, a poor sinner that has been redeemed by the blood of Christ, and I humbly believe and hope, has been made a partaker of the Spirit, will you blame me for being concerned for you, my brethren and my sisters, for you and I sprung from one father and mother, Adam and Eve, the common parents of us all; can you blame me for pouring out my soul, can you blame me for speaking a little home, when the Judge is just ready to mount the throne, when the books are open, when I see the elements melting with fervent heat, when I see all nature concurring to usher in the awful coming of the Son of God. Sinners in Zion, baptized heathens, professors but not possessors, formalists, believing unbelievers, talking of Christ, talking of grace, orthodox in your creeds, but heterodox in your lives, turn ye, turn ye, Lord help you to turn to him, turn ye to Jesus Christ, and may God turn you inside out to-night; may the power of the highest overshadow you, and may that glorious Father that raised Christ from the dead, raise your dead souls. Turn the text into a prayer, go home and say, for what purpose have I lived?

lived? into what have I been baptized? I have not so much as yet been baptized into Jordan; I have never led a life one day of reformation but when I was obliged to it: bless God that you are not now among the damned; bless God that you are not now howling in hell; bless the Lord that Jesus stands with pitying eyes, and outstretched arms to receive you now; will you go with the man? will you accept of Christ? will you begin to live now? may God say, Amen; may God pass by, not in anger but in love; may he, as he hath hitherto seen you in your blood, has said to you, live, and has preserved you in your natural state, may that same God of love, mercy, and life, pass by you, and cast the skirts of his love over you, and say to you dead sinners, come forth, live a life of faith on earth, live a life of vision in heaven; even so, Lord Jesus. Amen.

SERMON XIV.

Neglect of Christ the killing Sin.

JOHN v. ver. 40.

And ye will not come to me that ye may have life.

THE great apostle of the Gentiles, after he had set before the Hebrews the great cloud of witnesses of Old Testament believers, exhorts them to look higher, even to Jesus the common Saviour, and that not transiently, but earnestly and constantly, in his mediatorial character of humiliation, as enduring unheard of, unparalleled contradiction of sinners against himself; *least*, says he, *ye be weary, and faint in your minds.* If we had not such an example set before us, and brought to us by the Holy Ghost in a suffering hour, we should never hold out to the end: this was not the contradiction of the openly profane and scandalous, those that were without,

out, so much as from those that were within the pale of the church, even those to whom were committed the lively oracles of God, who had not only the very bible in their own hands, but were set apart to explain it to others. That the words of our text were spoken to them, appears from the preceeding verse, in which he bids them *search the scriptures*; as a person digs for a mine, or searches for some hidden treasure. The word bible, or book which I have in my hand, is well applied to the holy scriptures, because it is the book of God, written by him, that is, by his order, and by those who were inspired by him for that end; and yet, of all writings in the world, these are most neglected! God has condescended to become an author, and yet people will not read his writings. There are very few that ever gave this book of God, the grand charter of salvation, one fair reading through: though we profess to have assented to the truth of scripture, as our Lord said, *in them we think we have eternal life*, yet most read them as they would a proclamation, a romance, a play, or novels, that help only to bring them to the devil, but chuse not to read God's book, which is to be our guide to glory; *they are they*, says Christ, *which testify of me:* Lord God convert and change our hearts.

However, this was spoken in reference to the Old Testament, and certainly shows us, that Christ is the treasure hid in that field, yet as there are equal proofs of the divinity of the New Testament, the word Holy Scriptures include both, especially as Christ is the antitype of all the types, the Alpha and Omega, the beginning and the end of all divine revelation: would to God he was your Alpha and Omega too! Now, saith Christ, you pretend to reverence the scriptures; you that are set apart as persons learned in the scriptures, ye Scribes, ye lawyers, such as were mentioned in the gospel to-day. I fancy some people think, that when we read of lawyers in the scriptures, that we mean such lawyers as ours, who deal only in the civil and common law, but they were those that opened and explained the law to the people; these were the persons who thought and professed, that in them they had eternal life, that they testify of Christ the great Prophet that was promised in the scriptures to come into the world; yet, saith our divine master, to these very professors, these masters in Israel, *ye will not come to me that*

ye

ye may have life: though I am now present with you, though I am now come to explain the scriptures, and fulfil them, am now come to proclaim to you that life, that eternal life, which the scriptures declare were to be published and proclaimed by me, yet *ye will not come unto me that ye may have life.*

By eternal life we are to understand, all the blessings of a converted state, particularly the pardon of sins, not only before conversion but after. It is impossible but there should be sin every day and every hour in every professing person. My dear hearers, as I shall not have an opportunity for some time to speak to you, I don't chuse, especially when I am about to take my leave of you, to speak any thing that is severe, but I assure you without attempting to offend, with a broken heart I assure you, that this was the treatment Jesus Christ met with of old, and, God knows, this is the treatment Jesus Christ meets with now: *ye will not come to me that ye may have eternal life.*

If I am not mistaken, and I think I am not, the words suppose, that they and we are all dead in sin, for if we are not, I do not know why we need come to have life; and I mention this, because for want of believing and knowing

ing this, some that pretend to know Christ and to preach him, forget to lay the proper foundation, original sin; and that there is no ability or inclination in the heart of a natural man, so much as to do any thing spiritual; he is stupid and dead. But if we have eyes to see, if we have ears to hear, and if our hearts are not waxed hard, doubtless it would appear as clear to us as the sun shining in its meridian brightness, that man was dead till God breathed into him the breath of life, and then he became a living soul. I know some people believe that the words mean this, that God breathed into man, and he became a natural living soul, like other animals, but then they don't consider what a life God did breath into the soul, he breathed into it the life of God, a spiritual life was breathed into the soul; it is expressed in the strongest, but at the same time in the most concise terms that is possible, none but God, none but a man inspired by God, could say so much in so few words; it shows great skill in men to say so much in a little; what uninspired man ever wrote so as Moses did? Now Moses when he penned the scriptures, said, *God made man after his own image*, and you know ten thousand volumes

could not have said more than that. How long do you think it was that man continued in his original purity? I don't know that I ever yet heard, that any one thought he continued in his blessed state so long as from Saturday to Saturday. Mr. Boston, who, perhaps, is one of the best writers that ever Scotland produced, says, that there is an allusion in one of the Psalms to man's sudden fall, *Man being* born *in honour, continued not*; i.e. but a night before he fell. O much good may do those that boast of their free-will, that think they can stand by a power of their own, when father Adam, who had no corruption, did not stand a week, perhaps not two days; and how can we pretend to stand, let us have what grace we will, when that grace has so much corruption to oppose it? if Jesus Christ did not take care to secure our standing, we should fall to our ruin. Adam fell, and being our federal head, we fell in him. Why, says a Deist, and too many professors also, pray what business had God Almighty to make our fall or our standing depend on another? you will not object to this you church of England men, will you? then why have you god-fathers and god-mothers to promise for you? why have
we

we members of parliament to be the heads of the people, and what the parliament does, the people do, you have conſtituted them your heads and repreſentatives, you muſt ſtand and fall by them; ſo if you are bound for a perſon, you muſt ſtand and fall with him, muſt not you? I remember one of the miniſters that preached the morning exerciſes, when moſt, if not all the churches in this city, were filled with goſpel-preachers, till on Bartholomew-day near 2,500 of them in the whole were turned out, and the other miniſters that did not preach the goſpel continued till the plague came, and then they ran away, and left the pulpits to thoſe that were turned out, who were willing to go into them, though they expected the plague would ſeize them in preaching Chriſt there; one of thoſe miniſters ſays, ſuppoſe God had choſe all that were to be created, and to proceed from the loins of Adam, had been preſent, and that he ſhould have ſaid to them, I have been ſeven days employed in preparing the whole creation; I have made a garden, and will have one choſe by you to dwell in it, as my vicegerent and your repreſentative here below; here is Adam, the father of you all, whom I have bleſſed with a partner, that is bone of his bone, and flesh of his flesh, a creature like himself; all that I desire of your head and representative is, that he abstains from yonder tree, of every other tree in the garden he may freely eat except that; this I ordain as a test of his obedience, to see whether it is fulfilled, and you shall all stand or fall by this; who shall be the man? would they not all say, our first parent to be sure. O there is not a single man but would have chosen Adam to be their representative, they would rather stand and fall by him than by any body else; now pray why should we quarrel with him for acting in the manner we ourselves should have done, had we been in his situation? *God*, saith the apostle, *included all under sin.* What is sin but a breach, that is, a transgression of the law; *the wages of sin is death*; every transgression of the law incurs damnation. Have we eaten of the forbidden fruit? we must die, we are legally dead; and there is not a little child in the world that is not. It is enough to make the parents pray night and day for their children; there is not a child born but, to use the words of our own church, brings in with it corruption, which renders it liable to the wrath of

God

God forever. Then, say some, it is true what I have heard say of you, that there are little children in hell a span long; I never had such a thought in my life; I never believed that any infants, black or white, were damned in hell. I think a poor child, though it is born in a state of original sin, and I have often thought *that* is the reason why little children are seized with such terrible disorders as often carry them out of the world, with ten times more agony than parents feel; a great proof of man's offence. We see a poor little infant soon after it is born, in two or three months taken with fits, lie screaming and struggling, while the distressed parents are breaking their hearts, and wishing, though they love it dearly, that God would take it out of its pain. Is not this a strong proof that man is fallen from God? else who can tell what God designs hereby: however, I verily believe that by his grace he fits them for heaven. We have broken God's law, and are liable to eternal condemnation, we are therefore legally dead, every one of us without distinction; we are all upon a level, from the greatest king in the world, who has it in his power to write death or life upon the poor condemned malefactors; bring him to the

the bar of God's holy law, and it will tell him there, thou art the malefactor in the fight of God, thou thyself, and thus God is glorified. It is not greatness of station, nor external differences, that make a difference in the internal state of the soul. A nobleman may come with his star and garter to the king's bar, and be tried by his peers at Westminster-hall, and may be attended from the Tower by some of the king's officers, but whether a nobleman be tried at Westminster-hall, or a criminal in rags at the Old-Bailey, the law must be executed upon both: this is our state towards God, we have lived in trespasses and sins, are legally dead now; is that all? Dr. Taylor, of Norwich, says, that all the loss we have had by the fall is, that our misery is temporary. Alas! alas! when Arminians talk of the fall, you will find very few of them have courage enough to stab themselves. Conscience makes them cowards; they have lost all by Adam's fall. What death have we suffered, not only legally but spiritually dead; what do I mean by that? why, that we are deprived of that life of God in which we originally stood. Have you ever seen any body die? I have. Have you ever seen one of your friends die?

die? have you ever ſtole into the room, and looked but once at the dear object of your love, the partner of your life, but wait till the next day, and eſpecially in the ſummer ſeaſon, and ſee how changed! the laſt object I ſaw, put me in mind of the fall I ſaw nature in. O what a change! the glory is departed!

But beſides this legal death, there is a ſpiritual death, and the conſequence of that is eternal death; if I die in that ſtate I muſt die for ever; that is, I muſt be a creature living eternally baniſhed from God: if I be annihilated when I die, then, indeed, temporal death is all; but it is not ſo, I am to live in another world; the wiſeſt man upon earth tells us, that there is a future ſtate; and therefore by legal and ſpiritual death, I am liable to death eternal. I have the longer inſiſted on this, becauſe it is impoſſible to know, or to value that life that Jeſus Chriſt came into the world to impart to us and procure for us, without conſidering the nature of the death he delivers us from.

Now let us attend to what our Lord ſays, *Ye will not come to me that ye may have life;* in the tenth chapter he ſays, *I am come that they might have life, and that they might have it more*

more abundantly; now what life is that? to be sure, the life which a malefactor wants, who is tried by a Jury; why, he wants to have the chain taken off; what do you and I want? for we may want to eternity if we plead our innocence; there is not one of us but must plead guilty before God; well, what must I do? why, if ever I have life, I must be acquitted, something must pronounce me not guilty; my conscience says, guilty; why, then Jesus Christ came that we might have a legal life, that we might be acquitted from all that condemnation which we are under by our breaking his law; so far the remedy answers to the disease; but the remedy would not be extensive enough if that was all; therefore, it was an excellent answer a poor woman made at the Old-Bailey, I heard of it twenty years ago: she was brought sick to the bar to receive a pardon; the judge said, Woman, his majesty has given you a pardon: My lord, says she, I thank his majesty for a pardon, and you for pronouncing it, but that is not all I want; what my poor soul wants is, a pardon from Jesus Christ; what signifies a pardon from a judge, if I have a disease in me that will kill me? whether I am pardoned or not, I must have my disease cured,

cured, that the pardon may do me good. I thought it a strange plea of a man, a captain of a ship, that I heard tried some years ago for throwing a poor negro overboard; he asked the surgeon, do you think that the child will die? Sir, said he, it will not live above an hour; then, says he, you may let it down now: O, says the judge, you have murdered the child. I must have a pardon from my God, or I am damned; and if I have lost the divine image, which was the original dignity of man, I shall never get to glory without the restoration of that image I have lost by my sin. Spiritual life in the heart, is that which comes from Jesus Christ, and this is the life of God in the soul of man; it is not a metaphorical but a real thing, a resurrection to life by the power of Christ, *who is the resurrection and the life*, so there is a connection between a legal and a spiritual life; the type and antitype answers as face answers to face in water: thus as all in Adam have died, so all in Jesus Christ, the second Adam, are made alive. We are apt to think that such a one, and such a one, were sound Christians and gone to heaven, but there is a great deal of false charity in the world; without this life we are all undone. Now,

Now, my brethren, if this is the case, how must I have my life in glory? how must a dead creature be a Christian? how must a sinner that is spiritually dead have divine life? and how must a creature, every moment liable to death eternal, be made eternally alive? can any body answer that question? will reason tell me? no; will philosophy help me? no; for if *the world by wisdom knew not God*, surely, the world by wisdom knows not how to turn to God; therefore, you will find the greatest scholars the greatest fools, proudest deists, and most scornful atheists; for knowledge puffeth up; and if bare knowledge makes a Christian, the devil must be very good, he is the most knowing, and yet the most wicked. The only way to get this life restored, is to come to Jesus Christ; *ye will not come unto me*, saith our text, *that ye may have life*; implying, that without coming to him they cannot have life: *there is no other name given under heaven whereby we can be saved, but that of Jesus Christ. I am the way, the truth, and the life. I am the resurrection and the life*, saith the Lord. In order to have this life, we must come to Christ for it: I hope you don't think coming to Christ, means coming to see his person, that can never

be;

be: for our Lord talks of coming to him when he himself was the preacher, and they were all about him; though so many round him, yet there was but one that touched him. A great many people say, dear, if Christ was here, how would I caress him! I would let him in! when, perhaps, at the same time turn out one of his members. Would you like to see Jesus Christ with a parcel of boys and girls running before him, a parcel of poor fishermen with him, and Mary Magdalen, with a mob of poor people and publicans following him? we have got the same spirit the people had then, we should hoot at him and despise him, as the Pharisees did. A great many people think coming to Christ is to come to the sacrament; you know very well I love that privilege; and one of the greatest afflictions I have is, that my health will not permit me to attend all the ordinances; but thousands come to ordinances, that have no view of the God of ordinances in them, therefore you will find, that in all our public places it is as much the fashion to go to public worship about eleven o'clock, as any where else. They are not up time enough to their mattins; they go and say, we thank God, who has brought us to

the beginning of this day, and that when perhaps the clock strikes twelve, and they just up; thus people go to church as to a play, to see and be seen, and as soon as they go out of church, they ask where they are to go to next, and what party? Thousands go to church, or to meeting, and sacrament, and don't come to Christ: come and like this preaching, and numbers who are called fools for following us, eat the fragments that are left, that hear preaching, eat the fish and the loaves, and are only feasting upon shadows and not upon Christ: this should make us extremely careful to examine whether we ever came to Christ or no. A great moral preacher says of our preaching, when all their stock is out, then they cry come, come, come, and that is the burden of their song, say they; and I hope that will be the burden of our song till Christ says, *Come ye blessed of my Father*; what would you have us say? O, say you, bid a man do and live, so we will; and in the same sense Christ in the gospel says, thou art dead; what shall I do, says the man, to inherit eternal life? thou knowest our Lord said to him, Keep the law. Our Lord always spoke to the people in their own language; that is, thou
shalt

shalt love the Lord thy God with all thy heart; he began with morality at the right place, we begin at the fifth commandment. The great morality, says Dr. Young, is beginning with the love of God. *Thou shalt love thy neighbour as thyself; thou hast answered right*, says he, *do this, and thou shalt live.* Whoever loves the Lord God as he ought to do, with all his soul and strength, shall certainly live; but our Lord takes pains to convince him of his ignorance and folly; says he, *who is my neighbour?* as to the love of God, he had no thought of that. Thus we deceive our own souls, till Jesus Christ opens our eyes. What must we come to Christ for? to be acquitted; come to his blood to be pardoned; you must believe on him, not only with a bare speculative belief, that the devil has, and all the damned in hell, but to have his blood applied and brought home to the soul; we must come to him as the author and finisher of our faith. Did not you just now say, I believe in the Holy Ghost, the Lord and giver of life; and the form of baptism is in the name of the Father, Son, and Holy Ghost; it means, baptize them into the nature of the Father, Son, and Holy Ghost: and I remember about three or four and thirty

years

years ago, a friend mentioned that word in private conversation to me, we translate it, we believe in God; said he, we should translate it, *we believe it in God*, for we never do till God has put his faith in us, then we have in our souls a new life in Christ, then we live a life of faith; *the life I now live is by faith in the Son of God. I live, yet not I, but Christ liveth in me.* In order to this I must come to Jesus Christ, and believe on him for life eternal, the earnest of which eternal life I must have in my heart before I can be assured I do believe on him. O, my dear hearers, do we think of this, this is no new doctrine; I set out, blessed be God, with this doctrine. The second sermon I ever made, the second sermon I ever preached, was on these words, *He that is in Christ is a new creature:* I was then about twenty years and a half old. The next sermon I preached was upon, *Ye are justified*; the next sermon, *Ye are glorified*; which shows, that though I am near fifty-five years old, yet, I thank my God, I am so far from changing my principles, which I am sure I was taught by God's word and Spirit, that I am more and more confirmed, that if I was to die this moment, I hope I should have

strength

strength and courage given me to say, I am more convinced of the efficacy and the power of those truths which I preached when I was twenty years old, when I first preached them.

Now, my dear hearers, what could enter into the heart of any person in the world, to reject such a salvation as this? can you think that when a king saith to a prisoner, let him go, he would refuse it? there are some persons that refuse Christ. I remember when, by the bounty of the people here, we begged for the poor, one man went to the turnpike and said, this is Dr. Whitefield's bread and be damned. Human nature, what is it without Christ, the bread of life! We will not come to him that we may have life, though we may have it for asking; no, not for life eternal, as a free gift: we will not come to Christ and accept it at his hand; we *will* not: it is not said, we *shall* not, but we *will* not. Pray why will not people come to Christ to have life? because they do not think that they are dead, and do not want it; remember when you say, *you are rich and increased in goods*, that you know not, saith Christ, that *ye are poor and miserable, and blind and naked*. We do not see ourselves fallen creatures, we do
not

not know that: God give thee to know and feel, that *there is no name given under heaven whereby we can be saved, but Jesus Christ.* What, saith one, must I have inward feeling? what would the polite world do without feeling? do you think they would go to the playhouse and places of public diversion without feeling? if I can feel other things that do not concern religion, how can I come to God till I feel a need of him. We don't chuse to come to Christ, because we don't chuse to have him as a free gift; we don't like to come to him as poor and needy. I remember I heard an excellent minister of Christ in Scotland, one Mr. Wallis, of Dundee, preaching upon these words, *Behold I stand at the door and knock,* says he. Christ comes knocking at the door to come into your houses, but you will not come down to accept of his mercy. When the prodigal said, *I will arise and go to my Father, and will say unto him, I have sinned against heaven and in thy sight, and am no more worthy to be called thy son, make me as one of thy hired servants:* now you think that it was very humble in him, he who was a son of the head of the house, to be willing to be a servant. 'Tis true he says, I will go to my father's ther's house, but at the same time he says, I will work for my living, he shall not maintain me for nothing; but when he comes to his father, he is quite brought down, he says, *I have sinned against heaven and in thy sight;* the joyful father clasps him in his withered arms, and takes the poor ragged wanderer home. The lawyers and other Jews thought they were righteous, and therefore they would not come to Jesus Christ. Our Lord spoke of the Pharisees, who trusted in themselves that they were righteous, and would not come to him that they might have life; and if we trust in ourselves, neither shall we. Our Lord says, *I receive not honour from men. How can you come to him, that receive honour one of another? Honour to whom honour is due.* To such as are in power, whether in church or state, respect is due to their outward situation. I am for no levelling principles at all; but, my brethren, at the same time there is a fault, that we love to be applauded. There is no going to heaven, saith Mr. Gurnal, without wearing a fool's cap and a fool's coat, and there is no going to heaven without being accounted fools: so you see many professors follow the world, they have not courage enough to live in holy non-conformity to the world; and many people are frightned from Chrift, becaufe they would not be counted Methodifts; the fear of man has damned thoufands. You will not come to him, becaufe you cannot truft God, and then we love the world more than Chrift. *If any man love the world, the love of the Father is not in him.* If I had the management of people, their fhops would be open three or four hours before they are now; I do not want to hinder mens bufinefs; thofe that have moft money and moft power, if they acted as they ought to do, would be the greateft flaves to their fellow-creatures. When I talk of loving the world, I mean an inordinate love: I may live in the world, and not live upon it; my heart may be towards God: the love of the world is to be renounced, and therefore they will not come to Jefus Chrift they think, till they are going out of the world. If you are one of thofe who hate Chrift, why you are the man that will not come to him: why, fay you, does any body hate Chrift? pray hold your tongue, for fear of difcovering your ignorance : O, fay you, God forbid I fhould hate him. But, my dear foul, learn from this time forward, that every

one

one of us by nature hates Jesus Christ: we sent this message to him; we will not have this man to reign over us, we hate him because he is despised, we hate him because of the appearance of the people that are his followers, we hate him because of the narrowness of the way we are to pass in to him, because we must part with our lusts; we hate him because we must be non-conformists: I hate that rag of the whore of Babylon, O that form of prayer, O all that stuff, I thank God I was born a Dissenter, I love to be a Puritan, I don't love rites and ceremonies, no not in the church, and yet, perhaps, are more conformed to the world than numbers of the church, and have nothing but rites and ceremonies about their houses and families. What do we more than others? a churchman should prove himself a churchman, by having his articles, and keeping up the practice of religion; and a Dissenter should prove himself one, not by dissenting from the church, but from the *lusts of the flesh, the lust of the eye, and the pride of life,* and then we shall agree very well together, though one went to a place called a church, and another to a place called a meeting: would to God every soul now present would put this question

question to himself, Am I come to Christ, or am I not? There is a great number of persons here, you have heard of Providence calling me abroad, no doubt curiosity brings many of you here, to hear what the poor babler says: I tell you what I will say to you, that without you have an interest in the Son of God, you must be damned. *Examine yourselves whether you are in the faith*, whether your religion reaches any further than the church-door, whether you are the inward court worshippers: conscience, conscience, conscience, thou faithful monitor, God help thee to give a proper verdict. When I had the honour of opening lady Huntingdon's chapel, as I turned about I observed over my head were these words, *Earth, earth, earth, hear the word of the Lord:* O that every earthly soul may hear God's word this day. Don't be angry with me, I am now upon the decline of life, going toward threescore, surely now I may claim leave to speak to you freely; after next Sunday, perhaps, you may never hear me any more, though I do not intend to live abroad, but return, if please God, in a proper time, but long before that thou mayst be in hell or heaven. As the Lord lives, in whose name I speak,

speak, if you will not come to Christ to have life, you must come to his bar to hear him pronounce you damned to all eternity. If you come to him that you may have life, *Come, ye blessed*, will be the sentence there, but if you refuse now, *Depart, ye cursed*, will be your sentence then from the Lord, for in a little while he that shall come will come, and will not tarry. Hark! hark! don't you hear him, don't you hear him, don't you hear him yonder; hark! methinks I hear him, what does he say? see yonder, don't you see, good people, that yonder sun is darkened, and the moon turned into blood. O, *who can abide the day of his coming?* O, to think of his coming, may the sinner say, when I know his coming is only to damn my soul! How do the murderers dread the assizes, but pardoned sinners, pardoned criminals, are glad when they hear the high-sheriff coming: O, say they, I long to go to the bar, because I am going there only to plead the king's pardon. Happy, happy, happy you, that have come to this Jesus Christ that you might have life, that you might walk becoming him in your life and conversation. O, Christ will come, and come to you as his children; but God grant this life may

may be displayed in you and me more and more! If we are helped to know that Christ came that we might have life, and might have it more abundantly, O, pray that others may come, bring your children to Christ. I was pleased one day after I had been preaching on *Moses lifting up the serpent in the wilderness*, I think it was in New-England, I was taken up into a room to repose myself, there was a mantle-piece, representing the children brought in the arms of their parents to look at the brazen serpent: O may God help you to bring your children and your relations to view Christ. O Lord help my mother, my father, my child, my servant, to come to Jesus Christ that they may have life. The Lord help you to come, come young people. O I was charmed this morning, and every morning I give the sacrament, to see so many young men there crouding to the table; may the Spirit of God keep you near to Jesus Christ; and you young women, may God draw you nearer unto Christ. I remember when God touched my heart, and sent me down to see my friends in the country, I prayed God to bless me to those to whom I was called to dance and to play at cards with, and, blessed be God, he

blessed

blessed me to them all before I was twenty years of age, and after that he sent me to a prison, I there preached to a murderer, and some others, and, blessed be God, they came to Jesus Christ, and one of them went off most triumphantly. A poor creature, fourscore years of age, who has made it a practice to go and read to poor people, and to the prisoners, said, "Sir, I began late, but, by the help of God, I now work the harder for Jesus Christ." May he incline you to come, O young women and young men. There was a good woman who died sometime ago, whose last word I think was, I now go to my God. Will you come and go too, you old grey-headed sinners, that have one foot in the grave, God help you to go, God remove every obstacle; God grant that every mountain may be brought low, and a highway made into your hearts for Jesus Christ. Don't be angry with me; in a week or two I shall be tossing on the ocean, while you are hearing God's word here; while I am amidst storms and tempests, you will be upon the earth. Paul could stand the whipping, but it is not a whipping, but weeping, that breaks my heart; my greatest trial is, what if this sermon should help to sink these people

deeper

deeper in the pit, that makes my blood run cold. O that my sermon may never rise in judgment against you, my poor dear souls. I believe you find it hard when any of you are forced to be witnesses against your own children, your own friends, and whoever deals with the word with a disinterested spirit, must do it; the only way to prevent it, is to come to Christ; and if you cannot come, if you are sensible of it, God be praised; he will come to you if you cannot come to Christ, he will come and make you willing in the day of his power; that this may be the happy case, God grant to us all, for his name's sake. Amen.

SERMON

SERMON XV.

All Mens Place.

ECCLESIASTES vi. ver. 6.

Do not all go to one place?

I Remember an ingenious writer, who had been very copious in his publications, observed, that the best and most profitable were written after he was fifty years of age: it is supposed, then the judgment is ripened, and the genius is as it were advanced to maturity and knowledge; and experiences gathered when young, will be more useful in the decline of life, when grey hairs are seen here and there upon them. It is said indeed, that old men are twice children; but there are some whose geniusses are so very low that they cannot be twice children, because they are no better than children from their cradle to their grave; but this is not the case with God's children,

children, for upon a reflection of the wrong steps they have taken, if it proceeds from the sanctified sense of afflictions, they serve to make them more instructive in their latter day. This was the case of Solomon, though highly favoured when young, for the Lord appeared unto him twice, yet he fell most awfully, and had we not read of his recovery again, the doctrine of the final perseverance of the saints, must seem to fall to the ground, but we have reason to think that he was restored, and gave evidence of his recovery by writing in such a manner, that none could but one that knew much of God and himself; witness the book of Ecclesiastes, which in all ages of the church has been received with a peculiar respect. Ecclesiastes signifies a preacher, such Solomon was from his own experience, and exceeded by none but him *who spake as no man ever did*.

The chapter in which is the text, describes the vanity and misery of our present state, if unsanctified. *There is an evil*, saith he, *that I have seen under the sun, and it is common among men:* though he is going about to describe a monster, yet it is a monster that walks and stalks abroad, a man to whom God hath given riches, wealth, and honour, so that he
wanteth

wanteth nothing for his soul of all that he defireth, though God gives him not power to eat, this is vanity and a great difeafe. Was there ever a more ftriking defcription of an old covetous mifer, who leaves his wealth to fome perfon that fpends it fafter than the poor wretch got it? He goes on and fays, *If a man beget an hundred children, and live many years, fo that the days of his years be many, and his foul be not filled with good, and alfo that he have no burial, I fay, that an untimely birth is better than he, for he cometh in with vanity, and departeth in darknefs, and his name fhall be covered with darknefs. Moreover, he hath not feen the fun, nor known any thing; this hath more reft than the other.* And then though this creature fhould be fuppofed to live a thoufand years twice told, why, faith he, yet hath he feen no good, he has never been poffeffed of real good to make him happy here or hereafter, for, adds he, do not all go, both the abortive and the aged, young and old, high and low, rich and poor, whether bleffed with children, or have no children, whether like Lazarus, that beg their bread, or Dives, cloathed in purple and fine linen, and fare fumptuoufly every day, *Do not all go to one place?*

An important question! shall I propose it to you to-night? do you know what the wise man means when he offers this question to your consideration, *Do not all go to one place?* what can be the design of this? the thing, no doubt, here spoken of is death, the place here spoken of, no doubt, is the grave. An amazing consideration! part of the first sentence that the great and holy God ever denounced against fallen man, to one and all, *Dust thou art, and unto dust thou shalt return.* On account of our first parent's transgression, it is appointed unto all men, all sorts of men, all the inhabitants under heaven, once to die; and therefore the apostle saith, *Death hath passed upon all men, even upon those who have not sinned after the similitude of the transgression of Adam,* that is, who have not been guilty of actual sin. Can there be a stronger proof of the imputation of Adam's guilt, of original sin, or a more cutting trial that a tender father and nursing mother can undergo, than to see a dear little child just born, or but lent to the loving parents for a few months, taken away often in the greatest agonies that we can conceive? and if God, my dear hearers, has ever suffered your dear children suddenly

denly to be seized with convulsions, and continue in anguish and agonizing pains for many days together, you have had sufficient proof of it. A friend of mine in London, about thirty-two years ago, that was dotingly fond of every child he had, to whom I wrote a letter from Georgia, beginning with these words, Is your idol dead yet? for I thought it was such an idol that would soon go. The account he gave me the first time I saw him was, that the day before my letter was received, the child died in such agony and torture, that its excrements came out of its mouth, which made the fond and too indulgent parent wish to have rather died a thousand deaths himself, than that his child should die in such a way; and added, I was obliged to go to God, and desire him to take my darling away. What an awful proof are their sufferings, that children come into the world with a corruption that renders them liable to God's wrath and damnation, but the blood, the precious blood of Jesus Christ, it is to be hoped, cleanses them from the guilt and filth of sin. So any of you that have got children dead in infancy, O may you improve what I shall say by and by from the text, and pray and endeavour to go to that place,

place, where I hope you will see your children making a blessed constellation in the firmament of heaven: in this respect all go to the same place, some at the beginning of life, some at the middle, and some at the decline; and happy, happy they who go to bed soonest, if their souls are saved!

But, my dear hearers, in another case we may venture to contradict even Solomon; for if we consider the words of our text in another view, all do not go to one place; it is true, all are buried in the grave either of earth or water, but then after death comes judgment; death gives the decisive, the separating blow. Suppose then in our enlarging on the text, we should confine the word all to the unregenerate, and to those who are not born of God, these indeed, die when they will, all go to one place. If you should ask me, for I love dearly to have an inquisitive auditory, who I mean by unregenerate? who I mean by those that are not born of God? I answer, I do not mean all that only bear the name of Jesus Christ; I mention this, because a great many people think that all that are baptized, either when they are adult or when they are young, whether sprinkled or put under water, I believe

lieve a great many people think that all these go to heaven. I remember when I began to speak against baptismal regeneration in my first sermon, printed when I was about twenty-two years old, or a little more; the first quarrel many had with me was, because I did not say that all people who were baptized were born again; I would as soon believe the doctrine of transubstantiation. Can I believe that a person who gives no evidence of being a saint, from the time of his baptism to the time perhaps of his death, that never fights against the world, the flesh, and the devil, and never minds one word of what his god-fathers and god-mothers promised for him, can I believe that person is a real Christian? no, I can as soon believe, that a little wafer in the priest's hand, about a quarter of an inch long, is the very blood and bones of Jesus Christ, who was hung upon the cross without the gates of Jerusalem. I do believe baptism to be an ordinance of Christ, but at the same time, no candid person can be angry for my asserting, that there are numbers that have been baptized when grown up, or when very young, that are not regenerated by God's Spirit, who will all go to one place, and that place is where

there

there will be no water to quench that dreadful fire that will parch them with thirst. I am speaking out of a book which contains the lively oracles of God, and in the name of one who is truth itself, who knowing very well what he spoke, is pleased in the most solemn and awful manner to say, and that to a master in Israel, that *if a man be not born again of water and the Spirit, he cannot see the kingdom of God*; he can have no idea, no proper, no adequate notion of it, much less is he to expect to be happy eternally with God hereafter; and therefore as our Lord spoke to this man, give me leave to observe to you. I don't mean the Deists only by unregenerate sinners; I don't mean the profane mocker, who is advanced to the scorner's chair, nor your open profligate, adulterers, fornicators, abusers of themselves with mankind, these have damnation as it were written upon their foreheads with a sun-beam; and they may know that God is not mocked, for if they die without repenting of these things, they show they are in an unregenerate state, and will all go to one place: if any of you are going thither, may God stop you this night. But, my brethren, I will come closer; there are more unbelievers within

within the pale than without the pale of the church; let me repeat it again, you may think of it when I am tossing upon the mighty waters, there are more unbelievers within the pale of the church than without: all are not possessors that are professors, all have not got the thing promised, all are not partakers of the promise, that talk and bless God they have got the promised Saviour; I may have him in my mouth and upon my tongue, without having the thing promised, or the blessed promise in my heart. A moral man that can walk touching the law blameless, a person that thinks he is righteous, because he does not know why a person who has got no other religion but to go to a particular place of worship, values himself upon being a churchman or a diffenter; he is such a bigot, that he thinks no man will go to heaven but himself; these, however they may think themselves safe, will e'er long go to one place, whether they think so or no; they will be soon summoned to one bar, and the voice of the archangel sounding, *Arise, ye dead, and come to judgment*, will be the great alarm; the dead shall arise and appear before the Son of God, as Judge of all mankind; these, as well as the infidels, would gladly be excused; and as they once said, I pray to have me excused from coming to Christ, so they will fain be excused from appearing before, and being condemned by him, but they must all go to one place: and as they know not God, and are unacquainted with the divine life, they must hear and suffer the dreadful sentence, *Depart, ye cursed, into everlasting fire, prepared for the devil and his angels.* This is a thought, that if our hearts, my dear hearers, were properly awakened, would make our blood run cold: to be in a place of absence from God, a place where damned souls will be for ever cursing God and one another: give me leave to dwell upon it a little, and may it be blessed, under God, to awaken some careless person, who, perhaps, may be taking a walk to-night, and just step in to hear what the babler has to say while he is about to take his leave of the people. When I saw you from my study crowding to come in, when I saw you pushing forward, some to go up to the Tabernacle, or into the vestry, some to fill the area, and others to stand at the door, I thought how shall I manage with myself to-night, shall I endeavour to make these weep and cry, shall I not earnestly address so many precious

precious souls in a practical way, to bring them not to the preacher, but the preacher's master; knowing the terrors of the Lord, we would fain perfuade all to flee from this wrath to come. O awful thought! and yet it is a certain truth, all on earth muft go to one place; if we live like, and are devils here, we muft go to and be with them when we die for ever! A bleffed minifter of Chrift, in Scotland, told me a ftory he knew for truth, of a dreadful anfwer a poor creature gave on her death-bed, for the Scotch, except the people of New-England, are the moft knowing people in religious matters, perhaps any where; this perfon when dying was afked by a minifter, where do you hope to go when you die? fays fhe, I don't care where I go; what, fays he, don't you care whether you go to heaven or hell? no, fays fhe, I don't care whither I go; but, fays he, if you was put to your choice where would you go? fays fhe, to hell; to that he replied, are you mad, will you go to hell? yes, fays fhe, I will; why fo? fays he; why, fays fhe, all my relations are there. The dear minifter of Chrift preached after her death, told the ftory, and afked, is it not fhocking to hear a woman fay fhe would go to hell because her relations were there: why, you that are unregenerate must go to hell for all your unregenerate relations are there; your father the devil is there, all damned angels and damned spirits; your brothers and sisters are there; as they went one way here, so they must be banished from Jesus Christ to one place hereafter.

But I must close this mournful theme, it is too gloomy to dwell upon; blessed be God, I have another place to tell you of, and another sort of people to speak of, who shall all, as well as those I have spoken of, go to one place; perhaps, here are some of them; blessed is it to live in God. When death closes the eyes an actual separation is made, and instead of hearing, *Depart, ye cursed*, they will hear, *Come, ye blessed of my Father, inherit the kingdom prepared for you from the foundation of the world.* Our blessed master, and who speaks like him, gives us an awful view of Dives and Lazarus, the one feasting and fattening his body to the grave, not keeping one fast-day in a year, and the other starving at his gate, perhaps buried in the ditch, denied a grave by the parish, while this vile wretch, who died also, had a pompous funeral; there he was
carried

carried to one place; he was, perhaps, laid in state, two mutes attending round the coffin, while damned devils were gnawing his soul; he lift up his eyes in torment. Hark! don't you hear him, I will stop a little that you may: you ungodly ones, do not you hear your brother cry? he would not pray while alive, but hell makes him pray, not to God but to Abraham; *Father Abraham*, says he, *send Lazarus to dip the tip of his finger in water, and cool my tongue*; and I verily believe, the damned will have a sight of those that are in heaven, to let them know what a heaven, what a Christ, what a glory they have lost: God grant this may be none of your case, it will not be if you are of the number of those who are born from above, that are made new creatures in Christ Jesus; for by being born again from above, I mean receiving a principle of new life, imparted to our hearts by the Holy Ghost, changing you, giving you new thoughts, new words, new actions, new views, so that old things pass away, and all things become new in our souls. I know very well, that the doctrine of a divine influence is exploded: I have often told you, and I tell you again, now I am about going to another clime

for

for a-while, that the grand quarrel that our Lord Jesus Christ has with England, and I do not speak it as a prophet, or the son of a prophet, but as the Lord God liveth, in whose name I speak, for whose glory I am going abroad, and in whose fear I desire to die, if the Spirit of God and his divine influence is not more regarded in this land than it has been, wo, wo, wo to those that despise it, they may by and by, one day or other, wonder and perish. Blessed be God, there are a happy few who do regard it; and I am persuaded in my very soul, that the number in England, in Scotland, in Ireland, in Wales, and in America, does, and I pray it may, still greatly increase. Yet, notwithstanding the word of God does run and is glorified, how many are there at this day, that wilfully do despite to the Spirit of God, that hate the doctrine of the Spirit's divine influences; that if it were in their power, but we live under revolution principles, and are blessed with toleration, which is the bulwark of liberty of conscience, otherwise the street would run with the blood of both churchmen and dissenters, but whether the world will hear or forbear, blessed be God, when we speak of the

new

new birth, we do not speak of a cunningly devised fable; what our eyes have seen, what our hands have handled, and what our hearts have felt of the word of life, that declare we unto you. When I was sixteen years of age I began to fast twice a week for thirty-six hours together, prayed many times a-day, received the sacrament every Lord's-day, fasting myself almost to death all the forty days of Lent, during which, I made it a point of duty never to go less than three times a-day to public worship, besides seven times a-day to my private prayers, yet I knew no more that I was to be born again in God, born a new creature in Christ Jesus, than if I was never born at all. I had a mind to be upon the stage, but then I had a qualm of conscience; I used to ask people, pray can I be a player, and yet go to the sacrament and be a Christian? O, say they, such a one, who is a player, goes to the sacrament; though, according to the law of the land, no player should receive the sacrament, unless they give proof that they repent; that was archbishop Tillotson's doctrine: well then, if that be the case, said I, I will be a player, and I thought to act my part for the devil as well as any body;

body; but, blessed be God, he stopped me in my journey. I must bear testimony to my old friend, Mr. Charles Wesley, he put a book into my hands, called, the Life of God in the Soul of Man, whereby God shewed me, that I must be born again or be damned. I know the place; it may be superstitious, perhaps, but whenever I go to Oxford, I cannot help running to that place where Jesus Christ first revealed himself to me, and gave me the new birth. As a good writer says, a man may go to church, say his prayers, receive the sacrament, and yet, my brethren, not be a Christian. How did my heart rise, how did my heart shudder, like a poor man that is afraid to look into his account-books, lest he should find himself a bankrupt; yet shall I burn that book, shall I throw it down, shall I put it by, or shall I search into it? I did, and holding the book in my hand, thus addressed the God of heaven and earth: Lord, if I am not a Christian, if I am not a real one, God, for Jesus Christ's sake, show me what Christianity is, that I may not be damned at last. I read a little further, and the cheat was discovered; O, says the author, they that know any thing of religion, know it is a vital union

union with the Son of God, Christ formed in the heart; O what a ray of divine life did then break in upon my poor soul, I fell a writing to all my brethren, to my sisters, talked to the students as they came in my room, put off all trifling conversation, put all trifling books away, and was determined to study to be a saint, and then to be a scholar; and from that moment God has been carrying on his blessed work in my soul; and as I am now fifty-five years of age, going towards sixty, I tell you, my brethren, as I shall leave you in a few days, I am more and more convinced that this is the truth of God, and without it you never can be saved by Jesus Christ: all those born of God, whether when young or old, at the sixth, ninth, or eleventh hour, however separated from one another, through the grace of God, they shall all go to one place.

If you ask where that place is? I answer, blessed be God, to heaven; if you ask to whom they shall go? I answer, to the spirits of just men made perfect; and, what will be best of all, to Jesus Christ, the heavenly inheritance. If we were not to go to him, what would heaven be? if we were not to see him, what would glory be? I know some people think heaven is a fine place, so it is; but what makes it so, but the presence and joy of the God of glory? I would rather die a thousand deaths, than sacrifice my affections as I have done: after I had taken leave of all my friends some years ago at Deptford, I burst out into tears and said, Lord, I would not suffer all I feel for my friends but for thee, then returned to my friends and said, Now the bitterness of death is passed, I am going to be executed, God's will be done. Blessed be God, after death there are no separations, we shall all go to one place; ministers that could not preach in one pulpit, and Christians that could not agree with one another, blessed be God, shall by and by go to one heaven; whether they go to one place or no in this world, does not signify: says one, I go to the Dissenters; another, I go to church; and a great many Christians judge of one another as infidels, because they are not of one sentiment. A good woman came to me some years ago just as I had done preaching, some people love to be impertinent, what do you think, says she, of Cotton Mather and another minister, one said, I ought to receive the sacrament before my

expe-

experience was given in, the other said not, and I believe the angels were glad to carry them both to heaven. I said, good woman, I believe they have not talked about it since, for they will no more talk about these things. We have but one Father, one Holy Ghost, we have lived in one communion of faith; blessed be the living God, e'er long the angels shall come and call the elect from the east, the west, the north, and the south, to be at home with the Lord.

If this be the case, my brethren, it may support us under all the changes and partings of this mortal state. As I have been in a public character, I suppose I may venture to say, that no one has been called to such frequent partings from God's people as I have: I am going now the thirteenth time over the water; yes, I find what is said of St. Paul is true, he could bear a whipping, not a weeping: what mean you, says he, to weep and break my heart; he never said, whip me and break my back, no, no. All get to one place: what a blessed state! to see one's spiritual father, to see one's spiritual children, and hear them say, such and such a time God begat me to himself by your ministry! what a blessing will it be to hear them say, blessed be God, next to the Spirit I owe my coming here to that servant of thine! and with what ravishment will the minister say, behold me and the children thou hast given me! with what holy triumph will they all then cast their crowns at the foot of the Lamb! with what joy will they cry, grace, grace, when the top-stone is brought forth, and how will they then try who shall praise redeeming love and rich free grace in the highest strain! The difference here is you know, that we sing in parts, some sing treble, some tenor, and some base; what then? each part helps the other, were all to sing alike the harmony would not be compleat; however shocking it is in this world, all the differences that have been among the people of God, will only make us sing and unite us the better in a future state.

Well, my dear hearers, by this time then I hope you have began to ask, to what place am I going? Suppose now you reason thus; I have heard to-night that all unregenerate persons go to hell, and dwell among the damned; I have heard that all that are born again of God, and all that believe in Jesus Christ, whether Jew or Gentile, whether
bond

bond or free, all go to dwell with God, with angels, and the spirits of just men made perfect; I have heard the minister say, though he seems sometimes to ramble in his discourse, that we all go to one place, that is, the grave: I am hastening there, autumn is coming on, the fall of the leaf is approaching, a blast, occasioned by the sudden change of weather, or a surfeit, by feasting too luxuriantly on the fruits of God's bounty; another illness may take me to my long home. I hear of such-a-one's dying, and of such-a-one, perhaps in an apoplectic, perhaps in a paralytic fit: I am lusty and strong, I am glorying in my strength, but who knows but that may be only making me food for a fever; one would stand it better that was more emaciated than I am. If I should be taken this night, am I going the way to hell, or the way to heaven. Adrian, the emperor, cried out upon a time, *My trembling, dear departing soul, whither art thou going?* these were his words. Won't you hear an emperor preach, preach on his dying bed, when the silver cords of life are loosed? Conscience, conscience, conscience, thou candle of the Lord, may he help thee to light a poor sinner into a knowledge of himself. I

charge

charge thee in the name of our Lord Jesus Christ, in the name of that Saviour, in whose name and by whose power, I trust, I now preach; O conscience! thou faithful monitor, let every one hear their own. Come, if conscience was to speak what would it say? why, that if you are not acquainted with yourself and Christ, you are lost for ever. The Americans are the most hospitable people under heaven, they love to entertain strangers, who may be hereby kindly provided for without going to an inn: I always endeavoured to drop a word for Christ when I came to their houses. I remember Mr. Seeward, and some other good friends were with me; when I first got into the house, I began to talk of Christ; the master of it said, Sir, I believe you are right; I can't open a leaf in my bible, but I find I am no Christian: would to God all here minded the same leaf! May be, many here say, sir, I scorn your words; well, don't I? don't God tell you that won't do? you are a moral man, but don't love God; you don't get drunk, because it will make your head ach; you don't commit fornication and adultery, which is common among the great, and therefore they think God will not punish them

for

for it; perhaps you are not a fornicator, left you should stand in a sheet, though we have no discipline among us now; you don't do these things for fear of maintaining the bastard, or being taken up; but does your obedience proceed from love to God, to Christ; if not, may God convince you of your miserable state before you go hence.

But, blessed be God, there are numbers of dear souls here, that I hope e'er long to live in one place and to eternal ages with. All hail, my fellow Christians; all hail, my dear brethren and friends; all hail, ye that are children of one parent, born of one Spirit, and bring forth the fruits of the Holy Ghost in your conversation; yet a little while, and we must part; whether I die, or you die, blessed be God, one place shall e'er long hold us; in yonder blessed world we shall e'er long meet, and praise free grace; my brethren, we shall be then for ever with the Lord, for ever one with Christ; and if this be the case, let us comfort one another with these things; and if we are all going to one place, God, of his infinite mercy, keep us from falling out by the way. Don't say, I am of the Foundery; don't say, I am of the Tabernacle; don't
spend

spend your time in talking against John Wesley and George Whitefield; don't say, you go to the Tabernacle, I'll go to the chapel; no, don't speak of Paul and Cephas; God unite us more and more to Jesus Christ; and if you are going to heaven, God help you to travel a little faster than we do. My brethren, let us press forward toward the mark of the prize of our high calling in Christ Jesus. O that the God of love may fill us with such peace and such joy, that every storm, every trial, every temptation we meet with, may be over-ruled to good for us; all our afflictions, all our temptations, are to make heaven more desirable, and earth more loathsome.

If this is not the case with some of you, God convert you to-night. Help me, my dear Tabernacle and London hearers, help me, help me, help me for Jesus Christ's sake. You was once going to hell yourselves, for God's sake endeavour to stop those that are going there: pray for your unconverted friends. Young people, young people, that are going to hell giddily, may God stop you this night: was I to talk to you seriously, you would say as a young gentleman did, when I desired he would not swear; he turned to me and said,
Doctor,

Doctor, (I was no more a doctor then than now, and but young too) it is very hard you will not let a man go to hell his own way; if any of you are of this stamp, God grant he may not let you go to hell your own way, but go to heaven in God's way, in Christ's way. I am sure you are not happy; the devil never had a happy child in the world: O that God may turn your feet into the way of peace to-night: O that it may be with you as with a young man one night formerly: I remember I had about two hundred notes then; I came into moorfields this morning at six o'clock, says he, to meet my sweetheart, but, blessed be God, I met with Jesus Christ, my sweetheart: would to God you may do so, young men, to-night: when you have gone on to that place, O that it may be with you as it was with good Mr. Crane, who is appointed steward of the Orphan-house; he went once to see a play at Drury-lane, but that being full he went to Covent-garden, and that was so full he could not put his head in; well, says he, he told it me himself, and he is an Israelite indeed, one of the most honest men, perhaps, in the world, I will go and hear doctor Whitefield; there God reached his heart,

heart, and now he shines. I had letters yesterday or the day before from Georgia, that made my heart leap for joy; honest Mr. Wright, that ingenious, indefatigable man, and Mr. Crane, have gone on so well, and have managed the Orphan-house so well, that all letters from all parts give me a pleasure: would to God, one says, you could send ten thousand such people as Mr. Wright and Mr. Crane; would to God you could send a thousand such over, and an hundred preachers to preach Christ among us. O that curiosity may be over-ruled for good to some of you to-night: but I forgot myself, and can you blame me if I should detain you a little, tho' I am really afraid of unfitting myself for my voyage, if I tire myself before I go: to-morrow I am to go to see where I am to sleep. I intend, God willing, to have a sacrament here to-morrow, and another next Sabbath-day morning. I intend, God willing, to give you a parting word on Sunday evening, and give you notice of taking my last farewel in the week, for I must get a day or two to dispatch my private business, and be ready to go where my God calleth me.

I shall,

I shall, I think, be called to do something which I would, if possible, have avoided, and that is, as this place has been repaired, you see 'tis fresh done, which is expensive, and I am willing to leave every thing clear before I go, a collection must be made for defraying the charge. The world thinks I am very rich; a man, the other day, was so persuaded of my riches, that he sent me word, if I did not lay thirty pounds in such a place, I should be killed as sure as I am alive; but, blessed be God, I am alive yet; I do not fear dying suddenly, or being dispatched by a poignard, or a pistol to make a passage for my soul to flee to God. You may think, perhaps, I get a great deal by preaching here; and now I am going away, what do you think my stated allowance is for preaching at the Tabernacle? I have no more from this place than one hundred pounds a year; and I asked but last night how it stood, and instead of having a single sixpence, I was told there were fifty pounds arrears; well, said I, ungrateful as it is to me, I will make a collection to-night that all may be left free; and if others are left to make an advantage of it, may God make it a blessing. There are not six people in this place that I have

have had the value of a guinea of from January to Auguſt; nor have I had a guinea from all theſe ordinances towards bearing the expences of my voyage. When I come, my brethren, to heaven, you ſhall then know with what a ſpirit I have ſerved you; you ſhall then know that all I have done is to build places for others, where I hope God will meet you and your children when I am dead and gone. O that we may meet in one place, when God calls me hence: the Lord quicken you, the Lord ſtrengthen you, the Lord Jeſus Chriſt be with you, and grant that e'er long we may be where there ſhall be no more ſorrow, but we ſhall dwell with God and one another for ever; even ſo, Lord Jeſus Chriſt. Amen.

SERMON

SERMON XVI.

God a Believer's Glory.

ISAIAH lx. ver. 19.

And thy God thy Glory.

I LATELY had occasion to speak on the verse immediately following that of our text; but when I am reading God's word, I often find it is like being in a tempting garden, when we pluck a little fruit and find it good, we are apt to look after and pluck a little more, only with this difference, the fruit we gather below often hurts the body at the same time that it pleases the appetite, but when we walk in God's garden, when we gather fruit of the Redeemer's plants, the more we eat the more we are delighted, and the freer we are the more welcome; if any chapter in the bible deserves this character and description of an evangelical Eden, this does.

It

It is very remarkable, and I have often told you of it, that all the apoſtles preach firſt the law, and then the goſpel, which finds man in a ſtate of death, points out to him how he is to get life, and then ſweetly conducts him to it. Great and glorious things are ſpoken of the church of God in this chapter; and it ſtruck me very much this evening ever ſince I came into the pulpit, that the great God ſpeaks of the church in the ſingular number: how can that be, when the church is compoſed of ſo many millions gathered out of all nations, languages, and tongues? how is it, that God ſays thy maker and not your maker, that he ſpeaks of the church as though it conſiſted only of one individual perſon? the reaſon of it is this, and is very obvious, that though the church is compoſed of many members, they have but one Head, and they are united by the bond of one Spirit, by whom they have the ſame vital union of the ſoul with God; and therefore it teaches Chriſtians not to ſay to one another, *I am of Paul, I am of Apollos, or Cephas*, but to behave and live ſo, that the world may know that we all belong to one common Chriſt: God revive, continue, and increaſe this true Chriſtian love among us!

Of this church, thus collectively confidered, united under one head, the bleffed evangelical prophet thus fpeaks, *Violence fhall no more be heard in thy land, wafting nor deftruction within thy borders, but thou fhalt call thy walls falvation, and thy gates,* where the magiftrates affemble, and the people go in and out, *praife.* From this text, a great many good and great men have gathered what they call the Millenium, that Jefus Chrift is to come and reign a thoufand years on earth, but I muft acknowledge that I have always rejected a great many good mens pofitive opinion about the feafon when this ftate commences, and I would warn you all againft fixing any time; for what fignifies whether Chrift comes to reign a thoufand years, or when he comes, fince you and I are to die very foon; and therefore inftead of puzzling our heads about it, God grant we may live fo that we may reign with him for ever; and it feems to me, that whatfoever is faid of this ftate on earth, that the millenium is to be underftood in a fpiritual fenfe, as an emblem of a glorious, eternal, beatific ftate in the kingdom of heaven. *The fun fhall no more be thy light by day, nor for brightnefs fhall the moon give light unto thee,*

but

but the Lord shall be unto thee an everlasting light; and in order to prepare us for that light, and show us the nature of it, while we speak of it may it come with light and power to our souls. He adds in our text, *and thy God shall be thy glory:* this is spoken to all believers in general, but it is spoken to all fearful believers in particular; and I don't know that I can possibly close my poor, feeble ministration among you here, better than with these words; though, God willing, I intend, if he shall strengthen me this week, to give you a parting word next Wednesday morning; and O that what has been my comfort this day in the meditation on this passage, may be yours and mine to all eternity. He that hath an ear to hear let him hear what the evangelic prophet saith, *thy God thy glory*.

The Holy Ghost seems, as it were, particularly fond of this expression; when God published the ten commandments upon mount Sinai, he prefaced it thus, *I am the Lord*, and not content with that, he adds, *thy God;* and the frequency of it, I suppose, made Luther say, that *the gospel deals much in pronouns, in which consists a believer's comfort;* but if there were no other argument than this,

it

it would cut up that destructive principle by the very root that pretends to tell us that there is no such thing as appropriation in the Bible; that our faith is only to be a rational assent to the word of God, without a particular application of that word made to our souls: this is as contrary to the gospel, and to experience of every real saint, as light is contrary to darkness and heaven to hell. My brethren, I appeal to any of you, what good would it do you, if you had ten thousand notes wrote in large characters by the finest hand that can write in London; suppose you have got them, as many men have, and it is a very convenient way, that they were put into your little pockets made on the inside of your coat; suppose you should say, my coat is buttoned, I have all these here next my heart: when I come to look at them, I find there is not one note payable to me, they are all either forged, or payable to some body else, and therefore are good for nothing to me. All the promises of the gospel, all that is said of God and Christ, can do us no good, except that God and Christ is ours. The great question therefore is, whether the God we profess to believe in, is our God? not only, whether he is so in general, that the devils may say; but

whether

whether he is our God in particular. The devils can say, O God; but the devils cannot say, my God: that is a privilege peculiar to God's chosen people, who really believe on the Lord Jesus Christ: and therefore, my brethren, a deist cannot say, my God, my Christ, because he does not believe on that medium by which God becomes our God. That was a noble saying of Luther, " I will have nothing to do with an absolute God;" that is, I will have nothing to do with a God out of Christ. Now this is a deist's glory: Lord Bolingbroke values himself upon it, I am astonished at that man's infidelity and cowardice. I don't like those men that leave their writings to be published after their death: I love to see men bold in their writings: I like an honest man that will put out his writings while alive, that he may see what men can say against him, and then answer them; but it is meer cowardice to leave it to the world to answer for it, to set us a cavelling after they are got into the grave: says he, I will have nothing to do with the God of Moses; and I suppose the principles of that deist made one pretty near to him ask as soon as his breath was out of his body, where do you think he is gone to? another

other replies, where do you think but to hell. God grant that may not be the portion of any here!

The question then is, how God is our God; *thy God.* My brethren, our all depends upon it; what signifies saying, this is mine, and that is mine, if you cannot say, God is mine. The best thing that God has left in the New Testament, is himself: *I will be their God,* that is one of the legacies; and *a new heart also will I give them,* that is another; *I will put my laws in their mind, and write them in their hearts,* that is another: but all that is good for nothing, comparatively speaking, unless God has said at the same time, for they are all inseparable, *I will be their God, and they shall be my people.* Now how shall I know that God is my God? I am afraid, some people think there is no knowing; well then, if you think so, you set up a worship, and go and erect an altar, and instead of receiving God in the sacrament as yours, go and worship an unknown God. I am so far from believing, that we cannot know that God is ours, that I am fully persuaded of it, and would speak it with humility, and I would not chuse to leave you with a lie in my mouth, that I have known it for about thirty-five years as clear as the sun is in the meridian, that God is my God. And how shall I know it, my brethren? I would ask you this question, didst thou ever feel the want of God to be thy God? No body knows God to be their God that did not feel him to be his God in Christ: out of Christ, God is a consuming fire. I know there are a great variety of ways in peoples conversions, but still, my brethren, we must all feel our misery, we must all feel our distance from God, all feel that we are estranged from God, that we bring into the world with us a nature that is not agreeable to the law of God, nor possibly can be; we cannot be said to believe that God is our God, till we are brought to be reconciled to him through his Son. Can I say, a person is my friend, till I am reconciled to him? and therefore the gospel only is the ministration of reconciliation. Paul saith, *We beseech you as ambassadors of Christ, that you would be reconciled unto God:* this is to be the grand topic of our preaching; we are to beseech them, and God himself turns beggar to his own creatures to be reconciled to him: now this reconciliation is brought about by a poor sinner's being brought to Jesus Christ;

and

and when once he sees his enmity and hatred to God, feeling the misery of departing from him, and being conscious that he is obnoxious to eternal wrath, flies to Jesus as to a place of refuge, and expects only a reconciliation thro' the blood of the Lamb; without this, neither you nor I can say, God is my God: *there is no peace, saith my God, to the wicked.* The ministers of Christ must take care they don't preach an unknown God, and we must take care we don't pretend to live upon an unknown God, a God that is not appropriated and brought home to our souls by the efficacy of the Spirit. But, my brethren, we cannot say, God is our God, unless we are in Jesus Christ. Can you say, such a one is your father, unless you can give proof of it? You may be bastards, there are many bastards laid at Christ's door. Now, God cannot be my God, at least I cannot know him to be so, unless he is pleased to send into my heart the spirit of adoption, and to admit me to enjoy familiarity with Christ.

My brethren, I told you the other night that the grand controversy God has with England is for the flight put on the Holy Ghost. As soon as a person begins to talk of the work of the Holy Ghost, they cry, you are a methodist:

as soon as you speak about the divine influences of the Holy Ghost, O! say they, you are an enthusiast. May the Lord keep these methodistical enthusiasts amongst us to the latest posterity. Ignatius, supposed to have been one of the children that Jesus took up in his arms, in his first Epistle (pray read it) wrote soon after St. John's death, and we value nothing so authentic as what was wrote in the three first centuries, bears a noble testimony to this truth. When I was performing my first exercises at Oxford, I used to take delight to walk and read it, and could not help noting and putting down from time to time several remarkable passages. In the superscription of all his Epistles, I remember, he stiles himself *Theophoros*, i. e. Bearer of God*, and believed that those he wrote to, were so too. Some body went and told Trajan, that one Ignatius was an enthusiast, that he carried God about him: being brought before the emperor, who, though in other respects a good prince, was a cruel enemy to the Christians: but many a good prince does bad things by the influence of wicked counsellors, like our king Henry the Vth, who was brought in to persecute the poor Lollards,

* Deum ferens, *inspired, divine, holy*.

Lollards, for assembling in St. Giles's fields to hear the pure gospel, by false accusation of being rebels against him. Before such a prince was Ignatius brought; says Trajan, who is this that calls himself a *bearer of God?* says Ignatius, I am he, for which he quotes this passage, *I will dwell in them, and will walk in them, and they shall be my sons and daughters, says the Lord almighty.* The emperor was so enraged that, in order to cure him of his enthusiasm, he ordered him to be devoured by lions; at which Ignatius laughed for joy: O! says he, am I going to be devoured? and when his friends came about him, he almost danced for gladness; when they carried him to execution he smiled, and turning about, said, now I begin to be a martyr of Jesus Christ! I have heard that the lions have leaped from the martyrs, but when they come to me, I will encourage them to fall on me with all their violence. God give you such enthusiasm in a trying hour! This is to have God for our God: *he that believeth hath the witness in himself*, as it is written in this blessed word of God, and I hope it will be the last book that I shall read. Farewel father, farewel mother, farewel sun, moon, and stars! was the language of one of of the Scotch martyrs in king Charles's time, and it is amazing to me that even Mr. Hume (I believe) a professed deist, in his History of England mentions this as a grand exit, and also that seraphic soul Mr. Hervey, now with God, that the last words of the martyr were, Farewel thou precious Bible, thou blessed book of God. This is my rock, this is my foundation, it is now about thirty-five years since I have begun to read the Bible upon my pillow. I love to read this book, but the book is nothing but an account of the promises which it contains, and almost every word from the beginning to the end of it speaks of a spiritual dispensation, and the Holy Ghost, that unites our souls to God, and helps a believer to say, my Lord and my God! If you content yourselves with that, the devil will let you talk of doctrines enough : O you shall turn from Arminianism to Calvinism ; O you shall be orthodox enough, if you will be content to live without Christ's living in you. Now when you have got the Spirit, then you may say, God is mine. O this is very fine, say some, every body pretends to the Spirit: and then you may go on as a bishop once told a nobleman, My Lord, these methodists, say they, do all by the Spirit, so if the devil bids them murder any body, they will say, the Spirit bid them do it; and that very bishop died, how? why horrid! the last words he spoke were these, *The battle is fought, the battle is fought, the battle is fought, but the victory is lost for ever.* God grant, you and I may not die with such words as these. I hope you and I shall die and say, *The battle is fought, the battle is fought, the battle is fought, I have fought the good fight, and the victory is gained for ever.* Thus died Mr. Ralph Erskine, his last words were, Victory, victory, victory! and they that can call God their God, shall by and by cry, Victory, victory! and that for ever. God grant, we may all be of that happy number.

If we can call God our God, we shall endeavour by the Holy Ghost to be like God, we shall have his divine image stamped upon our souls, and endeavour to be followers of that God who is our Father: and this brings in the other part of the text, *thy God, thy Glory.* What is that? The greatest honor that a poor believer thinks he can have on earth, is to boast that God is his God. When it was proposed to David, that if he killed an hundred Philistines, he should have the king's daughter for his wife,

wife, and a very sorry wife she was, no great gain turned out to him: says he, *do you think it is a small thing to be the son-in-law to a king?* a poor strippling as I am here come with my shepherd's crook, what! to be married to a king's daughter, do you think that is a small thing? and if David thought it no small thing to be allied to a king by his daughter, what a great thing must it be to be allied to the Lord by one Spirit? I am afraid there are some people that were once poor that are now rich, that think it a great thing, that wish, O that my family had a coat of arms; some people would give a thousand pounds, I believe, for one. Coats of arms are very proper to make distinction in life, a great many people wear coats of arms that their ancestors got honourably, but they are a disgrace to them as they wear them on their coaches. But this is our glory, whether we walk or ride, whatever our pedigree may be in life, this is our honor that our God may be our glory. *O what manner of love is this,* saith one, *that the Lord doth bestow on us, that we should be called the sons of God!* born not of the will of man, born not of flesh, but born from above. O God grant that this may be your glory and mine!

My

My brethren, if God is our God and our glory, I'll tell you what we shall prove it by: whether we eat or drink, or whatever we do, we should do all to the glory of God. Religion, as I have often told you, turns our whole life into one continued sacrifice of love to God. As a needle, when once touched by a loadstone, turns to a particular pole, so the heart that is touched by the love of God, turns to his God again. I shall have occasion to take notice of it by and by, when I am aboard a ship: for as soon as I get on board, I generally place myself in one particular place under the compass that hangs over my head, I often look at it by night and by day; when I rise the needle turns to one point, when I go to bed I find it turns to the same point; and often, while I have been looking at it, my heart has been turned to God, saying, Lord Jesu, as that needle touched by the loadstone, turns to one point, O may my heart touched by the magnet of God's love, turn to him! A great many people think, they never worship God but when at church; and a great many are very demure on Lord's days, though many begin to leave that off. I know of no place upon the face of the earth where the Sabbath is kept as it is at Boston: if a single person was to walk in Boston streets in time of worship, he would be taken up; it is not trusted to poor insignificant men, but the justices go out in time of worship, they walk with a white wand, and if they catch any person walking in the streets, they put them under a black rod. O! the great mischiefs the poor pious people have suffered lately thro' the town's being disturbed by the soldiers! When the drums were beating before the house of Dr. Sawell, one of the holiest men that ever was, when he was sick and dying, on the sabbath day, by his meeting, where the noise of a single person was never heard before, and he begged that for Christ's sake they would not beat the drum; they damned and said, that they would beat to make him worse: this is not acting for the glory of God; but when a soul is turned to God, every day is a sabbath, every meal is a spiritual refreshment, and every sentence he speaks, should be a sermon; and whether he stays abroad or at home, whether he is on the exchange, or locked up in a closet, he can say, O God, thou art my God!

Now, my dear friends, can you, dare you say, that your God is your glory, and do you aim at glorifying the Lord your God: if your God is your glory, then say, *O God forbid that I should glory save in the cross of our Lord Jesus Christ, by whom the world is crucified to me, and I am crucified to the world.* What say you to that now? don't talk of God's being your glory, if you don't love his cross. If God is our glory, we shall glory not only in doing, but in suffering for him; we shall glory in tribulation, and count ourselves most highly honoured when we are called to suffer most for his great name sake. I might enlarge, but you may easily judge by my poor feeble voice this last week, that neither my strength of voice, or body, will permit me to be long to-night, and yet I will venture to give you your last parting salutation; and though I have been dissuaded from getting up to preach this night, yet I thought as my God was my glory, I should glory in preaching till I died. O that God may be all our glory! All our own glory fades away, there is nothing will be valuable at the great day but this, Thou art my God, and thou art my glory. It was a glorious turn that good Mr. Shepherd of Bradford mentions in one of his sermons, where he represents Jesus Christ as coming to judgment seated upon

upon his throne, in a sermon preached before some ministers. Christ calls one minister to him, Pray what brought you into the church? O, says he, Lord, there was a living in the family, and I was presented to it because it was a family living: stand thou by, says Christ. A second comes, What didst thou enter into the church for? O Lord, says he, I had a fine elocution, I had pretty parts, and I went into the church to shew my oratory and my parts: stand thou by, thou hast thy reward. A third was called, And what brought you into the church? Lord, says he, thou knowest all things, thou knowest that I am a poor creature, vile and miserable, and unworthy, and helpless, but I appeal to thee my glory, thou sittest upon the throne, that thy glory and the good of souls brought me there: Christ immediately says, Make room, men, make room, angels, and bring up that soul to sit near me on my throne. Thus shall it be done to all that make God their glory here below. Glorify God on earth, and he will glorify you in heaven. *Come, ye blessed of my Father, receive the kingdom prepared for you from the foundation of the world,* shall be your portion: and if so, Lord God almighty make us content to be

vilified

vilified whilst here, make us content to be despised while below, make us content to have evil things spoken of us, all for Christ's sake, yet a little while, and Christ will roll away the stone: and the more we are honoured by his grace to suffer, the more we shall be honoured in the kingdom of heaven. O that thought! O that blessed thought! O that soul transporting thought! it is enough to make us leap into a fiery furnace; in this spirit, in this temper, may God put every one of us.

If there be any of you that have not yet called God your God, may God help you to do so to-night. When I was reasoning within myself, whether I should come up, or whether it was my duty or not? I could not help thinking, who knows but God will bless a poor feeble worm to-night. I remember, a dear friend sent me word after I was gone to Georgia, "Your last sermon at the Tabernacle was blessed to a particular person;" I heard from that person to-day: and who knows but some may come to-day, and say, I will go and hear what the babler has to say? who knows but curiosity may be over-ruled for good? who knows but those that have served the lust of the flesh and the pride of life for
their

their god, may now take the Lord to be their God? O! if I could but see this, I think I could drop down dead for you.

My dear Christians, will you not help me to-night, you that can go and call God your God? go and beg of God for me, pray to heaven for me, do pray for those that are in the gall of bitterness, that have no God, no Christ to go to, and if they were to die to-night, would be damned for ever. O poor sinner, where is your glory then? where is your purple and fine linnen then? your purple robes will be turned into purple fire, and instead of calling God your God, will be damn'd with the devil: O think of your danger! *O earth, earth, earth, hear the word of the Lord!* If you never was awakened before, may the arrows of God, steep'd in the blood of Jesus Christ, reach your hearts now! Think how you live at enmity with God, think of your danger every day and every hour, your danger of dropping into hell; think how your friends in glory will leave you, and may this consideration, under the influences of the Holy Ghost, excite you to chuse God for your God! Tho' the sun is going down, tho' the shadow of the evening is coming on, God is willing, O man,

God

God is willing, O woman, to be a sinner's God, he has found out a way whereby he can be reconciled to you. I remember, when I saw a nobleman condemned to be hanged, the Lord High Steward told him, that however he was obliged to pass sentence on him, and did not know that justice would be satisfied but by the execution of the law in this world, yet there might be a way whereby justice might be satisfied and mercy take place in another: when I heard his Lordship speak, I wished that he had not only said, there might be a way, but that he had found out the way wherein God could be just, and yet a poor murderer coming to Jesus Christ should be pardoned.

You that can call God yours, God help you from this moment to glorify him more and more: and if God be your God and your glory, I am persuaded, if the love of God abounds in your hearts, you will be willing on every occasion to do every thing to promote his honor and glory, and therefore you will be willing at all times to assist and help as far as lies in your power to keep up places of worship, to promote his glory in the salvation and conversion of sinners; and I mention this because there is to be a collection this night; I would have chose, if possible, to have evaded this point, but as this Tabernacle has been repaired, and as the expence is pretty large, and as I would chuse to leave every thing unincumbered, I told my friends, I would undertake to make a collection, that every thing might be left quite clear: remember, it is not for me, but for yourselves, I told you on Wednesday how matters were; I am now going a thirteenth time over the water on my own expence, and you shall know at the great day what little, very little assistance I have had from those who owed, under God, their souls to my being here: but this is for the place where you are to meet, and where I hope God will meet you, when I am tossing on the water, when I am in a foreign clime. I think I can say thy glory, O God, calls me away, and as I am going towards sixty years of age, I shall make what dispatch I can, and I hope, if I am spared to come back, that I shall hear that some of you are gone to heaven, or are nearer heaven than you were. I find there is near 70l. arrears; I hope you will not run away, if you can say God is my glory, you will not push one upon another, as though you would loose yourselves in the croud, and say no body sees me;

me; but does not God Almighty see you? I hope you will be ready to communicate, and when I am gone that God will be with you; as many of you will not hear me on Wednesday morning. O may this be your prayer, O for Jesus Christ's sake, in whose name I preach, in whose strength I desire to come up, and for whose honor I desire to be spent, O do put up a word for me, it will not cost you much time, it will not keep you a moment from your business; O Lord Jesus Christ thou art his God! and, Lord Jesus Christ let him be thy glory! If I die in the waters, I shall go by water to heaven; if I land at the Orphan House, I hope it will be a means to settle a foundation for ten thousand persons to be instructed; and if I go by the continent, as I intend to do, I hope God will enable me to preach Christ; and if I return again, my life will be devoted to your service. You must excuse me, I cannot say much more, affection works; and I could heartily wish, and I beg it as a favour, when I come to leave you, that you will excuse me from a particular parting with you; take my public farewell; I will pray for you when in the cabin, I will pray for you when storms and tempests are about me; and this shall be my prayer for the dear people of the Tabernale, for the dear people of the Chapel, for the dear people of London, O God, be thou their God! and grant, that their God may be their glory. Even so, Lord Jesus! Amen.

SERMON

SERMON XVII.

Jacob's Ladder.

A FAREWEL SERMON.

GENESIS xxviii. ver. 12, &c.

And he dreamed, and behold, a ladder set upon the earth, and the top of it reached to heaven: and behold, the angels of God ascending and descending on it. And behold, the Lord stood above it, and said, I am the Lord God of Abraham thy father, and the God of Isaac: the land whereon thou liest, to thee will I give it, and to thy seed. And thy seed shall be as the dust of the earth; and thou shalt spread abroad to the west, and to the east, and to the north, and to the south: and in thee, and in thy seed shall all the families of the earth be blessed. And behold, I am with thee, and will keep thee in all places, whither thou goest, and will bring thee again into this land:

land: for I will not leave thee, until I have done that which I have spoken to thee of.

THE wife man observes, that *in the multitude of dreams there is many vanities*, being often the effects of a peculiar disorder of body, or owing to some disturbance of the mind. They whose nervous system has been long relaxed, who have had severe domestic trials, or have been greatly affected by extraordinary occurrences, know this to be true by their own experience; but however this may be, there have been, and possibly may be still, dreams that have no manner of dependance on the indisposition of the body, or other natural cause, but seem to bring a divine sanction with them, and make peculiar impressions on the party, though this was more frequent before the canon of scripture was closed, than now. God spoke to his people in a dream, in a vision of the night; witness, the subject of our present meditation, a dream of the patriarch Jacob's, when going forth as a poor pilgrim with a staff in his hand, from his father's house, deprived of his mother's company and instruction, persecuted by an elder brother, without attendants or necessaries,

cessaries, only leaning on an invisible power. I need not inform you in how extraordinary a way he got the blessing, which provoked his brother to such a degree, as determined him to be the death of Jacob, as soon as ever his aged father dropp'd: to what a height did this wicked man's envy rise when he said, *the days of mourning for my father will soon come*, and what then? why, though I have some compassion for the old man, and therefore will not lay violent hands upon my brother while my father is alive, yet I am resolved to kill him before my father is cold in his grave. This is the very spirit of Cain, who talked to his brother, and then slew him: this coming to the ears of his mother, she tells the good old patriarch her husband, who loving peace and quietness, takes the good advice of the weaker vessel, and orders Jacob to go to his mother's brother, Laban, and stay a little while out of Esau's sight, (perhaps out of sight out of mind) and by and by probably, said he, thou mayst come to thy father and mother again in peace and safety. Jacob, though sure of the blessing in the end, by his father's confirmation of it, yet prudently makes use of proper means; therefore he obeyed his

parents:

parents: and wo, wo be to those who think a parent's blessing not worth their asking for! Having had his mother's blessing, as well as his father's, without saying, I will try it out with my brother, I will let him know that I am not afraid of him, he views it as the call of God, and like an honest, simple pilgrim, went out from Beersheba towards Haran. Was it not a little unkind in his parents not to furnish him with some necessaries and conveniencies? When the servant was sent to fetch a wife for Isaac, he had a great deal of attendance, why should not Jacob have it now; his father might have sent him away with great parade; but I am apt to believe this did not suit Jacob's real, pilgrim spirit; he was a plain man, and dwelt in tents, when, perhaps, he might have dwelt under cedar roofs; he chose a pilgrim's life, and prudence directed him to go thus in a private manner, to prevent increasing Esau's envy, and giving the fatal blow.

Methinks, I see the young pilgrim weeping when he took his leave of his father and mother; he went on foot, and they that are acquainted with the geography of the place, say, that the first day of his journey he walked

not

not less than forty English miles; what exercise must he have had all that way! no wonder, therefore, that by the time the sun was going down, poor Jacob felt himself very weary, for we are told, ver. 11, *that he lighted on a certain place, and tarried there all night, because the sun was set.* There is a particular emphasis to be put upon this term, *a certain place*; he saw the sun going down, he was a stranger in a strange land. (You that are born in England can have very little idea of it, but persons that travel in the American woods can form a more proper idea, for you may there travel a hundred and a thousand miles, and go through one continued tract of tall green trees, like the tall cedars of Lebanon; and the gentlemen of America, from one end to the other, are of such an hospitable temper, as I have not only been told, but have found among them upwards of thirty years, that they would not let public houses be licensed, that they may have an opportunity of entertaining English friends: may God, of his infinite mercy, grant this union may never be dissolved.)

Well, Jacob got to a certain place, and perhaps he saw a good tree that would serve him for a canopy; however, this we are told, he tarried there all night becaufe the fun was fet, and he took of the ftones of that place and put them for his pillow, and laid down in that place to fleep; hard lodgings for him who was ufed to lie otherwife at home: I don't hear him fay, I wifh I was got back to my mother again, I wifh I had not fet out; but upon the hard ground and hard pillow he lies down; I believe never poor man flept fweeter in his life, for it is certainly fweet fleep when God is near us; he did not know but his brother might follow and kill him while he was afleep, or that the wild beafts might devour him; (in America, when they fleep in the woods, and I expect to have fome fuch fleeping times in them before a twelvemonth is over, we are obliged to make a fire to keep the beafts from us: I have often faid then, and I hope I fhall never forget it, when I rife in the morning, this fire in the woods that keeps the wild beafts from hurting us, is like the fire of God's love that keeps the devil from hurting us:) thus weary and folitary he falls afleep, and fweetly dreams, *and behold*; I don't remember many paffages of fcripture where the word, *behold*, is repeated fo many times in fo fhort a fpace a space as in the passage before us, doubtless, the Lord would have us particularly take notice of it, even us upon whom the ends of the world are come: Behold, *a ladder set upon the earth, and the top reached to heaven; and* behold, *the angels of God ascending and descending upon it; and* behold, *the Lord stood above it;* so here are three *beholds* in a very few lines. Was there any thing very extraordinary in that? perhaps the Deists would say, your patriarch was tired, and dreamed among other things of a ladder; yes, he did, but this dream was of God, and how kind was he to meet him at the end of the first day's journey, to strengthen and animate him to go forward in this lonesome pilgrimage!

This ladder is reckoned by some to denote the providence of God: it was let down as it were from heaven, particularly at this time to poor Jacob, that he might know that however he was become a pilgrim, and left his all, all for God's glory, that God would take care for his comfort, and give his angels charge over him to keep him in all his ways, which was denoted by the angels ascending and descending upon the ladder. Some think that particular saints and countries have particular guardian angels, and therefore that the angels that ascended were those that had the particular charge of that place, so far as Jacob had come; that the angels that descended were another set of angels, sent down from heaven to guard him in his future journey; perhaps, this is more a fancy than the word of God. However, I very much like the observation of good Mr. Burket, "Why should we dispute whether "every individual believer has got a particu- "lar angel, when there is not one believer "but has got guards of angels to attend him," which are a great deal better than a great many servants, that prove our plagues, and instead of waiting upon us make us wait upon them.

But, my dear hearers, I don't know one spiritual commentator, but agrees that this ladder was a type of the Lord Jesus Christ; and that as Jacob was now banished from his father's house, and while sleeping upon a hard, cold stone, God was pleased not only to give him an assurance that he would be with him in the way, but gave him a blessed sight of Jesus Christ, in whom Jacob believed.

A ladder you know is something by which we climb from one place to another; hence,

in

in condescension to our weak capacities, God ordered a ladder to be let down, to shew us that Christ is the way to heaven: *I am the way, the truth, and the life; I am the door*, says he; neither is there salvation in any other, for there is no other name given under heaven whereby we must be saved. The Deists, who own a God but deny his Son, dare go to a God out of Christ; but Jacob is here taught better: how soon does God reveal the gospel unto him; here is a ladder, by which God preaches to us; if you have a mind to climb from earth to heaven, you must get up by the Son of God; no one ever pointed out a proper way to heaven for us but himself. When Adam and Eve fell from God, a flaming sword turned every way to keep them from the tree of life; but Jesus alone is a new and living way, not only to the Holy of Holies below, but into the immediate presence of God; and that we might know that he was a proper Saviour, the top of it reached to heaven; if it had stopped short Jacob might have said, ah! the ladder is within a little way of heaven, but does not quite reach it; if I climb up to the top I shall not get there after all; but the top reached to heaven, to point out

out the divinity and exaltation of the Son of God; such a Saviour became us who was God, God over all, blessed for evermore: and therefore the Arian scheme is most uncomfortable and destructive; to talk of Christ as a Saviour that is not God, is no Christ at all. I would turn Deist to-morrow if I did not know that Christ was God; *but cursed is the man that builds his faith upon an arm of flesh.* If Christ is God, the Arians and Socinians, by their own principles, are undone for ever; but Jesus Christ is very God and very man, begotten (and not made) of the Father: God, of his infinite mercy, write his divinity deep in our hearts!

The bottom of the ladder reached to the earth; this points out to us the humiliation of the blessed Lord; for us men he came down from heaven; we pray to and for a descending God. All the sufferings which our Lord voluntarily exposed himself to, were that he might become a ladder for you and I to climb up to heaven by. Come down from the cross, say they, and we will believe thee; if he had, what would have become of us? did they believe on him when he was dead, buried, and risen again? no. Some people say,

if

if Chrift was here, O dear we fhould love him; juft as much as they did when they turned him out of doors, when he came down before. If he had come down from the crofs, they would have hung him up again: O that you and I might make his crofs a ftep to glory!

As the top of the ladder pointed out his exaltation, the bottom his humiliation, the two fides of the ladder being joined together, point out the union of the Deity and manhood in the perfon of Chrift; and that as this ladder had fteps to it, fo, bleffed be God, Jefus Chrift has found out a way whereby we may go, ftep after ftep, to glory. The firft ftep is the righteoufnefs of Chrift, the active and paffive obedience of the Redeemer; no fetting one foot upon this ladder without coming out of ourfelves, and relying wholly upon a better righteoufnefs than our own. Again, all the other fteps are the graces of the bleffed Spirit; therefore, you need not be afraid of our deftroying inward holinefs, by preaching the doctrine of the imputation of Chrift's righteoufnefs, that one is the foundation, the other the fuperftructure; to talk of my having the righteoufnefs of Chrift imputed to my foul,

without

without my having the holiness of Christ imparted to it, and bringing forth the fruits of the Spirit as an evidence of it, is only deceiving ourselves. I would never preach upon imputed righteousness, without speaking of inward holiness, for if you don't take a great deal of care, you will unawares, under a pretence of exalting Christ, run into Antinomianism, depths that Calvin never went into; probably, you will imbitter others spirits that don't agree with you, and at the same time hurt the fruits of the Spirit: may God give you clear heads, and at the same time warm hearts.

On the ladder Jacob saw the angels of God ascending and descending; what is that for? to shew that they are ministring spirits, sent forth to minister to them that shall be heirs of salvation; therefore we find them attending upon Christ. We do not hear much of them after the canon of scripture was closed, but as soon as ever Christ was born, the angels sang; till then we never hear of their singing below, as far as I can judge, since the creation; then the sons of God shouted for joy; but when Eve reached out her hand to pluck the fatal apple, and gave to Adam, earth groaned, and the angels hung, as it were, their harps upon

the

the willows; but when Chrift, the fecond Adam, was born, the angels fang at midnight, *Glory to God in the higheft.* I pray to God we may all die finging that anthem, and fing it to all eternity. After his temptations, they came and miniftred to him, as fome think, food for his body, and wifhed him joy and comfort in his foul ; and in his agonies in the garden, an angel ftrengthned him. After his refurrection two appeared again, one at the head and another at the foot of his fepulchre, to let thofe that looked into the fepulchre know, that they would not only wait upon the head but the foot ; and the angels are glad to wait upon the meaneft of the children of God. When our Lord departed, a cloud received him out of their fight, which probably was a cloud of angels: having led his difciples out of the city, he bleffed them, and then away he went to heaven: may that bleffing reft upon you and your children! This intimates that God makes ufe of angels to attend his people, efpecially when they are departing into eternity: perhaps, part of our entertainment in heaven will be, to hear the angels declare how many millions of times they have affifted and helped us. Our Lord fays, an-

gels

gels do there behold the face of the Father of his little ones; and therefore I love to talk to the lambs of the flock, and why should I not talk to them whom angels think it their honour to guard; and if it was not for this, how would any children escape the dangers they are exposed to in their tender age? it is owing to the particular providence of God, that any one child is brought to manhood; therefore I can't help admiring that part of the Litany, in which we pray, that God would take care not only of the grown people, but of children also: God take care of yours both in body and soul.

But what gave the greatest comfort to Jacob was, that the Lord was on the top of the ladder, which I do not know whether it would have been so, if Jacob had not seen God there. It comforts me, I assure you, to think, that whenever God shall call for me, I shall be carried by angels into Abraham's bosom; and I have often thought that whenever that time comes, that blessed, long longed-for moment comes, as soon as ever they have called upon me, my first question will be to them, where is my dear master? where is Jesus? where is that dear Emanuel, who has
loved

loved me with an everlasting love, and has called me by his grace, and have sent you to fetch me home to see his face? But I believe you and I shall have no occasion to ask where he is, for he will come to meet us, he will stand at the top of his ladder to take his pilgrims in; so God was at the top of the ladder, pray mind that. He appears not sitting, as he is often represented in heaven, but standing; as much as to say, here, here, Jacob, thy brother wants to kill thee; here thou art come out without a servant, art lying upon a hard bed, but here I am ready in order to preserve thee; I stand above, and I see thy weariness, I see the fatigue and hardships thou hast yet to undergo, though thou dost not see it thyself; thou hast thrown thyself upon my providence and protection, and I will give thee the word of a God that I will stand by thee; *the Lord stood above*; if he had said nothing, that would have been enough to have shewn his readiness to help.

But God speaks, *behold:* well might this be ushered in with the word *behold*; a ladder set on the earth, and *behold* the angels of God ascending and descending on it; and, above all, *behold* God speaking from it! what doth he say? *I am the Lord God of Abraham thy father.* Oh! happy they that can say, the Lord God of my father; happy you that have got fathers and mothers in heaven. I remember, about twenty-five years ago as I was travelling from Bristol, I met with a man on the road, and being desirous to know whether he was serious or not, I began to put in a word for Christ, (and God forbid I should travel with any body a quarter of an hour without speaking of Christ to them) he told me what a wicked creature he had been; but, sir, says he, in the midst of my wickedness people used to tell me, you have got a good many prayers upon the file for you, your godly father and mother have prayed very often for you; and it was the pleasure of God he was wrought upon, and brought to Christ. Lay in a good stock for your children, get a good many prayers in for them, they may be answered when you are dead and gone. *I am the God of Abraham thy father*, not thy grandfather; to put him in mind what an honour God would put upon him, to make him as it were the father of the church. Though you have many instructors, says Paul, you have but one Father: *and the God of Isaac, the land whereon*

whereon thou liest, to thee will I give it, and to thy seed. Amazing! amazing! you know very well when persons buy or come to an estate, they usually take possession of it by some ceremony, such as receiving or taking up a piece of dirt, or twig, in their hand, as a sign of their title. Now, says God, poor Jacob, thou dost little think that this very spot of ground that thou liest on to-night, cold and stiff, I intend to give to thee, and thy posterity, for an inheritance. O my brethren, live all to God, and God will give all to you: who would have thought of this, probably Jacob did not: it is as if God took a pleasure in seeing his dear children lie on such hard ground; if he had been on a feather-bed, he might not have had such a visit: thou shalt have now a God to lean upon, *to thee will I give it, and to thy seed, which shall be as the dust of the earth, and thou shalt spread abroad to the west, and to the east, and to the north, and to the south; and in thee, and in thy seed, shall all the families of the earth be blessed.* Thus did heaven balance the loss of the comforts of his father's house, by the discovery of his and his offspring's prosperity, by an interest in the promised seed.

My particular circumstances call me to observe, and I believe God has done it on purpose to encourage me, that faith, resting on the promise, is easily resigned to the loss of present good, whereas worldly hearts consider prosperity as a portion, they don't care if the devil takes them hereafter, so they have it now; and that makes carnal people wonder how we can give up things in this world, for the sake of those not yet born; but it is to glorify God, and lay a foundation for others happiness. Here God gives Jacob to know, that hereafter his seed should spread on the east, west, north, and south, his branches should multiply, and at last from his loins should Jesus Christ come; what for? *in whom all the families of the earth should be blessed:* God Almighty grant we may be blessed in him.

Then if Jacob should say in his heart, hast thou no promise for me? here is another *behold* comes in; *Behold, I am with thee, and will keep thee in all places whither thou goest.* What a word is this! thou hast nobody with thee, nothing but a staff, (he could not carry much upon his back, like a poor soldier with a napsack behind, and a little bread in his pocket)

pocket) well, faith God, I do not despise thee because thou art destitute, but I love thee the better for it; thy brother Esau longs to kill thee, but if Esau stabs thee he shall stab thy God first; I will not only be with thee now, but I will watch every step thou takest, *I will be with thee in all places whither thou goest:* as much as to say, Jacob, thou art a pilgrim, thy life is to be a moving life, I don't intend thou shalt settle and keep in one place; thy life is to be a life of changes, thou art to move from place to place, but *I will be with thee in all places whither thou goest,* and thereby it shall be known that I am Jacob's God, and also by my bringing thee again into this land. He not only assures him of a succesful journey, whither he was now going, but promises to bring him back once more to see his dear father and mother, and relations again; *I will bring thee back to this land*; and to confirm his faith and hope, the great God adds, *I will not leave thee till I have done that I have spoken to thee of*; that is, all the good he had just now promised. Some people promise, but they cannot do it to-day, and they will not do it to-morrow. I have known the world, and have rung the changes

of

of it ever since I have been here; but, blessed be God, an unchangeable Christ having loved his own, he loved them to the end; *I will not leave you till I have performed all things I have promised you:* may this promise come upon you and your children, and all that God shall call.

Thus spake the great Jehovah to poor Jacob, just setting out to a strange land, knowing not whither he went; but now God speaks not only to Jacob, but he speaks to you; and, blessed be the living God, he speaks to me also, less than the least of all; and as my design is (though I cannot tell but this may be the last opportunity) to speak something to you about my departure; yet, brethren, my grand design in preaching to you is, to recommend the Lord Jesus Christ to your souls; and, before I go, to make a particular, personal application. Give me leave, therefore, to ask you, it may be the last time I may ask many of you, whether you have ever set your foot upon this blessed ladder, the Son of God? I ask you in the name of the Lord Jesus Christ, in the name of the Father, Son, and Holy Ghost, did you ever set your foot, I say, upon this ladder? that is, did you ever

yet

yet believe on Jesus Christ, and come to him as poor lost sinners, relying upon no other righteousness than that of the Son of God? perhaps, if you was to speak, some of you would say, away with your ladder; and what will you do then? why, say you, I will climb to heaven without it; what ladder will you climb upon? O, I think to go to heaven because I have been baptized, that ladder will break under you; what, a ladder made of water, what are you dreaming of? no; O, I think I shall go to heaven because I have done nobody any harm; what, a ladder made of negative goodness, no; I think to go, you'll say, by good works; a ladder made of good works, that has not Christ for its bottom, what is that? I think, say you, to go to heaven by my prayers and fastings; all these are good in their place: but, my brethren, don't think to climb to heaven by these ropes of sand. If you never before set your foot on Christ, this blessed ladder, God grant this may be the happy time.

I have been praying before most of you were up I believe, that God would give me a parting blessing. I remember, soon after I left England last, that a dear Christian friend told

told me, that there was one woman, who came only out of curiosity, that dated her conversion from hearing my last sermon; and, I bless God, I never once left England, but some poor soul has dated their conversion from my last sermon. When I put on my surplice, to come out to read the second service, I thought it was just like a person's being decently dressed to go out to be executed; I would rather, was it the will of God, it should be so, than to feel what I do in parting from you, then death would put an end to all; but I am to be executed again and again, and nothing will support me under the torture, but the consideration of God's blessing me to some poor souls. Do pray for me, ye children of God, that God would give us a parting blessing. God help you, young people, to put your foot on this ladder; don't climb wrong: the devil has got a ladder, but it reaches down to hell; all the devil's children go down, not up; the bottom of the devil's ladder reaches to the depths of the damned, the top of it reaches to the earth; and when death comes, then up comes the devil's ladder to let you down; for God's sake come away from the devil's ladder; climb, climb, dear young men. O it

O it delighted me on Friday night at the Tabernacle, when we had a melting parting sacrament; and it delighted me this morning to see so many young men at the table; God add to the blessed number! Young women, put your feet upon this ladder; God lets one ladder down from heaven, and the devil brings another up from hell. O, say you, I would climb up God's ladder, I think it is right, but I shall be laughed at; do you think to go to heaven without being laughed at? the Lord Jesus Christ help you to climb to heaven; come, climb till you get out of the hearing of their laughter. O trust not to your own righteousness, your vows, and good resolutions.

Some of you, blessed be God, have climbed up this ladder, at least are climbing; well, I wish you joy, God be praised for setting your feet on this ladder, God be praised for letting down this ladder: I have only one word to say to you, for Jesus Christ's sake, and your own too, climb a little faster; take care the world does not get hold of your heels. It is a shame the children of God don't climb faster; you may talk what you please, but God's people's lukewarmness is more provoking to him than all the sins of the nation. We cry out against the sins of the land, would to God we did cry out more of the sins of the saints; *I will spue you out of my mouth, because you are lukewarm,* says Christ; and if any of you say you cannot climb because you are lame-footed, look to Jesus Christ, my dear friends, and your affliction shall make you climb; and if any of you are coming down the ladder again, the Lord Jesus Christ bless the foolishness of preaching to help you up again. O, say you, I am giddy, I shall fall; here, I will give you a rope, be sure lay hold of it; just as the sailors do when you go aboard a ship, they let down a rope, so God lets down a promise: climb, climb, then, till you have got higher into a better climate, and God shall put his hand out by and by when you get to the top of the ladder to receive you to himself. Blessed be the living God, I hope and believe I shall meet many of you by and by.

And now, my brethren, it is time for me to preach my own funeral sermon; and I would humbly hope that, as a poor sinner, I may put in my claim for what God promised Jacob; and I do put in, with full assurance of faith that God will be with me. I am now going, for the thirteenth time, to cross the Atlantic:

Atlantic: when I came from America laſt, I took my leave of all the Continent, from the one end of the provinces to the other, except ſome places which we had not then taken; I took my leave for life, without the leaſt deſign of returning there again, my health was ſo bad; and the proſpect of getting the orphan-houſe into other hands made me ſay when I firſt came over, I have no other river to go over than the river Jordan. I thought then of retiring, for I did not chuſe to appear when my nerves were ſo relaxed that I could not ſerve God as I could wiſh to do; but as it hath pleaſed God to reſtore my health much, and has ſo ordered it by his providence, that I intend to give up the orphan-houſe, and all the land adjoining, for a public college. I wiſhed to have had a public ſanction, but his grace the late archbiſhop of Canterbury put a ſtop to it; they would give me a charter, which was all I deſired, but they inſiſted upon, at leaſt his grace and another did, that I ſhould confine it totally to the Church of England, and that no extempore prayer ſhould be uſed in a public way in that houſe, though Diſſenters, and all ſorts of people, had contributed to it: I would ſooner cut my head off than
betray

betray my trust, by confining it to a narrow bottom; I always meant it should be kept upon a broad bottom, for people of all denominations, that their children might be brought up in the fear of God: by this means the orphan-house reverted into my hands; I have once more, as my health was restored, determined to pursue the plan I had fixed on; and, thro' the tender mercies of God, Georgia, (which about thirty-two years ago was a total desolate place; and when the land, as it was given me by the House of Commons, would have been totally deserted, and the colony have quite ceased, had it not been for the money I have laid out for the orphan-house, to keep the poor people together) that colony is rising to a most amazing height, by the schemes now going on, public buildings are erecting. I had news last week of the great prosperity of the negroes; and I hope by the twenty-fifth of March, which is the day, the anniversary day, I laid the first brick, in the year 1739; I say, I hope by that time all things will be finished, and a blessed provision will be made for orphans and poor students that will be brought up there; it will be a blessed source of provision for the children of God in another part of the world.

This

This is the grand design I am going upon; this is my visible cause; but I never yet went to them, but God has been pleased to bless my ministration among them; and therefore after I have finished the orphan-house affair, I intend to go all along the Continent by land, (which will keep me all the winter and spring) and when I come to the end of it, which will be Canada and New-England, then I hope to return again to this place; for, let people say what they will, I have not so much as a single thought of settling abroad on this side eternity; and I am going in no public capacity, I shall set out like a poor pilgrim, at my own expence, trusting upon God to take care of me, and to bear my charges; and I call God to witness, and I must be a cursed devil and hypocrite, to stand here in the pulpit and provoke God to strike me dead for lying, I never had the love of the world, nor never felt it one quarter of an hour in my heart, since I was twenty years old. I might have been rich: but though the Chapel is built, and I have a comfortable room to lie in, I assure you I built it at my own expence, it cost nobody but myself any thing. I have a watch-coat made me, and in that I shall lie every night

night on the ground, and may Jacob's God bless me. I will not say much of myself, but when I have been preaching, I have read and thought of those words with pleasure, *Surely this is the house of God. And I will bring thee again to this land.* Whether that will be my experience or not, blessed be God, I have a better land in view; and, my dear brethren, I do not look upon myself at home till I land in my Father's kingdom; and if I am to die in the way, if I am to die in the ship, it comforts me that I know I am as clear as the sun, that I go by the will of God; and though people may say, will you leave the world? will you leave the Chapel? O, I am astonished that we cannot leave every thing for Christ; my greatest trial is, to part with those who are as dear to me as my own soul; and however others may forget me, as thousands have, and do forget me, yet I cannot forget them: and now may Jacob's God be with you; O keep close to God, my dear London friends; I do not bid you keep close to Chapel, you have done so always: I shall endeavour to keep up the word of God among you in my absence; I shall have the same persons that managed for me when I was out last, and they sent

me

me word again and again, by letter, that it was remarkable, that the Tottenham-court people were always present when ordinances were there.

You see I went upon a fair bottom; I might have had a thousand a year out of this place if I had chose it; when I am gone to heaven you will see what I have got on earth *; I do not like to speak now, because it may be thought boasting; but I am sure there are numbers of people here, if they knew what I have, would love me as much as they now hate me. When we come before the great Judge of quick and dead, while I stand before him, God grant you may not part with me then, it will be a dreadful parting then, it will be worse then to go into the fire, to be among the devil and his angels; God forbid it! God forbid it! God forbid it! O remember that my last words were, come, come to Christ; the Lord help you to come to Christ; come to Christ, come to Jacob's God; God give you faith like Jacob's faith.

You that have been kind to me, that have helped me when I was sick, some of whom are

---

* The greatest part of the substance this man of God left behind him, which was not much, was bequeathed to him by deceased friends.

are here that have been very kind to me; may God reward you, my friends, and God forgive my enemies; God, of his infinite mercy, bleſs you all; you will be amply provided for, I believe, here; may God ſpread the goſpel every where; and may God never leave you, nor forſake you. Even ſo, Lord Jeſus. Amen and Amen.

SERMON

SERMON XVIII.

The Good Shepherd.

A FAREWEL SERMON.

JOHN x. ver. 27, 28.

My sheep hear my voice, and I know them, and they follow me. And I give unto them eternal life, and they shall never perish, neither shall any pluck them out of my hand.

IT is a common, and, I believe, generally speaking, my dear hearers, a true saying, that bad manners beget good laws. Whether this will hold good in every particular, in respect to the affairs of this world, I am persuaded the observation is very pertinent in respect to the things of another; I mean bad manners, bad treatment, bad words, have been over-ruled by the sovereign grace of God, to produce and to be the cause of the best sermons that were ever delivered from the mouth of the God-man, Christ Jesus.

One would have imagined, that as he came cloathed with divine efficience, as he came with divine credentials, as he spake as never man spake, that no one should have been able to have resisted the wisdom with which he spake; one would imagine they should have been so struck with the demonstration of the Spirit, that with one consent they should all own, that he was *that prophet that was to be raised up like unto Moses.* But you seldom find our Lord preaching a sermon, but something or other that he said was cavilled at; nay, their enmity frequently broke through all good manners; they often, therefore, interrupted him whilst he was preaching, which shows the enmity of their hearts long before God permitted it to be in their power to shed his innocent blood. If we look no farther than this chapter, where he represents himself as a good shepherd, one that laid down his life for his sheep; we see the best return he had, was to be looked upon as possessed or distracted; for we are told that there was a division therefore again among the Jews for these sayings, and many of them said, *he hath a devil and is mad, why hear ye him?* If the master of the house was served so, pray what are the ser-

servants to expect? Others, a little more sober-minded, said, *these are not the words of him that hath a devil*; the devil never used to preach or act in this way. *Can a devil open the eyes of the blind?* So he had some friends among these rabble. This did not discourage our Lord, he goes on in his work; and we shall never, never go on with the work of God, till, like our master, we are willing to go through good and through evil report; and let the devil see we are not so complaisant as to stop one moment for his barking at us as we go along.

We are told, that our Lord was at Jerusalem at the feast of the dedication, and it was winter; the feast of dedication held, I think, seven or eight days for the commemoration of the restoration of the Temple and Altar after its profanation by Antiochus: now this was certainly a mere human institution, and had no divine image, had no divine superscription upon it; and yet I don't find that our blessed Lord and Master preached against it; I don't find that he spent his time about this; his heart was too big with superior things; and I believe when we, like him, are filled with the Holy Ghost, we shall not entertain our audiences with disputes about rites and ceremonies, but shall treat upon the essentials of the gospel, and then rites and ceremonies will appear with more indifference. Our Lord does not say, that he would not go up to the feast, for, on the contrary, he did go there, not so much to keep the feast, as to have an opportunity to spread the gospel-net, and that should be our method not to follow disputing; and it is the glory of the Methodists, that we have been now forty years, and, I thank God, there has not been one single pamphlet wrote by any of our preachers about the non-essentials of religion.

Our Lord always made the best of every opportunity; and we are told, *he walked in the temple in Solomon's porch.* One would have thought the Scribes and Pharisees would have put him in one of their stalls, and have complimented him with desiring him to preach, no, they let him walk in Solomon's porch; some think he walked by himself, nobody choosing to keep company with him. Methinks, I see him walking and looking at the temple, and foreseeing within himself how soon it would be destroyed; he walked pensive, to see the dreadful calamities that would come

come upon the land, for not knowing the day of its visitation; and it was to let the world see he was not afraid to appear in public: he walked, as much as to say, have any of you any thing to say to me? and he put himself in their way, that if they had any thing to ask him, he was ready to resolve them; and to shew them, that though they had treated him so ill, yet he was ready to preach salvation to them.

In the twenty-fourth verse we are told, *Then came the Jews round about him, and said unto him, how long dost thou make us to doubt?* They came round about him when they saw him walking in Solomon's porch; now, say they, we will have him, now we will attack him. And now was fulfilled that passage in the Psalms, *they compassed me about like bees* to sting me, or rather like wasps. Now, say they, we will get him in the middle of us, and see what sort of a man he is; we will see whether we can't conquer him; they came to him and they say, *how long dost thou make us to doubt?* Now this seems a plausible question, *how long dost thou make us to doubt?* Pray how long, sir, do you intend to keep us in suspense? Some think the words will bear this
inter-

interpretation; pray, sir, how long do you intend thus to steal away our hearts? they would represent him to be a designing man, like Absalom, to get the people on his side, and then set up himself for the Messiah; thus carnal minds always interpret good mens actions. But the meaning seems to be this, they were doubting concerning Christ; doubting Christians may think it is God's fault that they doubt, but God knows it is all their own. *How long dost thou make us to doubt?* I wish you would speak a little plainer, sir, and not let us have any more of your parables; pray let us know who you are, let us have it from your own mouth; *if thou be the Christ tell us plainly*; and I don't doubt but they put on a very sanctified face and looked very demure; *if thou be the Christ tell us plainly*, intending to catch him: if he does not say he is the Christ, we will say he is ashamed of his own cause; if he does tell us plainly that he is the Christ, then we will impeach him to the governor, we will go and tell the governor that this man says he is the Messiah; now we know of no Messiah but what is to jostle Cæsar out of his throne. The devil always wants to make it believed that God's people,

people, who are the most loyal people in the world, are rebels to the government under which they live; *if thou be the Christ tell us plainly.* "Our Lord does not let them wait long for an answer; honesty can soon speak: *I told you and ye believed not: the works that I do in my Father's name, they bear witness of me.* Had our Lord said, I am the Messiah, they would have taken him up; he knew that, and therefore he joined *the wisdom of the serpent* with *the innocence of the dove*; says he, I appeal to my works and doctrine, and if you will not infer from them that I am the Messiah, I have no further argument. *But,* he adds, *ye believe not, because ye are not of my sheep.* He complains twice; for their unbelief was the greatest grief of heart to Christ: then he goes on in the words of our text, *My sheep hear my voice, and I know them, and they follow me. And I give unto them eternal life, and they shall never perish, neither shall any pluck them out of my hand.* My sheep hear my voice; you think to puzzle me, you think to chagrin me with this kind of conduct, but you are mistaken; you don't believe on me, because you are not of my sheep. The great Mr. Stodart, of New-England,

land, (and no place under heaven produces greater divines than New England) preached once from these words, *but ye believe not, because ye are not of my sheep*; a very strange text to preach upon to convince a congregation, yet God so blessed it, that two or three hundred souls were awakened by that sermon: God grant such success to attend the labours of all his faithful ministers.

My sheep hear my voice, and they follow me. It is very remarkable, there are but two sorts of people mentioned in scripture; it does not say the Baptists and Independents, nor the Methodists and Presbyterians; no, Jesus Christ divides the whole world into but two classes, sheep and goats: the Lord give us to see this morning to which of these classes we belong.

But it is observable, believers are always compared to something that is good and profitable, and unbelievers are always described by something that is bad, and good for little or nothing.

If you ask me why Christ's people are called sheep? as God shall enable me, I will give you a short, and I hope it will be to you an answer of peace. Sheep, you know, generally love to be together; we say a flock of sheep,

sheep, we don't say a herd of sheep; sheep are little creatures, and Christ's people may be called sheep, because they are little in the eyes of the world, and they are yet less in their own eyes. O some people think if the great men were on our side, if we had king, lords, and commons on our side, I mean if they were all true believers, O if we had all the kings upon the earth on our side, suppose you had; alas! alas! do you think the church would go on the better? why, if it was fashionable to be a Methodist at court, if it was fashionable to be a Methodist abroad, they would go with a bible or a hymn-book instead of a novel; but religion never thrives under too much sun-shine. *Not many mighty, not many noble are called, but God hath chosen the foolish things of the world to confound the wise, and God hath chosen the weak things of the world to confound the things which are mighty.* Dr. Watts says, here and there I see a king, and here and there a great man in heaven, but their number is but small.

Sheep are looked upon to be the most harmless, quiet creatures that God hath made: O may God, of his infinite mercy, give us to know that we are his sheep, by our having this blessed temper infused into our hearts by the Holy Ghost. *Learn of me*, saith our blessed Lord; what to do, to work miracles? no; *Learn of me, for I am meek and lowly in heart.* A very good man, now living, said once, if there is any one particular temper I desire more than another, it is the grace of *meekness*, quietly to bear bad treatment, to forget and to forgive; and at the same time that I am sensible I am injured, not to be overcome of evil, but to have grace given me to overcome evil with good. To the honour of Moses it is declared, that he was the meekest man upon earth. Meekness is necessary for people in power; a man that is passionate is dangerous; every governor should have a warm temper, but a man of an unrelenting, unforgiving temper, is no more fit for government than Phaeton to drive the chariot of the sun, he only sets the world on fire.

You all know, that sheep of all creatures in the world are the most apt to stray and be lost; Christ's people may justly, in that respect, be compared to sheep; therefore, in the introduction to our morning service, we say, *We have erred and strayed from thy ways like lost sheep*. Turn out a horse, or a dog,

and

and they will find their way home, but a sheep wanders about, he bleats here and there, as much as to say, dear stranger, shew me my way home again: thus Christ's sheep are too apt to wander from the fold; having their eye off the great shepherd, they go into this field, and that field, over this hedge and that, and often return home with the loss of their wool.

But at the same time sheep are the most useful creatures in the world; they manure the land, and thereby prepare it for the seed; they clothe our bodies with wool, and there is not the least part of a sheep but is useful to man: O my brethren, God grant that you and I may, in this respect, answer the character of sheep. The world says, because we preach faith we deny good works; this is the usual objection against the doctrine of imputed righteousness, but it is a slander, an impudent slander. It was a maxim in the first reformers time, that tho' the *Arminians* preached up good works, you must go to the *Calvinists* for them. Christ's sheep study to be useful, and to clothe all they can; we should labour with our hands, that we may have to give to all those that need.

Believers confider Chrift's property in them; he fays, *My fheep:* O bleffed be God for that little, dear, great word *My.* We are his by eternal election: *the fheep which thou haft given me,* fays Chrift. They were given by God the Father to Chrift Jefus, in the covenant made between the Father and the Son from all eternity. They that are not led to fee this, I wifh them better heads; though, I believe, numbers that are againft it have got better hearts: the Lord help us to bear with one another where there is an honeft heart.

He calls them my fheep, they are his by purchafe. O finner, finner, you are come this morning to hear a poor creature take *his laft farewel;* but I want you to forget the creature that is preaching, I want to lead you farther than the Tabernacle; where do you want to lead us? why, to Mount Calvary, there to fee at what an expence of blood Chrift purchafed thofe whom he calls his own; he redeemed them with his own blood, fo that they are not only his by eternal election, but alfo by actual redemption in time; and they were given to him by the Father, upon condition that he fhould redeem them by his heart's blood. It was a hard bargain, but Chrift

Christ was willing to strike the bargain, that you and I might not be damned for ever.

They are his, because they are enabled in a day of God's power voluntarily to give themselves up unto him; Christ says of these sheep especially, that *they hear his voice, and that they follow him.* Will you be so good as to mind that? here is an allusion to a shepherd: now in some places in scripture, the shepherd is represented as going after his sheep*; that is our way in England) but in the Eastern nations, the shepherds generally went before; they held up their crook, and they had a particular call that the sheep understood. Now, says Christ, *My sheep hear my voice. This is my beloved Son,* saith God, *hear ye him.* And again, *the dead shall hear the voice of the Son of God, and live:* now the question is, what do we understand by hearing Christ's voice?

First, we hear Moses' voice, we hear the voice of the law; there is no going to Mount Zion but by the way of Mount Sinai, that is the right straight road. I know some say, they don't know when they were converted; those are, I believe, very few: generally, nay I may say almost always, God deals otherwise.

Some

---

* 2 Sam. vii. 8.   Psal. lxxviii. 71.

Some are, indeed, called sooner by the Lord than others, but before they are made to see the glory of God, they must hear the voice of the law; so you must hear the voice of the law, before ever you will be savingly called unto God. You never throw off your cloak in a storm but you hug it the closer, so the law makes a man hug close his corruptions*; but when the gospel of the Son of God shines into their souls, then they throw off the corruptions which they have hugged so closely; they hear his voice saying, Son, daughter, be of good cheer, thy sins, which are many, are all forgiven thee. *They hear his voice*; that bespeaks the habitual temper of their minds: the wicked hear the voice of the devil, the lusts of the flesh, the lusts of the eye, and the pride of life; and Christ's sheep themselves attended to them before conversion; but when called afterwards by God, they hear the voice of a Redeemer's blood speaking peace unto them, they hear the voice of his word and of his Spirit.

The consequence of hearing his voice, and the proof that we do hear his voice, will be to follow him. Jesus said unto his disciples,

If

---

* Rom. vii. 7, 8, 9.

Ser. XVIII. *The Good Shepherd.*

If any man will come after me, let him deny himself, and take up his cross and follow me. And it is said of the saints in glory, that *they followed the Lamb whithersoever he went.* Wherever the shepherd turns his crook, and the sheep hear his voice, they follow him; they often tread upon one another, and hurt one another, they are in such haste in their way to heaven. Following Christ, means following him through life, following him in every word and gesture, following him out of one clime into another. *Bid me come to thee upon the water,* said Peter: and if we are commanded to go over the water for Christ, God, of his infinite mercy, follow us! We must first be sure that the Great Shepherd points his crook for us: but this is the character of a true servant of Christ, that he endeavours to follow Christ in thought, word, and work.

Now, my brethren, before we go farther, as this is the last opportunity I shall have of speaking to you for some months if we live; some of you, I suppose, don't chuse in general to rise so soon as you have this morning; now I hope the world did not get into your hearts before you left your beds; now you are here, do let me intreat you to enquire

whether

whether you belong to Christ's sheep or no. Man, woman, sinner, put thy hand to thy heart and answer me, didst thou ever hear Christ's voice so as to follow him, to give up thyself without reserve to him? I verily do believe from my inmost soul, and that is my comfort now I am about to take my leave of you, that I am preaching to a vast body, a multitude of dear, precious souls, who, if it was proper for you to speak, would say, Thanks be unto God, that we can follow Jesus in the character of sheep, though we are ashamed to think how often we wander from thee, and what little fruit we bring unto thee; if that is the language of your hearts, I wish you joy; welcome, welcome, dear soul, to Christ. O blessed be God for his rich grace, his distinguishing, sovereign, electing love, by which he has distinguished you and me. And if he has been pleased to let you hear his voice, through the ministration of a poor, miserable sinner; a poor, but happy pilgrim, may the Lord Jesus Christ have all the glory.

If you belong to Jesus Christ, he is speaking of you; for, says he, *I know my sheep.* I know them, what does that mean? why, he knows their number, he knows their names,

he

he knows every one for whom he died; and if there was to be one missing for whom Christ died, God the Father would send him down again from heaven to fetch him. *Of all*, saith he, *that thou hast given me, have I lost none.* Christ knows his sheep; he not only knows their number, but the words speak the peculiar knowledge and notice he takes of them; he takes as much care of each of them, as if there was but that one single sheep in the world. To the hypocrite he saith, *Verily, I know you not*; but he knows his saints, he is acquainted with all their sorrows, their trials and temptations; he bottles up all their tears, he knows their domestic trials, he knows their inward corruptions, he knows all their wanderings, and he takes care to fetch them back again. I remember I heard good Dr. Marryat, who was a good market-language preacher, once say at Pinner's-hall, (I hope that pulpit will be always filled with such preachers) *God has got a great dog to fetch his sheep back*, says he. Don't you know that when the sheep wander, the shepherd sends his dog after them to fetch them back again? so when Christ's sheep wander, he lets the devil go after them, and suffers him to bark at them, who, instead of driving them farther off, is made a means to bring them back again to Christ's fold.

There is a precious word I would have you take notice of, *I know them*; that may comfort you under all your trials. We sometimes think that Christ does not hear our prayers, that he does not know us; we are ready to suspect that he has forgotten to be gracious; but what a mercy it is that he does know us. We accuse one another, we turn devils to one another, are accusers of the brethren, and what will support two of God's people when judged by one another but this, Lord, thou knowest my integrity, thou knowest how matters are with me?

But, my brethren, here is something better, here is good news for you; what is that? say you; why, *I give unto them eternal life, and they shall never perish, neither shall any pluck them out of my hand.* O that the words may come to your hearts with as much warmth and power as they did to mine thirty-five years ago. I never prayed against any corruption I had in my life, so much as I did against going into holy orders, so soon as my friends were for having me go; and bishop Benson was

pleased

pleased to honour me with peculiar friendship, so as to offer me preferment, or do any thing for me: my friends wanted me to mount the church betimes, they wanted me to knock my head against the pulpit too young; but how some young men stand up here and there and preach, I don't know how it may be to them; but God knows how deep a concern entering into the ministry and preaching was to me; I have prayed a thousand times till the sweat has dropped from my face like rain, that God, of his infinite mercy, would not let me enter the church before he called me to, and thrust me forth in his work. I remember once in Gloucester, I know the room, I look up at the window when I am there and walk along the street; I know the window, the bedside, and the floor upon which I have laid prostrate: I said, Lord, I cannot go, I shall be puffed up with pride, and fall into the condemnation of the devil; Lord, don't let me go yet; I pleaded to be at Oxford two or three years more; I intended to make an hundred and fifty sermons, and thought I would set up with a good stock in trade however; but I remember praying, wrestling, and striving with God; I said, I am undone, I am

unfit

unfit to preach in thy great name, send me not, pray, Lord, send me not yet. I wrote to all my friends in town and country, to pray against the bishop's solicitation, but they insisted I should go into orders before I was twenty-two. After all their solicitation these words came into my mind, *nothing shall pluck you out of my hand.* O may the words be blessed to you, my dear friends, that I am parting with, as they were to me when they came warm upon my heart; then, and not till then, I said, Lord, I will go, send me when thou wilt. I remember when I was in a place called Dover-Island, near Georgia, we put in with bad winds; I had an hundred and fifty in family to maintain, and not a single farthing to do it with, in the dearest part of the king's dominions; I remember, I told a minister of Christ now in heaven, I had these words once, sir, *Nothing shall pluck you out of my hand.* O, says he, take comfort from them, you may be sure God will be as good as his word, if he never tells you so again. And our Lord knew his poor sheep would be always doubting they should never reach heaven, therefore, says he, *I give to them eternal life, and they shall never perish.*

Here

Here are in our text three blessed declarations, or promisses:

First. *I know them.*

Second. *They shall never perish*; though they often think they shall perish by the hand of their lusts and corruptions; they think they shall perish by the deceitfulness of their hearts; but Christ says, *they shall never perish.* I have brought them out of the world to myself, and do you think I will let them go to hell after that. *I give to them eternal life*; pray mind that; not I will, but I do. Some talk of being justified at the day of judgment, that is nonsense; if we are not justified here, we shall not be justified there. He gives them eternal life, that is, the earnest, the pledge, and assurance of it; the indwelling of the Spirit of God here, is the earnest of glory hereafter.

Third. *Neither shall any pluck them out of my hand.* He holds them in his hand, that is, he holds them by his power, none shall pluck them thence; there is always something plucking at Christ's sheep, the devil, the lusts of the flesh, the lusts of the eye, and the pride of life, all try to pluck them out of Christ's hand. O my brethren, they need not pluck us, for we help all three to pluck ourselves out of the hand of Jesus; but *none shall pluck them out of my hand*, says Christ. *I give to them eternal life. I am going to heaven to prepare a place for them, and there they shall be.* O my brethren, if it was not for keeping you too long, and too much exhausting my own spirits, I could call upon you to leap for joy; there is not a more blessed text to support the final perseverance of the saints; and I am astonished any poor soul, and good people I hope too, can fight against the doctrine of the perseverance of the saints; what if a person say they should persevere in wickedness? ah! that is an abuse of the doctrine; what, because some people spoil good food, are we never to eat it? But, my brethren, upon this text I can leave my cares, all my friends, and all Christ's sheep to the protection of Christ Jesus's never-failing love.

I thought this morning, when I came here riding from the other end of the town, it was to me like coming to be executed publicly; and when the carriage turned just at the end of the walk, and I saw you running here, O thinks I, it is like a person now coming just to the place where he is to be executed: when I went up to put on my gown, I thought it

was

was just like dressing myself to be made a public spectacle to shed my blood for Christ; and I take all heaven and earth to witness, and God and the holy angels to witness, that tho' I had preferment enough offered me, that tho' the bishop took me in his arms, and offered me two parishes when I was but twenty-two years old, and always took me to his table; though I had preferment enough offered me when I was ordained, thou, O God, knowest, that when the bishop put his hand upon my head, I looked for no other preferment than publickly to suffer for the Lamb of God: in this spirit I came out, in this spirit I came up to this metropolis. I was thinking when I read of Jacob's going over the brook with a staff, that I would not say so much, but I came up without a friend, I went to Oxford without a friend, I had not a servant, I had not any one to introduce me; but God, by his Holy Spirit, was pleased to raise me up to preach for his great name's sake: through his Divine Spirit I continue to this day, and feel my affections are as strong as ever towards the work, and the people of the living God. The congregations at both ends of the town are dear to me; God has honoured me to build this and the other place; and, blessed be his name, as he called me to Georgia at first, and I left all London affairs to God's care, when I had most of the churches in London open for me, and had twelve or fourteen constables to keep the doors, that people might not crowd too much; I had offers of hundreds then to settle in London, yet I gave it up for God, to go into a foreign clime; and I hope with that same single intention I am going now.

When I came from America last, I thought I had no other river to pass over but the river Jordan, I remember I told you so; and as the orphan-house was then to be given, I thought, out of my hands, I then intended to retire into some little corner, and pray when I could not preach, my spirits were so low, and my nerves and animal frame so weak, but God, of his infinite mercy, has renewed my strength, and is pleased to raise my spirits, so that I find my heart is willing to go here or there, wherever God shall call.

The orphan-house being turned into a college is a matter of great consequence; you that have not been in America can't tell, but I heartily wish, I am neither a prophet, nor
the

the son of a prophet, and I hope none of us will ever be driven to America for an asylum, where God's people were driven from this land an hundred years ago: clouds are growing thick, and if a spirit of moderation does not prevail among governors and governed, what but confusion must happen to persons who strive one with another, and are making sport for the devil by destroying one another? may the great and gracious God avert every impending storm; and by diffusing a spirit of moderation and of a sound mind, and by keeping his people close to himself, avert those storms, those terrible judgments, that we have reason to expect from our repeated provocations. I am going now to settle the orphan-house upon a proper basis; I go now in the fall, that I may be in Georgia in the winter, which is fine weather there. The twenty-fifth of March is the anniversary of the day on which I laid the first brick of the orphan-house; by that time, I hope, all the buildings will be finished, and the plantation settled; and then I hope to go and preach along the continent to New-England, and from thence I intend, if God permit me, to return

return to my dear London and English friends again.

I have blessed news from the orphan-house; one writes me word, Would to God you could send a thousand such as you have sent, Mr. Dixon, and his wife, that have been old servants there; Mr. Wright, Mr. Crayne, and Mr. Wright's brother, and those that have been employed with them to carry on the work of the Lord; and I cannot think but God intends to lay a foundation for a blessed seminary for Christ: Lord Jesus, hear our prayers upon that account.

Now I must come to the hardest part I have to act: I was afraid when I came out from home, that I could not bear the shock, but I hope the Lord Jesus Christ will help me to bear it, and help you to give me up to the blessed God, let him do with me what he will. This is the thirteenth time of my crossing the mighty waters; it is a little difficult at this time of life; and though my spirits are improved in some degree, yet weakness is the best of my strength: but I delight in the cause, and God fills me with a peace that is unutterable, which nobody knows, and a stranger intermeddles not with: into his

his hands I commend my spirit; and I beg that this may be the language of your hearts, Lord, keep him, let nothing pluck him out of thy hands. I expect many a trial while I am on board, satan always meets me there; but that God which has kept me, I believe will keep me. I thank God, I have the honour of leaving every thing quite well and easy at both ends of the town; and, my dear hearers, my prayers to God shall be, that nothing may pluck you out of Christ's hands. Witness against me, if I ever set up a party for myself; did ever any minister, or could any minister in the world say, that I ever spoke against any one going to any dear minister? I thank God, that he has enabled me to be always strengthning the hands of all, though some have afterwards been ashamed to own me. I declare to you, that I believe God will be with me, and will strengthen me; and I believe it is in answer to your prayers, that God is pleased to revive my spirits: may the Lord help you to pray on. If I am drowned in the waves I will say, Lord, take care of my London, take care of my English friends, let nothing pluck them out of thy hands.

And

And as Christ has given us eternal life, O my brethren, some of you, I doubt not, will be gone to him before my return; but, my dear brethren, my dear hearers, never mind that; we shall part, but it will be to meet again forever. I dare not meet you now, I can't bear your coming to me to part from me, it cuts me to the heart and quite overcomes me, but by and by all parting will be over, and all tears shall be wiped away from our eyes. God grant that none that weep now at my parting, may weep at our meeting at the day of judgment; and if you never were among Christ's sheep before, may Christ Jesus bring you now. O come, come, see what it is to have eternal life; don't refuse it; haste, sinner, haste away: may the great, the good shepherd, draw your souls. Oh! if you never heard his voice before, God grant you may hear it now; that I may have this comfort when I am gone that I had last, that some souls are awakened at the parting sermon. O that it may be a farewel sermon to you; that it may be a means of your taking a farewel of the world, the lusts of the flesh, the lusts of the eye, and the pride of life. O come,

Ser. XVIII. *The Good Shepherd.*

O come, come, come, to the Lord Jesus Christ; to him I leave you.

And you, dear sheep, that are already in his hands, O may God keep you from wandering; God keep you near Christ's feet; I don't care what shepherds keep you, so as you are kept near the great shepherd and bishop of souls. The Lord God keep you, lift up the light of his countenance upon you, and give you peace. Amen.

F I N I S.

☞ These SERMONS being entered in the Hall-Book of the Company of Stationers, whoever presumes to pirate them will be prosecuted.

www.ingramcontent.com/pod-product-compliance
Lightning Source LLC
Chambersburg PA
CBHW022106300426
44117CB00007B/607